CW00539515

Focus on Courage

The 59 Victoria Crosses
of The Royal Green Jackets

Sergeant William Gregg of The Rifle Brigade, the first person to be awarded a VC, DCM and MM, receives his VC from His Majesty King George V, Colonel-in-Chief of The King's Royal Rifle Corps, at a field investiture at Headquarters Third Army at Frohen-le-Grand, France, on 9 August 1918. The King is wearing a black armband in mourning for his cousin, the Tsar of Russia, and the Tsar's family, who were assassinated on 16/17 July 1918.

Focus on Courage

The 59 Victoria Crosses
of The Royal Green Jackets

by
Lieutenant-General Sir Christopher Wallace KBE DL
and Major R.D. Cassidy MBE

Published by
The Royal Green Jackets Museum Trust
2006

Published by The Royal Green Jackets Museum Trust,
Peninsula Barracks, Winchester, Hampshire, SO23 8TS, UK

A catalogue record for this book is available from
The British Library

ISBN 0-9549370-1-5

Maps drawn by Bob Thorn
Designed by Columns Design Limited, Caversham, Reading, Berkshire
Indexed by Tehuti Knowledge Services Limited, Arnold, Nottinghamshire
Printed and bound by Cromwell Press Limited, Trowbridge, Wiltshire

Contents

List of Illustrations and Maps

Note: Every effort has been made to trace the origin and give attribution to illustrations that are not sourced from within the Regiment. Where thanks are due, especially to Kenneth Petrie whom we have been unable to trace (see back cover), they are readily given.

Illustrations

vii

Abbreviations

A Cpl	Acting Corporal
ADC	Aide-de-Camp
BEF	British Expeditionary Force
Bgr	Bugler
Bt	Brevet
Bt.	Baronet
Capt	Captain
CB	Companion of the Order of the Bath
CBE	Commander of the Order of the British Empire
CGM	Conspicuous Gallantry Medal
CMG	Companion of the Order of St Michael and St George
Cpl	Corporal
CSgt	Colour-Sergeant
CSM	Company Sergeant-Major
CVO	Commander of the Royal Victorian Order
DCM	Distinguished Conduct Medal
DSO	Distinguished Service Order
Ensn	Ensign
GBE	Knight Grand Cross of the Order of the British Empire
GC	George Cross
GCB	Knight Grand Cross of the Order of the Bath
GCMG	Knight Grand Cross of the Order of St Michael and St George
GOC	General Officer Commanding
Hon.	Honourable
KBE	Knight Commander of the Order of the British Empire
KCB	Knight Commander of the Order of the Bath
KCMG	Knight Commander of the Order of St Michael and St George
KRRC	King's Royal Rifle Corps
LI	Light Infantry
LCpl	Lance-Corporal
LSgt	Lance-Sergeant
Lt	Lieutenant

Abbreviations

Lt-Col	Lieutenant-Colonel
LRB	London Rifle Brigade
Maj	Major
MBE	Member of the Order of the British Empire
MC	Military Cross
MM	Military Medal
MVO	Member of the Royal Victorian Order
OBE	Officer of the Order of the British Empire
Oxf & Bucks LI	Oxfordshire and Buckinghamshire Light Infantry
QVR	Queen Victoria's Rifles
RB	Rifle Brigade
RGJ	Royal Green Jackets
Rfn	Rifleman
Sgt	Sergeant
TA	Territorial Army
RAMC	Royal Army Medical Corps
RMC	Royal Military College
VC	Victoria Cross
2Lt	Second Lieutenant

The Royal Green Jackets Family Tree

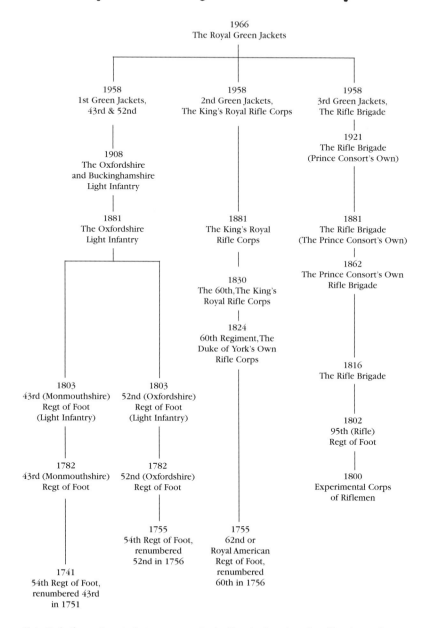

1966
The Royal Green Jackets

1958
1st Green Jackets,
43rd & 52nd

1958
2nd Green Jackets,
The King's Royal Rifle Corps

1958
3rd Green Jackets,
The Rifle Brigade

1921
The Rifle Brigade
(Prince Consort's Own)

1908
The Oxfordshire
and Buckinghamshire
Light Infantry

1881
The Oxfordshire
Light Infantry

1881
The King's Royal
Rifle Corps

1881
The Rifle Brigade
(The Prince Consort's Own)

1862
The Prince Consort's Own
Rifle Brigade

1830
The 60th, The King's
Royal Rifle Corps

1824
60th Regiment, The
Duke of York's Own
Rifle Corps

1816
The Rifle Brigade

1803
43rd (Monmouthshire)
Regt of Foot
(Light Infantry)

1803
52nd (Oxfordshire)
Regt of Foot
(Light Infantry)

1802
95th (Rifle)
Regt of Foot

1782
43rd (Monmouthshire)
Regt of Foot

1782
52nd (Oxfordshire)
Regt of Foot

1800
Experimental Corps
of Riflemen

1755
54th Regt of Foot,
renumbered
52nd in 1756

1755
62nd or
Royal American
Regt of Foot,
renumbered
60th in 1756

1741
54th Regt of Foot,
renumbered 43rd
in 1751

Note: Only the regiments that were once in the Regular Army's order of battle are shown.
For information about the Territorial regiments see pages xvii–xviii.

Total Number of VCs Awarded: 1854–2005

Event	Dates	Total Number of VCs Awarded	Number Awarded to Green Jackets
Crimean War	1854–6	111	8
Indian Mutiny	1857–9	182	16
Small Wars (excl South African War)	1860–1913	151	6
South African War	1899–1902	78	4
First World War	1914–18	628	23
Between the Two World Wars	1919–38	11	–
Second World War	1939–45	182	2
Since the Second World War	1946 onwards	12	–
		1355	**59**

VCs Awarded to the Antecedent Regiments of The Royal Green Jackets

Event	Oxf & Bucks LI	KRRC	RB	Total
Crimean War			8	**8**
Indian Mutiny	3	9	4	**16**
Small Wars 1864–1903[1]	1	3	2	**6**
South African War		2	2	**4**
First World War[2]	2	9	12	**23**
Second World War		1	1	**2**
Total	6	24	29	**59**

Note:

[1] New Zealand, Canada, Zululand, Egypt, Sudan and Somaliland.
[2] Includes Regular, Service and Territorial battalions – see page 92.

The orders, decorations and medals of General Sir Walter Congreve
VC KCB CVO (top two rows) and his son, Major W. La T. Congreve
VC DSO MC (bottom row), the first person to be awarded a VC, DSO and
MC. General Congreve and his son, Billy, both served in The Rifle Brigade.
They are one of three pairs of fathers and sons to be awarded VCs and the
only pair to have served in the same Regiment. (RGJ Museum)

The Royal Green Jackets For Valour Roll

† = Posthumous   ᵉ = Elected by Ballot

Rfn F. Wheatley
Sebastopol 1854
RB

Lt the Hon. H.H. Clifford
Inkerman 1854
RB

Lt W.J.M. Cuninghame
Sebastopol 1854
RB

Lt C.T. Bourchier
Sebastopol 1854
RB

Rfn J. Bradshaw
Sebastopol 1855
RB

Rfn R. Humpston
Sebastopol 1855
RB

Rfn R. McGregor
Sebastopol 1855
RB

Lt J.S. Knox
Sebastopol 1855
RB

Rfn S. Turner
Delhi 1857
KRRC

CSgt S. Garvin
Delhi 1857
KRRC

Ensn A.S. Heathcoteᵉ
Delhi 1857
KRRC

CSgt G. Wallerᵉ
Delhi 1857
KRRC

Rfn W.J. Thompsonᵉ
Delhi 1857
KRRC

Rfn J. Divane (Duane)ᵉ
Delhi 1857
KRRC

Bgr W. Suttonᵉ
Delhi 1857
KRRC

LCpl H. Smith
Delhi 1857
52nd LI

Bgr R. Hawthorne
Delhi 1857
KRRC

Ensn E.A. Lisle
   Phillipps†
Delhi 1857
KRRC

Capt H. Wilmot
Lucknow 1858
RB

Rfn D. Hawkes
Lucknow 1858
RB

Cpl W. Nash
Lucknow 1858
RB

Rfn V. Bambrick
India 1858
KRRC

Rfn S. Shaw
India 1858
RB

Pte H. Addison
India 1859
43rd LI

Capt F.A. Smith
New Zealand 1864
43rd LI

Rfn T. O'Hea
Canada 1866
RB

Bt Lt-Col R.H. Buller CB
Zululand 1879
KRRC

Rfn F. Corbett (Embleton)
Egypt 1882
KRRC

Lt P.S. Marling
Sudan 1884
KRRC

Capt W.N. Congreve
S. Africa 1899
RB

Lt the Hon. F.H.S. Roberts[†]
S. Africa 1899
KRRC

Rfn A.E. Durrant
S. Africa 1900
RB

Lt L.A.E. Price-Davies DSO
S. Africa 1901
KRRC

Bt Maj J.E. Gough
Somaliland 1903
RB

Lt J.H.S. Dimmer
Belgium 1914
KRRC

Lt J.F.P. Butler
W. Africa 1914
KRRC

CSM H. Daniels
France 1915
RB

A Cpl C.R. Noble[†]
France 1915
RB

2Lt G.H. Woolley
Belgium 1915
QVR

LSgt D.W. Belcher
Belgium 1915
LRB

Rfn W. Mariner (Wignall)
France 1915
KRRC

2Lt S.C. Woodroffe[†]
Belgium 1915
RB

Rfn G.S. Peachment[†]
France 1915
KRRC

Cpl A.G. Drake[†]
Belgium 1915
RB

Bt Maj W. La T. Congreve
DSO MC[†]
France 1916
RB

Sgt A. Gill[†]
France 1916
KRRC

2Lt G.E. Cates[†]
France 1917
RB

CSM E. Brooks
France 1917
Oxf & Bucks LI

Sgt E. Cooper
Belgium 1917
KRRC

Sgt W.F. Burman
Belgium 1917
RB

Sgt A.J. Knight
Belgium 1917
Post Office Rifles

Rfn A.E. Shepherd
France 1917
KRRC

LCpl J.A. Christie
Palestine 1917
Finsbury Rifles

LSgt J.E. Woodall
France 1918
RB

Sgt W. Gregg
DCM MM
France 1918
RB

Rfn W. Beesley
France 1918
RB

LCpl A. Wilcox
France 1918
Oxf & Bucks LI

xiv

Rfn J. Beeley[†]   Lt-Col V.B. Turner
N. Africa 1941   N. Africa 1942
KRRC   RB

Two VCs have been awarded to Medical Officers attached to Green Jacket battalions:

Capt H.S. Ranken[†], RAMC attached KRRC, France 1914
Lt G.A. Maling, RAMC attached RB, France 1915

Four VCs have been awarded to officers with previous service in one of the antecedent regiments of The Royal Green Jackets:

Capt the Hon. A.H.A. Anson, 84th Regiment, formerly RB, Delhi 1857
Capt F.O. Grenfell, 9th Lancers, formerly KRRC, Belgium 1914
Lt-Col A.D. Borton DSO, 2nd/22nd London Regiment, formerly KRRC, Palestine 1917
Lt J.H. Grayburn[†], The Parachute Regiment, formerly Oxf & Bucks LI, Arnhem 1944

One VC has been awarded to an officer who later served in one of the antecedent regiments of The Royal Green Jackets:

Capt A.M. Toye MC, Oxf & Bucks LI, formerly Middlesex Regiment, France 1918

Notes:

1. Ranks and decorations were those held at the time of the act of gallantry for which the VC was awarded.
2. Privates in the KRRC and RB were known as Riflemen, although the rank was not formally approved until 1923.

Introduction

This year marks the 150th Anniversary of the institution of the Victoria Cross, an event to be followed in February 2007 by the creation of a new regiment, The Rifles, merging The Royal Green Jackets and Light Infantry. We therefore felt that now, prior to the merger, was just the moment to chronicle for posterity in a single book the extraordinary acts of bravery of the 59 members of the Regular, Service and Territorial battalions of the antecedent regiments of The Royal Green Jackets who have been awarded a VC, Britain's highest award for gallantry in the presence of the enemy. It is a record of which the Regiment is hugely proud; no other Infantry regiment in the British Army prior to the current round of mergers and amalgamations has been able to lay claim to a greater number. However, we are wary about focusing on figures. First, we do not want to imply that there is or ought to be a league table recording the number of VCs awarded to each regiment, for, while fortune may favour the brave, it is not always the most deserving that receive their due. Secondly, 'the numbers' game' risks unbecoming argument about legitimacy and eligibility, complicated by the frequency with which the organisation of the British Army and the titles and affiliations of regiments have changed. There is also plenty of scope for idle interpretation and ambiguity, since the historical record is not always accurate. Thirdly, the idea that VCs are won in gladiatorial competition with others runs counter to the acts of selflessness with which VC awards are associated and the modesty and motives of the recipients. Thus, it is as well to know that the cognoscenti never refer, except inadvertently, to VCs being won; they are awarded.

Having made these points, we believe that we must offer some explanation about those whom we have included within our constituency of antecedent regiments of The Royal Green Jackets.

First, there are the Regular regiments – The Oxfordshire and Buckinghamshire Light Infantry (43rd and 52nd), The King's Royal Rifle Corps (60th) and The Rifle Brigade. The principal changes in their titles over the past 250 years, culminating in the creation of The Royal Green Jackets in 1966, are recorded on the Family Tree at page x. However, in writing this book, we have tended to use the regimental titles with which the majority of readers will be most familiar and not necessarily the title which would be historically correct.

Secondly, there are the Service battalions formed during the First World War in response to Lord Kitchener's appeal, as Secretary of State for War, for volunteers to serve their Country. As a result, The Oxfordshire and Buckinghamshire Light Infantry, The King's Royal Rifle Corps and The Rifle Brigade all expanded to include varying numbers of Service battalions, each bearing the title of their parent regiment.

Thirdly, there are the Territorial battalions, with which the Regular regiments have been affiliated since the Cardwell Reforms of 1881. However, there have been many changes in these affiliations over the years as Territorial battalions have come and gone. We have, therefore, concerned ourselves only with those relating to the First World War, as no VCs were awarded to our Territorials during any other conflict.

During the First World War, there were two Territorial battalions linked to The Oxfordshire and Buckinghamshire Light Infantry – the 4th Battalion, The Oxfordshire and Buckinghamshire Light Infantry, and the 1st Buckinghamshire Battalion. Each of these battalions, confusingly, sent two battalions overseas during the First World War – the 1st/4th and 2nd/4th, and the 1st/1st and 2nd/1st.

In the case of The King's Royal Rifle Corps and The Rifle Brigade it was more complicated. In 1881, as a part of the Cardwell Reforms, a number of Rifle Volunteer Corps in London were designated Volunteer battalions of either The King's Royal Rifle Corps or The Rifle Brigade. On 1 April 1908 a new Territorial Force was created, reinforcing the affiliations in the Counties, but removing the links in London, where a new regiment, The London Regiment, was formed. This Regiment assumed command of all the Territorial battalions in London, with The King's Royal Rifle Corps and The Rifle Brigade ceasing to have any formal connection with them. In July 1916 the pre-1908 designations were restored, although the battalions retained their London Regiment titles until 1922. Technically, therefore, The King's Royal Rifle Corps and The Rifle Brigade were without Territorial battalions between 1 April 1908 and July 1916. However, the Green Jackets have always chosen to ignore this aberration in War Office decision-making, not least because many of these battalions were as proud, if not more proud, of their Green Jacket heritage than their Regular counterparts. It would be heresy, too, to suggest that the likes of Queen Victoria's Rifles, Queen's Westminster Rifles or London Rifle Brigade were anything other than Green Jacket Territorial regiments.

In sum, six Territorial battalions of The London Regiment were linked to The King's Royal Rifle Corps during the First World War and five to The Rifle Brigade. Again, confusingly, each battalion sent two battalions overseas, mostly to the Western Front, for example, the 1st/6th and 2nd/6th. For completeness the full list is:

Territorial battalions of The King's Royal Rifle Corps

6th (City of London) Battalion (City of London Rifles)
9th (County of London) Battalion (Queen Victoria's Rifles)
11th (County of London) Battalion (Finsbury Rifles)
12th (County of London) Battalion (The Rangers)
15th (County of London) Battalion (Prince of Wales's Own Civil Service
    Rifles)
16th (County of London) Battalion (Queen's Westminster Rifles)

Territorial battalions of The Rifle Brigade

5th (City of London) Battalion (London Rifle Brigade)
8th (City of London) Battalion (Post Office Rifles)
10th (County of London) Battalion
17th (County of London) Battalion (Poplar & Stepney Rifles)
25th (County of London) (Cyclist) Battalion

Having explained the constituency of antecedent regiments, we would like to stress that this book is neither a Regimental history nor a history of conflict or campaigning in the 19th and 20th Centuries. While it seeks to place the heroism of each of our 59 VC recipients in a wider context, its focus is on the acts of gallantry which each performed. We also want the book to be a ready source of reference for those seeking biographical details about each VC recipient, although lack of space precludes the inclusion of all the information available. For those wishing to know more, there is a wealth of material available in the public domain, much of which has been accessed during preparation of this book. We have also included some new information gleaned from The Royal Green Jackets Museum Archives and elsewhere.

This book has been written with a wider readership in mind, and not just those in the Regiment. Chapter 1 is devoted to a description of the circumstances leading to the institution of the VC and the changes introduced thereafter, with the original Royal Warrant reproduced at Appendix B, a detailed description of the Cross at Appendix C and frequently asked questions answered at Appendix D. Hopefully, those with little or no knowledge will find the book as interesting to read as those who have made a study of the VC over many years.

Lastly, no Introduction would be complete without an expression of thanks to all those who have assisted in making publication of this book possible, especially Roy Trustram Eve, who has acted as our business manager and occasional critic. We would also like to thank all those who have helped us with our research, particularly Mrs Didy Grahame, Secretary of the Victoria Cross and George Cross Association; Lieutenant-Colonel Ian Hywel-Jones, co-ordinator of the Victoria Cross and George Cross Project; Miss Diana Condell, Senior Curator, Medals at the Imperial War Museum, London; George Caldwell, author; Rajesh Rampal in Delhi;

and the Museum staff, Ken Gray, Stewart Morris and Christine Pullen. We are, too, very grateful to the Imperial War Museum for permitting us to include a number of photographs from the Museum's photographic archive, and to Mary Rose de Lisle and Gerard de Lisle for allowing us to reproduce documents and a painting relating to Ensign E.A. Lisle Phillipps VC. We also thank Bob Thorn for drawing the maps; Andy Sollars for contributing at no cost the photographs of the medal groups that illustrate this book; Krys Bottrill for indexing the book; and Columns Design for their expert help and advice. Above all, we want to thank the Directors of RAB Capital plc, an asset management company quoted on the Alternative Investment Market, Tim Stephenson and Audrey Hanmer, descendants of General Sir Walter Congreve VC and Major Billy Congreve VC, and Henry Parker, great-great nephew of General Sir Redvers Buller VC, and his father, Peter Parker, for their very generous contributions towards underwriting the costs of publication of this book, thus enabling more of the sale proceeds to accrue to the Regimental Museum. We are also very grateful to others for their donations and for the grants received from The Royal Green Jackets Administrative Trustees, the 43rd and 52nd Club, the Celer et Audax Club (KRRC), the John Bodley Trust (RB), and the 4(V) RGJ Trustees.

Christopher Wallace
Chairman
RGJ Museum Trustees
Winchester, June 2006

Ron Cassidy
Curator
RGJ Museum (1989-98)

HRH Prince Albert, the Prince Consort, Colonel-in-Chief of The King's Royal Rifle Corps 1850–2 and Colonel-in-Chief of The Rifle Brigade 1852–61, who, together with Her Majesty Queen Victoria, played a leading role in the institution of the Victoria Cross

Chapter 1
The Evolution of the Victoria Cross[1]

Origins

On 19 December 1854 Captain G.T. Scobell,[2] Member of Parliament for Bath, stood up in the House of Commons to propose the motion: 'That an humble address be presented to Her Majesty [Queen Victoria] praying that she would be graciously pleased to institute an "Order of Merit" to be bestowed upon persons serving in the Army or Navy for distinguished and prominent gallantry during the present [Crimean] war and to which every grade and individual, from the highest to the lowest, in the United Services, may be admissible.'[3]

The idea was not new and is better attributed to the Duke of Newcastle, the Secretary of State for War, who probably first raised the matter with Prince Albert, Queen Victoria's husband, during a visit to Windsor Castle on 11/12 November 1854. Meanwhile, and prior to Captain Scobell's motion in the House, *The Times* and its war correspondent, William Howard Russell, were reporting not only the deficiencies of the British Army's command and logistics arrangements in the Crimea and the suffering of the troops, but also the inadequacies of the existing system of rewarding the gallantry of officers and soldiers in the front line. In a leader on 5 December 1854, *The Times* commented: 'After every battle appears a solemn document, according the meed of praise to those who distinguished themselves in it. … In the [London] Gazette we published on Monday, Lord Raglan named *all* the Generals of Division and Brigade, and *all* their staff. As a record of service, nothing could be less to the purpose. The battle of Inkerman [5 November 1854] was fought and won entirely by the battalion officers and soldiers. It is called in the camp "The Soldiers' Victory". In such a conflict we would think that the battalion officers and even the most prominent soldiers should be named – certainly not that they should be omitted, while officers on the staff, even not engaged, are duly enumerated …'[4]

At the start of the Crimean War in March 1854 there were three principal means of rewarding the actions of individuals in battle – by bestowing one of the gradations of the Order of the Bath,[5] promotion by brevet, or mention in the field despatch of the Commander-in-Chief. However, only officers of the rank of Major and above in the Army and Commander and above in the Navy, who had been mentioned in despatches, were eligible for the Order of the Bath, the number of appointments to which, being an Order, was limited by Statute. Furthermore, because commanders-in-chief were unwilling to discriminate between individuals, appointments tended to be seen as appendages of rank. Promotion by brevet was useful but subject to the criticism that virtually all those rewarded in this manner were not company officers in the line but held staff appointments. A mention in despatches was subject to both shortcomings; it was indiscriminate and almost entirely confined to staff officers. The arrangements also contrasted unfavourably with the awards available to those serving in the Armed Forces of other countries. In France, for example, all ranks performing acts of heroism were eligible to receive the Legion of Honour, while from 1837 Indian soldiers in the service of the Honourable East India Company were eligible to receive the Indian Order of Merit.[6]

On 4 December 1854 a step towards improving the situation occurred with the institution by Royal Warrant of the Distinguished Conduct Medal (DCM) for which non-commissioned ranks in the Army were eligible, to be followed nine months later by the introduction of the Conspicuous Gallantry Medal (CGM) for non-commissioned ranks in the Navy. Junior officers, however, remained ineligible for either the Order of the Bath or the DCM/CGM. The introduction of the DCM also did nothing to stem the growing clamour to institute a British equivalent to the Indian Order of Merit, as is evident from Captain Scobell's motion in the House only a fortnight after the DCM was instituted. Reassured that the Duke of Newcastle was already seized by the need, Scobell withdrew his motion. His intervention, though, did spur the Duke into action.

After spending much of Christmas and the New Year drafting some initial rules for a new award, the Duke of Newcastle wrote to Prince Albert on 20 January 1855 stating that it was his belief that: 'The value attached by soldiers to a little bit of ribbon is such as to render any danger insignificant and any privation light if it can be attained, and I believe that great indeed would be the stimulus and deeply prized the reward of a Cross of Military Merit.'[7] Two days later the Prince, illustrating his considerable interest in the subject, responded with a well-argued memorandum detailing his thoughts on the matter and, importantly, signalling his support for the introduction of 'a small cross of merit for *personal deeds of valour*'.[8] This was sufficient to embolden the Duke to announce in the House of Lords on 29 January 1855 that: 'Her Majesty has been advised to institute a Cross of Merit which will be open to all ranks in future. It is not intended … that this new Order shall in any way affect the present Order of the Bath, but that a separate and distinct Cross of Military Merit shall be given, … which, I hope, will be an object of ambition to every individual in the service, from the General who commands down to the privates in the ranks. My Lords, I cannot say that the rules for this new Cross are entirely matured, for the subject requires a great deal of consideration.'[9]

On the following day, 30 January 1855, the Duke of Newcastle's direct involvement in this matter was abruptly ended. Following a vote in the House of Commons to establish a Select Committee 'to enquire into the [terrible] condition of our army before Sevastopol, and into the conduct of those departments of the Government whose duty it has been to minister to the wants of the army',[10] Lord Aberdeen, the Prime Minister, resigned to be replaced by Lord Palmerston. Lord Panmure was appointed Secretary of State for War.

Lord Panmure quickly discovered that the Duke of Newcastle's comment to their Lordships on 29 January that 'I cannot say that the rules for this new Cross are entirely matured' was somewhat of an understatement, as it was not until late December 1855 that a draft Warrant was submitted to the Queen for her preliminary approval. On 28 December Prince Albert responded, stating that he had gone through the draft carefully together with the Queen, marking it in pencil with their comments. Their most fundamental observation was that acts of gallantry should be recognised by bestowal of a decoration and not by admission to an Order. The suggestion that the new award should be titled the 'Victoria Cross' was written in the margin. Various suggestions were also proposed for a motto with a note that: 'The Motto should *explain the decoration* and exclude the possibility of its object being misunderstood.' An idea of Prince Albert's that the Warrant should include provision for selection by election was added. In a note at the end of the draft, the Prince wrote:

> *A most important case has been left unnoticed, viz, where a body of men, say a Brigade, a Regiment, a Company, &c may have performed a deed of valour superior to any an individual could perform and influencing the fate of a field or even campaign: in such a case it would not do to refuse the Cross on account of there being too many brave men, and yet to give it to all of them would not answer the purpose of the institution. In such a case the deed might be rewarded by a certain number of Crosses being given to the whole body participating in it, leaving to a 'jury' of those engaged to select the proper representatives. I even hope that this will be the common case. For instance, the maintenance of the Sandbag Battery at Inkerman, the charge of Balaclava, the storming party of the Quarries, 7 Jun, &c. These are deeds more valuable than the throwing of a shell out of a Battery, or carrying a wounded Officer off the Field.*[11]

On 30 December 1855 Lord Panmure responded in true courtier-like fashion that: 'Her Majesty and Your Royal Highness have greatly improved this reward for military exploits by changing its character from an "order" to a "decoration". I will have the warrant redrafted with the alterations proposed ....'[12] In his book, *The Evolution of the Victoria Cross*, M.J. Crook offers the opinion that: 'It is from this point in time that it is justifiable to refer to the new award as the Victoria Cross and to lay the choice of name and style of the decoration to the credit of Prince Albert.'[13]

Thereafter progress was relatively swift with the final version of the Warrant instituting the Victoria Cross (VC) signed by The Queen at Buckingham Palace on 29 January 1856.

The Royal Warrant of 29 January 1856

The Royal Warrant, which was published in *The London Gazette* on 5 February 1856, is reproduced in full at Appendix B.[14] Of note, the preamble emphasised Queen Victoria's wish that the VC 'should be highly prized and eagerly sought after by the Officers and Men of Our Naval and Military Services'.

Clause 1 ordained that the 'Escroll' or motto to be inscribed on the Cross would be 'For Valour'. This resulted from comments made by the Queen on 5 January 1856 after seeing two design drawings of the proposed VC with the motto 'for the brave'. In her response she stated: 'The motto would be better "For Valour" than "for the brave", as this would lead to the inference that only those are deemed brave who have got the Cross.'[15]

Clause 2 stated that the medal ribbon would be red for the Army and blue for the Navy. Following the formation of the Royal Air Force on 1 April 1918, red was prescribed for all three Services, an order applied retrospectively and enshrined in an amending Warrant issued in 1920.

Clause 3 required a register to be kept of all awards. This became known as the VC Register, which remains in use today.

Clause 4 made provision for a Bar to be attached to the medal ribbon of individuals receiving a second VC award. Three Bars have been awarded since the VC was instituted.

Clause 5 ordained that only those who performed some signal act of valour or devotion 'in the presence of the enemy' would be eligible for an award.[16] However, on 10 August 1858 a Royal Warrant was issued permitting awards for instances of conspicuous courage and bravery under circumstances of extreme danger not before the enemy. This subsequently gave rise to six awards, including to Rifleman O'Hea (RB), before the provision was withdrawn in 1881.

Clause 6 stated that conspicuous bravery and not, for example, rank, length of service or wounds, would be the only justification for an award.

Clause 7 permitted an award to be conferred 'on the spot' when the act was performed in the sight of a senior commander.

Clause 8 permitted a senior commander to recommend an individual for an award when the act had not been witnessed by him but reported to him by a more junior commander and proved to his satisfaction.

Clauses 9, 10 and 11 covered the rules for notification, publication and investiture of awards. Queen Victoria, however, was soon to establish, at the first VC investiture on 26 June 1857, the subsequent practice of the ruling Monarch decorating individuals in person whenever possible and practicable.

Clause 12 applied only to the Navy.

Clause 13 covered the rules for election by ballot in the circumstances envisaged by Prince Albert in his response to Lord Panmure on 28 December 1855, with the number of awards dictated by the size of the unit involved. Among the first to benefit from this provision were five members of the 1st/60th, KRRC, as a result of the recapture of Delhi during the Indian Mutiny in 1857.

Clause 14 initiated a Special Pension of £10 per annum for non-commissioned ranks in receipt of an award, plus a further £5 when awarded a Bar. In 1890 this was changed to allow officers who were awarded a VC prior to commissioning to retain their pension. All officers did not become eligible for the Special Pension, now known as an Annuity, until 1 August 1959.[17] The annuity, which is subject to regular review, presently amounts to £1,495 tax-free (May 2006).

Clause 15 ordained that a VC recipient 'convicted of Treason, Cowardice, Felony or of any infamous Crime' would be liable to have his name erased from the VC Register and to forfeit his annuity. Initially Clause 15 was strictly applied, with relatively minor offences resulting in eight erasures, including Rifleman Bambrick (KRRC) and Rifleman Corbett (KRRC). On such occasions the War Office also sought return of the medal. However, King George V felt very strongly that a VC should never be forfeited, stating that 'even were a VC to be sentenced to be hanged for murder, he should be allowed to wear his VC on the scaffold'.[18] As a result, there has been no case of forfeiture since 1908, with the names of those who were erased from the Register, although never formally reinstated, restored to the roll of recipients.

There have been other changes to the rules governing the award of the VC since its inception. Some merit particular mention.

The latest Royal Warrant recoding the conditions of award of the VC, dated 30 September 1961, ordains that 'the Cross shall only be awarded for most conspicuous bravery, or some daring or pre-eminent act of valour or self-sacrifice or extreme devotion to duty in the presence of the enemy'. It further states that those making recommendations for an award 'shall call for such description, conclusive proof as far as the circumstances of the case will allow, and attestation of the act as he may think requisite, and if he approve he shall recommend the grant of the Decoration …'. Contrary to the belief of some, there is no statutory provision requiring acts to be witnessed by a minimum number of officers or attested by sworn statements. In other words, a degree of latitude exists concerning the extent to which the act is proven, although the threshold governing the burden of proof very sensibly remains high for such a pre-eminent award.

Although the original Royal Warrant of 29 January 1856 did not expressly exclude posthumous awards, Lord Panmure ruled against awarding VCs posthumously, stating that: 'It was an *order* for the living.'[19] Instead, in circumstances in which a potential recipient was killed, an arrangement was introduced permitting a Memorandum to be inserted in *The London Gazette* announcing that had the named person survived he would have been recommended for a VC. Six such entries were made between 1859 and 1897, including one for Ensign Lisle Phillipps (KRRC).[20] However, in 1902 King Edward VII assented to the award of posthumous VCs to six persons killed while performing acts of gallantry in the South African War. Subsequently, on 15 January 1907, he was persuaded, on grounds of fairness, to assent to posthumous awards to the six persons named in the Memoranda between 1859 and 1897. Thereafter, recommendations for posthumous awards were accepted.

Over the years, eligibility for the award of a VC has changed. In October 1857 it was extended to include members of the Honourable East India Company, but not native Indians, who had to wait until 1911 to become eligible. Members of the Colonial Forces in New Zealand and other parts of the Empire were included in 1867. Servicewomen have always been eligible, although no awards to women have yet been made.

The Cross

While Prince Albert dominated in helping to shape the terms of the original Royal Warrant, Queen Victoria led on matters to do with the design of the Cross, with Messrs Hancock of Bruton Street, London, a firm of gold and silversmiths founded in 1849, responsible for production.[21]

The Queen expressly wished the design of the VC to be simple and unpretentious. It was not only as a result of her suggestion that the motto 'For Valour' was adopted, but other details as well. Commenting on a specimen proof submitted to her in early February 1856, she stated: 'The Cross looks very well in form, but the metal is ugly; it is copper and not bronze and will look very heavy on a red coat with the Crimson Ribbon. Bronze is, properly speaking, gun-metal; this has a rich colour and is very hard; copper would wear very ill and would soon look like an old penny.'[22]

After the submission of further proofs, the Queen finally gave her approval to the design of the VC on 3 March 1856. On the following day the War Office placed an order with Messrs Hancock for the manufacture of 106 VCs. Quoting M.J. Crook again:'It was, no doubt, the receipt of this mass order which forced Mr Hancock to adopt the process of casting in manufacturing the VC, the metal employed being so tough that it broke the dies when striking was attempted.'[23]

The Victoria Cross (obverse) – actual size

A further year was to pass before *The London Illustrated News*, on 7 March 1857, first published a picture of a VC, with the first Crosses not worn in public until the inaugural investiture by Queen Victoria on 26 June 1857. (See Appendix C for additional information about the design and manufacture of VCs.)

Selection

Royal Assent to the Warrant instituting the VC and its subsequent publication in early February 1856 immediately prompted the War Office and the Admiralty to seek clarification on a number of points. In particular, the Warrant did not specify the start date for the award, a matter resolved by Lord Panmure on 20 February 1856 when he ruled 'that it is not intended that services rendered previous to the commencement of the present [Crimean] war shall be considered as coming within the limits of the new decoration'.[24] Shortly afterwards the first moves in the quest for candidates for the award were initiated, but the response was slow.

On 30 March 1856 the Treaty of Paris formally bringing the Crimean War to a close was signed. As more and more British troops returned to England sporting Crimean War Medals,[25] so impatience to hasten the award of VCs increased. On 27 June 1856 Captain Scobell asked in the Commons 'whether arrangements for the distribution of the "Victoria Order of Valour" were completed, or nearly so, and whether it would be brought into operation at an early period'.[26] On 21 July the Queen wrote to Panmure: 'Now that the Queen's Crimean Army has almost entirely arrived in this country, the Queen wishes to remind Lord Panmure of the "Victoria Cross"; these distinctions always have the most effect when they are given without delay, ...'[27] Panmure, however, elected to await the return of Sir William Codrington, the British Commander-in-Chief in the Crimea, before, on 5 September, writing to The Duke of Cambridge, the Commander-in-Chief at Horse Guards, urging him to hasten the collection of the names of those recommended for the VC. Horse Guards, in turn, sought nominations from commanding officers, with submissions required on special forms issued for the purpose.

Although most, if not all, commanding officers would have been aware since the Duke of Newcastle's announcement in the House of Lords on 29 January 1855 of the intention to introduce the VC, and some may have been keeping lists, it took time to gather the required names. A Board of senior officers then met in December to screen the nominations and to make recommendations to the Commander-in-Chief, who forwarded them to Lord Panmure on 2 February 1857. He, in turn, forwarded them to the Queen on 15 February stating that: 'The list for the Army is incomplete, but as it will take some time to receive the names from the regiments abroad, both HRH The Duke of Cambridge and Lord Panmure think that it is better at once to proceed with this first list.'[28]

First List of VC Recipients, 24 February 1857

The list of candidates was heavily pruned during the screenings that took place before submission to the Queen; for example, only two out of an initial 32 nominations from the 55th (Westmorland) Regiment were gazetted, two out of 32 from the 57th (West Middlesex) Regiment and two out of 38 from the 77th (East Middlesex) Regiment. Meanwhile, the absence of nominations from some regiments suggested that their commanding officers either had not appreciated the significance of the award or were too idle to fill in the forms.

When the final list was put before The Queen, her interest in the citations was evident from her comment that reference to 'a panic' occurring in the ranks during one particular gallant action should be removed. The Monarch's interest was similarly demonstrated in 1918 when King George V took exception to a citation describing Germans as 'Huns'.

Of the 86 names put before the Queen, she approved all except one, as she considered the individual's act of gallantry to have been of questionable morality. The remaining 85 names, 27 Navy and 58 Army, including eight from The Rifle Brigade, were published in a *Supplement to The London Gazette* on 24 February 1857. All were Crimean War veterans.

First VC Investiture, 26 June 1857

Out of a total of 111 officers and non-commissioned ranks awarded VCs for acts of gallantry during the Crimean War, Queen Victoria decorated sixty-two, 14 Navy and 48 Army, including all eight from The Rifle Brigade, at the inaugural investiture held in Hyde Park on 26 June 1857.

By all accounts it was a grand affair, with 9,000 troops present, including the 2nd Battalion, The Rifle Brigade, and its band. The Battalion travelled from Aldershot very early in the morning to be there and in the evening proceeded to Liverpool, where the men embarked the following day for Dublin. Lieutenant Knox VC (RB), who lost an arm in the Crimea, was the Parade Adjutant.

At 7 a.m. a crowd of about 100,000 people started to gather. At 9 a.m. the troops formed up on the parade ground with the 62 VC recipients in line in front of them. Max Arthur in his book, *Symbol of Courage*, best describes what followed:

> *With the military dignitaries assembled, at 9.55 a.m. a flash from the field batteries and a heavy boom announced the approach of the Queen's cortege through the Hyde Park Corner gate. Queen Victoria rode between Prince Albert and her future son-in-law, Prince Frederick William of Prussia. With precision timing, as the royal party approached, the whole assembled force presented arms as the Queen inspected her troops.*
>
> *The sixty-two newly made Victoria Crosses were laid out on a scarlet-covered table, in front of the Queen, who, unexpectedly, decided to remain on horseback throughout the investiture. As each name was called, the man stepped forward, the army recipients saluting and the naval men removing their hats. Lord Panmure passed the medals to the Queen as she pinned them on to the specially provided loop of cord which each man wore to make the fixing easier. In ten minutes it was done.*[29]

The eight VC recipients from The Rifle Brigade were the last to be decorated. The troops then marched past in slow and quick time before the Queen and her cortége returned to Buckingham Palace. The Queen later wrote in her diary:

The first VC investiture, Hyde Park, 26 June 1857. Painting by George Houseman Thomas.

The Royal Collection © 2006, Her Majesty Queen Elizabeth II

A thick heavy morning. - Full of agitation for the coming great event of the day, viz: the distribution of the 'Victoria Cross'. - Breakfast early, and ½ p.9 we went down and mounted our horses, I, in my full uniform, riding 'Sunset'. The whole was conducted in full state. Several interesting circumstances combined to make this day, an important one. It was, in the 1st place, the solemn inauguration of the new and honourable order of valour, - also the day of Albert's new title [Prince Consort] *becoming known and the 1st time I had ever ridden on horse-back, at a great Review in London, ... It was a beautiful sight, & everything admirably arranged. ... The heat [was] very great, but I felt it less than I had expected. ... It was indeed a most proud, gratifying day.*[30]

By the time of the investiture over two and a half years had elapsed since the idea of 'an order of valour' was first proposed; indeed, without the personal interest and involvement of Queen Victoria and Prince Albert the VC might never have been introduced. However, it was soon to become a much coveted and cherished award and a visible sign that the recipient had performed an act or acts of individual heroism that frequently captured the public's imagination. There can be no doubt, too, that the institution of the VC filled a void and that its introduction served, and continues to serve, its purpose admirably.

The deeds of the eight members of The Rifle Brigade who received their VCs at the hands of The Queen in Hyde Park on 26 June 1857 are described in the next chapter.

The George Cross

On 24 September 1940 King George VI authorised the institution of the GC 'for acts of the greatest heroism or of the most conspicuous courage in circumstances of extreme danger'. He was moved to do so by his wish to recognise individual acts of outstanding bravery by the civilian population during

the Blitz – Nazi Germany's bombing of British cities in 1940. Since these acts were not performed 'in the presence of the enemy', they were ineligible for the award of a VC.

Prior to the inception of the GC several gallantry awards existed for civilians and service personnel who performed acts of great heroism in circumstances other than battle, including the Empire Gallantry Medal instituted in 1922, the Albert Medal for saving life on land and sea (1866), and the Edward Medal: Mines and Industry for saving life in mines and quarries (1907), but none matched the prestige and distinction of the VC.

The GC is the civilian equivalent of the VC, and second only to the VC in the Order of Precedence of Orders, Decorations and Medals conferred by the Crown. It is only awarded for deliberate acts of exceptional heroism in circumstances where the danger of death is

The George Cross (obverse)

considerable and when the individual concerned is aware of the threat to his or her own life. It may be awarded posthumously. It may also be awarded more than once, in which case a Bar is added to the ribbon. Service personnel are eligible to receive the GC in circumstances when the award of a VC would be inappropriate.

The medal, which is suspended from a dark blue ribbon, consists of a plain silver cross with the Royal cipher 'GVI' in the angle of each limb. In the centre is a medallion showing St George and the Dragon, surrounded by a circular band inscribed *For Gallantry*. The reverse is plain and bears the name of the recipient and the date of the award.

Since its institution and as at 1 May 2006, 157 GCs have been awarded, just over two-thirds to Service personnel and just over half posthumously. The total includes two 'collective' GCs, one to the Island Fortress of Malta in 1942 and the second to the Royal Ulster Constabulary in 1999. There have been no Bars. Four GCs have been awarded to women. Two brothers from the same family (Booker) have received GCs, and one brother from the same family (Seagrim) has been awarded a VC and another the GC.

In 1940 all living holders of the Empire Gallantry Medal were instructed to exchange their award for the GC. In 1971 living holders of the Albert Medal and Edward Medal were invited to do the same. A total of 245 exchanges took place, including the exchange of an Albert Medal by Lance-Corporal Sidney Williams of the 1st/6th (City of London) Battalion, The London Regiment (City of London Rifles), a Territorial battalion of The King's Royal Rifle Corps. Lance-Corporal Williams received his Albert Medal for saving the life of a colleague by entering and rescuing him from a burning gunpowder store in France on 4 January 1918 (*London Gazette*, 30 August 1918). He is the only member of an antecedent regiment of The Royal Green Jackets to have received a GC, albeit through exchange.

Chapter 2
The Crimean War: 1854–6

Origins

For at least 200 years prior to the Crimean War, Russia sought to expand its empire southwards and gain access to the Mediterranean. In 1783 Catherine the Great annexed the Crimea including the Black Sea port of Sebastopol (Sevastopol). Turkey, however, with its capital at Constantinople, continued to control passage through the Bosphorous and Dardanelles straits. By 1852 Turkey, dubbed 'the sick man of Europe', seemed ripe for invasion. In July 1853, Russia took advantage of a dispute over the custody of holy places in Jerusalem to occupy Moldavia and Wallachia, two provinces in modern Romania, which were then under Turkish suzerainty. After Russia ignored ultimatums to withdraw, Turkey declared war on Russia on 23 October 1853. Just over a month later, on 30 November, a strong Russian flotilla surprised and destroyed a weak Turkish squadron in Sinope harbour.

Throughout 1853 Britain and France became increasingly concerned about Turkey's survival and the threat to trade, including with India, which the presence of Russian vessels in the Eastern Mediterranean would pose. Warships were ordered to the Dardanelles and, on 3 January 1854, British and French fleets entered the Black Sea. Concurrently, preparations were initiated for the despatch of troops should further diplomatic efforts fail to avert conflict. On 22 February the first members of a British Expeditionary Force (BEF) to be commanded by Lord Raglan left England for Malta. Still Russia refused to withdraw from Moldavia and Wallachia. On 28 March 1854 Britain declared war on Russia, France having done so the day before. Britain, France and Turkey then signed treaties of alliance committing each to act in concert with the other against Russia, but with their forces remaining under independent, national command.

After staging at Malta, the BEF proceeded to Gallipoli, where, by the end of May, 18,000 British and 22,000 French troops had arrived. In June the force was transported to Varna to bolster the Turkish presence in Bulgaria. In July the Russians withdrew from Moldavia and Wallachia, but by then the die was cast. On 16 July Lord Raglan received a despatch from the Duke of Newcastle, the Secretary of State for War in London, dated 29 June, directing him to capture Sebastopol and to take or destroy the Russian fleet. This caused some consternation among British commanders as no invasion plan existed, logistic shortcomings abounded, cholera was prevalent (affecting 8% of the force by early August), and there was little time to achieve success before the onset of winter. Nevertheless, and contrary to his better judgement, Lord Raglan felt bound to comply.

On 24 August the BEF, consisting of five infantry divisions and one cavalry division, began embarkation at Varna and, on 2 September, set sail for the Crimea. On 13 September the Turks surrendered Eupatoria. On 14 September, some 63,000 French, British and Turkish troops (26,000 British) started to disembark in Calamita (Kalamita) Bay at a spot 30 miles north of Sebastopol. On 19 September, after four days of unloading, the Allies began advancing south towards Sebastopol. However: 'The plan for a swift coup de main went badly wrong, and the invaders were condemned to besieging their quarry from exposed upland to the south during biting winter conditions, as the ranks of men and horses were decimated. A long campaign under such privation not having been anticipated, the supply, transport and medical arrangements woefully broke down. Before peace settled over the hills, valleys and shattered remains of Sevastopol [in March 1856], approximately 22,000 British, a minimum 80,000 French, possibly 10,000 Turks, 2,000 Sardinians and more than 100,000 Russians had perished.'[1]

Regimental Involvement

Among the troops in the Crimea were the 1st and 2nd Battalion, The Rifle Brigade (1 and 2 RB).

2 RB had been in England since returning from Canada in June 1852. The Battalion was one of the first to be warned for service in the Crimea, embarking at Portsmouth on 24 February 1854 and remaining with the BEF until landing in Calamita Bay with The Light Division under Lieutenant-General Sir George Brown on 14 September.

1 RB, having returned to England from South Africa in January 1854, left for the Crimea on 14 July, reinforced by 100 men from the 60th, KRRC. Sailing via Malta and Constantinople, the Battalion reached Varna on 6 September. Departing soon afterwards, 1 RB landed in Calamita Bay with the 4th Division under command of Major-General Sir George Cathcart on the same day as 2 RB.

Each battalion, on departure from England, numbered nearly 1,000 officers and men, organised in eight Service companies and equipped with the new Minié rifle. During the campaign the establishment of each battalion was increased, first, to twelve companies and, then, to sixteen, and the Minié rifle exchanged for the long Enfield.

No other battalions from the antecedent regiments of The Royal Green Jackets took part in the Crimean War.

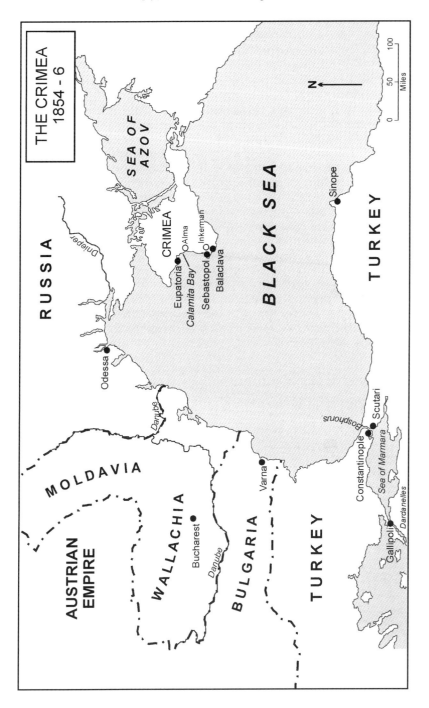

The Crimean War: 1854-6

THE CRIMEA
1854 - 6

RUSSIA

SEA OF AZOV

CRIMEA

Eupatoria
Calamita Bay
Alma
Inkerman
Sebastopol
Balaclava

Sinope

BLACK SEA

TURKEY

Odessa

Dnieper

N

100
50
0
Miles

Danube

MOLDAVIA

WALLACHIA

Bucharest

Danube

BULGARIA

Varna

AUSTRIAN
EMPIRE

TURKEY

Bosphorus
Constantinople
Scutari

Sea of Marmara

Dardanelles

Gallipoli

Main Events

Battle of the Alma, 20 September 1854

The River Alma was the second of four rivers to be crossed on the Allied advance from Calamita Bay to Sebastopol and an obvious feature on which to base a defensive line as the river and the ground on the north (allied) side were dominated by high ground on the south (Turkish) side. On 20 September, as the British advanced some three miles inland from the Black Sea, the Turks could be seen occupying a number of fortified redoubts on the far side of the river. As the British neared the river, they were increasingly subject to heavy artillery fire. 2 RB, skirmishing ahead of The Light Division in two wings, under command of Lieutenant-Colonel A.J. Lawrence and Major W.S.R. Norcott, hastened to ford the river and, in company with the 19th (1st Yorkshire) Regiment, assaulted uphill, successfully driving the Russians from one of their main positions, known as the Great Redoubt. As they did so, Colonel Lawrence, Major Norcott and Lieutenant Ross (Adjutant) had their horses shot from under them. However, no sooner had success been achieved when a staff officer, mistakenly fearing a Russian counter-attack, ordered withdrawal, an error requiring a further attack on the Great Redoubt later in the day by the Highland and Guards Brigades. During the battle 2 RB suffered 11 killed and 39 wounded.

Lord Raglan in his despatch praised the conduct of 2 RB, stating that the capture of the Great Redoubt was 'materially aided by the advance of four

2 RB fording the River Alma at the head of The Light Division prior to the Battle of the Alma on 20 September 1854. Painting by Louis Johns.

companies of the Rifle Brigade under Major Norcott'. Sir George Brown later recommended Norcott for the VC without success, declaring that 'Major Norcott's conduct on that occasion was not only conspicuous for the whole Division, but attracted the notice of the enemy; for the Officer in command of the [nearby] Russian battery, who was subsequently made prisoner, informed Lord Raglan, that he had laid a gun specially for "the daring officer in the dark green uniform on the black horse".'[2]

While 2 RB was in action at the forefront of the battle, the 4th Division, including 1 RB, remained in reserve.

Siege of Sebastopol Begins, 27 September 1854

After the Battle of the Alma, the Allies continued their advance on Sebastopol and, on 27 September 1854, started to occupy the high ground to the south of the town and besiege it. Before they were able to do so, the Russians split their forces, retaining 30,000 troops on garrison duties and deploying a field army with a further 30,000 troops in the hinterland to the east of Sebastopol to threaten the Allied flanks and lines of communication. There was also a civilian population of 38,000 within Sebastopol. The British, meanwhile, chose to use Balaclava, some eight miles south of Sebastopol, as their supply port.

Believing that an assault on Sebastopol without preliminary bombardment was out of the question, the Allies entrenched while the guns were emplaced. It was during this period, on 12 October 1854, that Rifleman Wheatley of 1 RB carried out the action, which later resulted in the award of a VC.

Rifleman F. Wheatley VC

(Later Rifleman F. Wheatley VC DCM)

Rifleman Francis Wheatley was born in July 1821 in Ruddington, Nottinghamshire. He enlisted in 1 RB on 5 November 1839 and had already served with the Battalion in 1846-7 and 1852-3 during the South African (Kaffir) wars. He arrived with 1 RB in the Crimea on 14 September 1854 and, on the day before the action which gave rise to his VC, was commended, and later received a DCM, for gallant conduct in the trenches outside the Redan at Sebastopol – a strongly fortified triangular earthwork occupied by the Russians.

The citation for Wheatley's VC, published in a *Supplement to The London Gazette* on 24 February 1857, is extremely brief, stating: 'For throwing a live shell over the parapet of the trenches.' The Regimental History provides a little, but not a lot, more detail.

On the 12th [October] *Private Francis Wheatley of the 1st Battalion, being on duty in the trenches when a live shell fell among the party, having unsuccessfully endeavoured to knock out the fuse with the butt of his rifle, took up the shell with great deliberation and flung it over the parapet. It had scarcely fallen outside when it exploded. For this act of valour he afterwards received the Victoria Cross and the cross of the Legion of Honour.*[3]

Bearing in mind Prince Albert's rather disparaging comments in December 1855 about awarding a VC for 'throwing a shell out of a Battery' (see page 3), it is perhaps surprising that Rifleman Wheatley's action survived the screening process that led ultimately to his award. So be it. He survived the War and was discharged from the Army in April 1861. He then entered the service of the author of the Regimental History, Sir William Cope, Bt., becoming the lodge-keeper at Sir William's home at Bramshill Park in Hampshire. He died four years later in Westminster Hospital on 21 May 1865, aged 43.

Battle of Balaclava, 25 October 1854

Rifleman Wheatley's action preceded both the Battle of Balaclava and Inkerman, which were soon to follow. From the middle of October the Riflemen of 1 and 2 RB 'were nightly thrown out in advance of the intrenchments; whatever regiments found the duties, they formed a line of double sentries, to watch and report any suspicious movements in the place'.[4]

On 17 October the Allies began what was to become known as the First Bombardment of Sebastopol, which was to last for a week but to no great effect, with the Russians responding in kind. Meanwhile, Lord Raglan was becoming increasingly concerned about the threat posed by the Russian field army to the British lines of communication and the port at Balaclava. On 25 October the Russians advanced and battle was joined, culminating at 11 a.m. in Lord Cardigan's celebrated but disastrous Charge of the Light Brigade. The Russians, however, were prevented from seizing Balaclava and in December, as winter set in, they withdrew from the positions they had occupied.

During the later stages of the battle, 1 RB was deployed to prevent a Russian break-through of the British positions, but was not greatly involved. 2 RB was not involved at all.

Battle of Inkerman,[5] 5 November 1854

On 5 November the Russians launched a major assault to dislodge the British from their positions on the high but broken ground immediately to the east of Sebastopol. Over 57,000 Russians from within the garrison of Sebastopol and from their field army were committed to the attack, which initially fell upon the British 2nd Division. Both 1 RB with the 4th Division and three companies of 2 RB with The Light Division quickly deployed to support the 2nd Division.

Two companies of 2 RB under Captain F.R. Elrington were soon engaged in stopping a column of Russians infiltrating the British positions through a ravine. Quoting from the Regimental History: 'Captain Elrington, with two companies of the 2nd Battalion, at once attacked them, and drove them down at the point of the bayonet; they retreated by the bottom of the ravine, and did not again make their appearance in that part of the fight. ... These companies under Elrington lost 5 men killed and 10 wounded in this gallant affair.'[6] Captain Elrington was later recommended for the VC, but Sir George Brown refused to forward the recommendation on the grounds that the 2nd Battalion had not been engaged in the Battle of Inkerman!

Meanwhile, 1 RB became involved in the main battle and remained so throughout the day in a series of hard-fought close-quarter encounters which resulted in the Battalion suffering 28 killed and 33 wounded, of whom a number later died. The Divisional Commander, Sir George Cathcart, was also killed.

Although no members of 1 or 2 RB were awarded a VC at Inkerman, one was awarded to Lieutenant Clifford.

Lieutenant the Hon. H.H. Clifford VC

(Later Major-General Sir Henry Clifford VC KCMG CB)

Lieutenant Henry Clifford was born at Irnham Hall, Lincolnshire, on 12 September 1826, the third son of the 7th Baron (Lord) Clifford of Chudleigh, and educated at Stonyhurst College. After purchasing his commission, he served with 1 RB in 1846-7 and 1852-3 during the South African (Kaffir) wars. On return to England, the Commanding Officer of 1 RB, Colonel Buller, became a brigade commander in The Light Division and Lieutenant Clifford was appointed his ADC. He was present at the Alma and at Balaclava before taking part at the Battle of Inkerman.

Clifford's VC citation, published in the same *Supplement to The London Gazette* of 24 February 1857 as Rifleman Wheatley's, is almost as brief, stating: 'For conspicuous courage at the Battle of Inkerman [5 November 1854], in leading a charge and killing one of the enemy with his sword, disabling another, and saving the life of a soldier.'

Clifford himself provided a fuller account of the action in a letter written on the following day to 'Dear Relations and Friends'.

Yesterday morning at daybreak, fire of Musketry was heard to our extreme right; we turned out 18 Officers and 656 Sergeants, Drummers, Rank and file of the 88th and 77th Regt, all we had at our Brigade in Camp (the remainder being in the Trenches), and under the command of Sir G. Brown and General Buller marched off in the direction of the firing, which became more and more serious, cannon opening and shell bursting in the lines of the Division which is about a quarter of a mile on our right.

Brevet Major the Hon. H.H. Clifford VC on horseback near Sebastopol, 1856

A watercolour by Major the Hon. H.H. Clifford VC entitled 'The Advanced Trench'

On reaching the ground of the 2nd Division it was evident from the roll of musketry the enemy was in great force and had driven back our Picquets. Most unfortunately the weather was very foggy, and we could only be guided by the sound of the firing. When about 50 yards from the crest of the hill in our front, over which the attack was being made, we formed into line, the 88th Regiment on the right and the 77th Regiment on the left; we brought our right up so that our left might rest on a large and deep ravine. We moved quickly on in the direction of the shots, which from the way they whistled past, and the great report made by the discharge, I was sure must be very close.

On reaching the left brow of the hill, I saw the enemy in great numbers in our front, about 15 yards from us; it was a moment or two before I could make General Buller believe that they were Russians. 'In God's name,' I said, 'fix bayonets and charge.' He gave the order and in another moment we were hand to hand with them. Our line was not long enough to prevent the Russians outflanking our left, which was unperceived by the 77th, who rushed on, with the exception of about a dozen, who, struck by the force on our left and who saw me taking out my revolver, halted with me.

'Come on,' I said, 'my lads!' and the brave fellows dashed in amongst the astonished Russians, bayoneting them in every direction. One of the bullets in my revolver had partly come out and prevented it revolving and I could not get it off. The Russians fired their pieces within a few yards of my head, but none touched me. I drew my sword and cut off one man's arm who was in the act of bayoneting me and a second seeing it, turned round and was in the act of running out of my way, when I hit him over the back of the neck and laid him dead at my feet. About 15 of them threw down their arms and gave themselves up and the remainder ran back and fell into the hands of the 77th returning from the splendid charge they had made and were killed or taken prisoners.

Out of the small party with me (12), 6 men were killed and 3 wounded, so my escape was wonderful.[7]

The way in which Clifford conducted himself caught the eye of General Brown, who was later to write of Clifford, that he was 'universally admitted to be one of the most gallant and most promising young officers in the Army'.[8] After promotion to Captain on 29 December 1854, he became Deputy Assistant Quarter Master General of The Light Division, continuing to serve in the Crimea until the end of the War, by which time he had been appointed Brevet Major. In addition to the VC, he was awarded the French Legion of Honour and the Order of Medjidie – the Turkish equivalent to the Legion of Honour.

After the Crimean War Clifford served in China (1857-8) as Assistant Adjutant General during the Second China War, returning to England with the rank of Brevet Lieutenant-Colonel. Further staff appointments followed, with the award of a CB on 2 June 1869 and promotion to Major-General in 1877. During the South African (Zulu) War of 1879 he commanded the lines of communication. He was mentioned in despatches and awarded a KCMG on 19 December 1879. In 1882 he was appointed to command Eastern District at Colchester, but was diagnosed with cancer and obliged to retire. He died at the family home, Ugbrooke Park, Chudleigh, in Devon, aged 56, on 12 April 1883.

Apart from his VC, Clifford is especially remembered for the excellence of the watercolours he painted during his time in the Crimea (see pages 20 and 25). In 1907 his cousin, Ensign E.A. Lisle Phillipps, was awarded a retrospective posthumous VC for his gallantry with the 1st/60th, KRRC, at Delhi in 1857.

Siege of Sebastopol Continues, November 1854

Meanwhile, conditions around Sebastopol were rapidly worsening.

For some days after the battle of Inkerman the Riflemen were engaged in burying the dead. Their other duties also were very severe. … Even when other regiments were in the trenches they furnished a party a hundred yards in front; and wherever there was an alarm or a position to be stormed the green-jackets were in request. During this time and while the duties were so constant, the men suffered much also from scarcity of rations. And even those issued were such that the men could scarcely use. Until the end of December the coffee was served out green; there were no vegetables for a considerable time; the biscuit when the weather was wet, was mouldy; and fuel was scarcely to be procured. Even such supplies as were in Balaklava were but scantily brought up owing to want of transport.[9]

Such conditions, however, did not bring an end to the fighting. On 20 November two more members of 1 RB took part in an action resulting in both being awarded a VC.

Lieutenant C.T. Bourchier VC
(Later Colonel C.T. Bourchier VC)

Lieutenant W.J.M. Cuninghame VC
(Later Colonel Sir William Cuninghame, Bt., VC)

Lieutenant Claude Bourchier was born in Devon on 22 April 1831 and was commissioned in The Rifle Brigade on 10 April 1849. He served with 1 RB in 1852–3 during the South African (Kaffir) War. Lieutenant William Cuninghame[10] was born in Ayr, Scotland, on 20 May 1834 and, after attending Harrow School, was commissioned in The Rifle Brigade on 11 March 1853. Both officers accompanied 1 RB to the Crimea and were present at the battles at the Alma, Balaclava and Inkerman. The citation for each in the *Supplement to The London Gazette* of 24 February 1857 is worded exactly the same: 'Highly distinguished at the capture of the Rifle Pits, 20th November, 1854. His gallant conduct was recorded in the French General Orders.'

The Regimental History provides a full account of the action on 20 November.

The Russian riflemen [defending Sebastopol] *having established themselves in front of the left attack along some rising ground, annoyed our working parties as well as those of the French on the opposite side of the ravine by their fire. Lord Raglan determined to drive them back and to take possession of the pits. These pits, caverns, or 'ovens', as they were called by the men, are formed by the decay of softer portions of the rock between the harder strata, leaving caves in the sides of the hill. The duty of driving the Russians from them was confided to the 1st Battalion; and on November 20 a party consisting of Lieutenant Henry Tryon, in command, with Lieutenants Bourchier and Cuningbame, 4 sergeants and 200 rank and file, was detailed to carry it into execution. It was kept a secret what the service was to be till the party fell in about four o'clock in the afternoon. Then Tryon wheeled them round him and told the men what they were wanted for. He said that he intended to drive the Russians out, and that he was sure that they could do it. And right well they did it. Marching down to the trenches they lay down till dark. They then advanced stealthily, creeping along the broken ground which led first down a slight incline, and then up towards the enemy, who were completely surprised by the attack. Fifty men under Tryon formed the storming column; 50 the supports under Bourchier and 100 the reserve under Cuningbame. Eventually these parties became practically one. They quickly drove the Russian riflemen from their cover, though supported by a heavy column of Russian infantry. The occupants of the pits were evidently surprised. But soon the guns bearing on the pits poured grape and canister on the Riflemen, who had no cover, for the pits were open on the enemy's side. In the moment of taking possession of the pits the gallant Tryon fell shot in the head; Bourchier, who succeeded to the command of the party, maintained his advantage; and Cuningbame greatly distinguished himself by the energy with which he repulsed an attempt to turn the left flank of the advanced party, and thereby ensured the success of the capture. Repeatedly during that long night did the Russians attempt to retake the pits; sometimes by sending forward strong columns, sometimes by creeping up a few at a time, and when they got near making signals for their companions to come on. But this handful of Riflemen, under the command of these two young officers, bravely withstood them, and held the position until relieved next day by another party of the Battalion. In this affair Lieutenant Tryon and 9 men were killed, and 17 men were wounded.*[11]

It does not take much imagination to speculate that, if Lieutenant Tryon had survived, he, too, would assuredly have been awarded a VC. Unfortunately, the Memorandum procedure, which secured a posthumous VC for Ensign E.A. Lisle Phillipps (see pages 48-9), was not followed and the opportunity missed.

In addition to the VC, both Bourchier and Cuninghame were awarded the Turkish Order of Medjidie. Bourchier also received the French Legion of Honour. A third officer, Lieutenant Lennox of the Royal Engineers, received a VC for the same action.

Following his gallantry, Bourchier was promoted to Captain on 29 December 1854 and to the rank of Major in 1855. He later served in India, including at Lucknow during the Indian Mutiny, and on the North-West Frontier in 1863. He retired as a Colonel on full pay in 1869, becoming an ADC to Queen Victoria. He died at Hove on 11 November 1877, aged 46, from 'softening of the brain'.

Cuninghame, meanwhile, was promoted to Captain in 1856, later transferring to the 21st (Royal Scots Fusiliers) Regiment. In 1870 he succeeded his father as ninth Baronet, and from February 1874 to April 1880 was the Member of Parliament for the Borough of Ayr. He died near Lowestoft, aged 63, on 11 November 1897.

Siege of Sebastopol Continues, Winter 1854/5

The actions of Lieutenant Bourchier and Cuninghame took place at the beginning of a terrible winter for the troops in the Crimea. By the end of November 1 and 2 RB were suffering greatly from cholera and dysentery. After leaving England nearly 1,000 strong, and despite a draft of 154 men, 1 RB could only muster 275 all ranks fit for duty. Additionally, as is evident from one of Lieutenant Clifford's watercolours reproduced opposite:

> *The clothing which the Riflemen brought out from England being worn or torn by hard service, they presented a strange appearance. The greatcoat was always worn, and the blanket, with a hole cut through for the head, was put on under it. Over their shoulders they wore Cathcart's oilskins[12]; and sand-bags, pieces of knapsacks, anything that would bend, were wrapped round the legs by way of gaiters. Some had loose Russian boots, which were worn over the trousers; for the cold was intense and food and fuel scanty, and everything that could give warmth, for comfort it could not be called, was pressed into service. ... Some articles of warm clothing were indeed supplied; such as jerseys, drawers, blankets, socks and mitts; but these were not in sufficient quantities.*[13]

A watercolour by Major the Hon. H.H. Clifford VC entitled 'Rifleman'

During the winter the Riflemen spent seven hours out of every twenty-four in the trenches, spending the remaining time in tented lines to the rear. In January, amidst driving snow, the first steps were taken to build makeshift wooden huts in place of the tents. By mid-March the weather was improving. The tempo of operational activity, much reduced during the winter, increased.

On 22 April 1855 three Riflemen in 2 RB – Bradshaw, Humpston and McGregor – took part in an action in an area forward of the Redan known as the Quarries, not far from Rifleman Wheatley's action six months previously (see page 17), which resulted in all three being awarded a VC.

Rifleman J. Bradshaw VC
(Later Corporal J. Bradshaw VC)

Rifleman R. Humpston VC

Rifleman R. McGregor VC

Background information about Rifleman Joseph Bradshaw, Robert Humpston and Roderick McGregor is sketchy. Bradshaw was an Irishman, born in County Limerick in September 1835, enlisting in 1853. Humpston was an Englishman, born in Derby in 1832. His enlistment date is not known. McGregor was a Scot, born near Inverness in 1822. He enlisted in The Rifle Brigade on 23 June 1842 and between June 1847 and May 1851 was sentenced six times to periods of detention varying from five to seven weeks.

The first part of the VC citation for Rifleman Bradshaw and Rifleman Humpston in the *Supplement to The London Gazette* of 24 February 1857 is worded exactly the same: 'A Russian Rifle Pit, situated among the rocks overhanging the Woronzoff Road, between the 3rd parallel, Right Attack, and the Quarries (at that period in possession of the enemy), was occupied every night by the Russians, and their Riflemen commanded a portion of the Left Attack, and impeded the work in a new battery then being erected on the extreme right front of the 2nd parallel, Left Attack.'

Rifleman Bradshaw's citation then states: 'It [the Russian Rifle Pit] was carried in daylight on the 22nd of April, 1855, by two Riflemen, one of whom was Private Bradshaw; he has since received the French War Medal. The Rifle Pit was subsequently destroyed on further support being obtained.' In Rifleman Humpston's citation, his name is substituted for Bradshaw's with the statement 'he received a gratuity of 5*l*. [pounds], and was promoted', without reference to the French War Medal, which he did not receive. There no other record of his promotion, which it must be presumed he did receive.

Rifleman McGregor's VC citation, also published in the *Supplement to The London Gazette* of 24 February 1857, is totally different and refers to another date. It reads: 'For courageous conduct when employed as a sharpshooter in the advanced trenches in the month of July, 1855; a Rifle Pit was occupied by two Russians, who annoyed our troops by their fire. Private McGregor crossed the open space under fire, and taking cover under a rock, dislodged them, and occupied the pit.'

The author of the Regimental History, Sir William Cope, sought to clarify McGregor's action by stating: 'In the official notification of the grant of the Victoria Cross, MacGregor [*sic*] is said to have performed this act of valour "in the month of July"; but I have been repeatedly assured by Bradshaw that he, Humpston and MacGregor were together, and won their crosses on this occasion.'[14] He also describes the action in greater detail.

> *On April 22 a bandsman of the 2nd Battalion named Wright, who was on duty in the trenches, going to fetch water from a well in front of the advanced trench near the Quarries, was killed; it being impossible to throw up any cover near the well in consequence of the rockiness of the soil. This man being a great favourite of his comrades, a number of them rushed out determined to drive out the Russian riflemen, by whose fire he had fallen, from the pits which they occupied. Three men, Bradshaw, Humpston and MacGregor, were the first to reach them, and drove the Russians out, killing some while a few escaped. For this gallant deed these three Riflemen received the Victoria Cross, Bradshaw being also decorated with the French War Medal.*[15]

Cope's account, seemingly reliant only on the word of Rifleman Bradshaw, is credible but not conclusive. There are those who continue to argue that, whether or not McGregor took part in the action with Bradshaw and Humpston on 22 April, he must have taken part in a subsequent action in July 1855 and it was for the later action that he received his VC and not the earlier one. It is strange, though, that the author of McGregor's VC citation is so imprecise about the date in July. This adds weight to the doubt surrounding whether an action in July 1855 ever took place; there is no known record of it elsewhere. Thus, the Regiment, over many years, has chosen to accept Bradshaw's word, as reported by Cope, and to believe that the citation is wrong.

After the Crimean War, all three Riflemen served in India during the Indian Mutiny, Bradshaw being promoted to Corporal. McGregor was also promoted to Corporal on 22 January 1858 but was reduced in rank to Rifleman in March 1863. He was discharged on 17 November 1863 as unfit for further military service. Notwithstanding his disciplinary breaches he was in receipt of one good conduct badge.

Little is known about Bradshaw, Humpston or McGregor once they left the Army, Bradshaw dying, aged 40, at Woolwich on 21 March 1875, Humpston, aged 52, in Derby on 22 December 1884, and McGregor, aged 66, in Scotland on 9 August 1888.

Siege of Sebastopol Continues, April to June 1855

Meanwhile, on 9 April 1855 the Second Allied Bombardment of Sebastopol took place, to be followed by the Third Bombardment on 6 June. On the following day, 7 June, 2 RB took part in a successful assault on the Quarries. On 17 June the Fourth Bombardment began, to be followed on 18 June by a major but unsuccessful British attempt to capture the Redan, the three sides of which were 70 yards long, 15 feet high and fronted by a ditch 20 feet wide and 14 feet deep, giving a total height for escalade of some 30 feet. It was here that Lieutenant Knox of 2 RB performed the second of two acts resulting in the award of a VC.

Lieutenant J.S. Knox VC

(Later Brevet Major J.S. Knox VC)

Lieutenant John Knox was a Glaswegian, born on 30 September 1828, who, because he was very tall for his age, managed to enlist in the Scots Fusilier Guards, aged $14\frac{1}{2}$, on 15 May 1843. He was later promoted Sergeant, accompanying the Battalion to the Crimea and performing the first act of gallantry recorded in his VC citation at the Battle of the Alma. He was at Balaclava and Inkerman, after which Prince Albert, Colonel-in-Chief of The Rifle Brigade, hearing of Knox's conspicuous gallantry, offered him a commission in The Rifle Brigade, which he was glad to accept.

His VC citation in the *Supplement to The London Gazette* of 24 February 1857 is worded: 'When serving as a Serjeant[16] in the Scots Fusilier Guards, Lieutenant Knox was conspicuous for his exertions in reforming the ranks of the Guards at the Battle of the Alma. Subsequently, when in the Rifle Brigade, he volunteered for the ladder-party in the attack on the Redan, on the 18th of June [1855], and (in the words of Captain Blackett, under whose command he was,) behaved admirably, remaining on the field until twice wounded.'

Space does not permit inclusion of a more detailed account of his act of gallantry with the Scots Fusilier Guards at the Battle of the Alma. However, his own vivid account of storming the Redan, which most probably understates his bravery and the role he performed, is worthy of record, not least for the description it offers of the event.

At daybreak [18 June 1855] *the French began the attack,* [pre-empting] *the English waiting for the signal to advance. The Russians were all the time preparing to receive us warmly. At last, about 5 a.m., the flag was hoisted, and away we went, meeting a powerful fire, sweeping us down in all directions. At starting we were only a short two hundred yards from the Redan; on leaving the trench, I met* [Captain] *Blackett with a smashed leg moving back on his hips and hands. The command then fell to me, but not a dozen men were left to lead. These I led up to the Abattis; then taking a rifle from a dead Rifleman, I fired several shots at the enemy, all the time talking to Capt. Foreman, in command of the sharpshooters, about what ought to be done, both deciding there was nothing for it but to remain until shot over. My rifle was aimed at a Russian when I was struck in the left arm, the weapon falling to the ground, upon which poor Foreman remarked, 'You are wounded'. I replied, 'I fancy I am'. He offered me some brandy; this I declined. Having a stout handkerchief ready for the work, he took it, and by chance placed himself in front of me and bound up the wound. At that instant a shower of grape-shot passed; he was struck dead, falling on my feet speechless, the spirit gone. I remained standing, strange to say. Having had enough I retired. A short distance off a grape-shot caught the broken arm and lodged in the arm. Still I kept my feet and walked on into our trenches, there tumbling over through loss of blood. … Walking out of the battle got me back before the doctors had any of them work to do. They were waiting for a job, soon removed the arm from the socket under chloroform, without any pain or trial to me. Seven days after I was out of bed, walking about none the worse man, although only one arm left.*[17]

In addition to the VC, Knox was awarded the French Legion of Honour. Subsequently, both the Scots Fusilier Guards and The Rifle Brigade have laid claim to him as one of their own; indeed VC records often list him as a member of the Scots Fusilier Guards and not The Rifle Brigade. Suffice it to observe that, while he undoubtedly served in both regiments, *The London Gazette* clearly states him to be a member of 2 RB.

Despite losing an arm Knox continued to serve in the Army, becoming Acting Paymaster at the Depot in Winchester in January 1856. He was also the Parade Adjutant at the first VC investiture in Hyde Park on 26 June 1857. After promotion to Captain in 1858 he specialised in musketry, serving as a Musketry Officer at the Depot, in Gibraltar and at Portsmouth before retiring from the Army as a Brevet Major in 1872. He immediately became Governor of Cardiff Prison and subsequently of Kirkdale and Hull prisons before retiring from the Prison Service in 1892. He died, a much loved and respected member of the Regiment, at Cheltenham on 8 January 1897, aged 68.

Siege of Sebastopol Continues, July 1855 Onwards

The attack on the Redan, in which Lieutenant Knox had taken part, proved a costly affair. 1 RB suffered nine killed and 11 wounded; 2 RB lost 26 killed and 81 wounded. Allied attempts to capture Sebastopol intensified, with each side regularly probing the defences of the other and being rebuffed.

Soon another incident took place in 2 RB. Quoting from the Regimental History:'On 3 July Captain Fyers was coming off picquet in the advanced works with about 400 men. They were retiring by a zig-zag which by some oversight of the Engineers was directly enfiladed by a Russian gun. As soon as the men were well in the *boyau* [communication trench] a round shot was fired, which, bounding along, knocked down 13 men, of whom 8 were killed or died of their wounds. The wounded were removed by Fyers, Colour-Sergeant Kemp, and some soldiers of another regiment who came to their assistance.'[18] Captain Fyers later recommended Colour-Sergeant Kemp for a VC, but he did not receive it.

On 17 August the Allies launched their Fifth Bombardment and on 5 September the Sixth. On 8 September a further British attempt to capture the Redan failed, although French success elsewhere led to the Russians abandoning the Redan on the following day. However, despite the tightening Allied encirclement of Sebastopol, Russian resistance continued and, as winter approached for a second time, diplomatic efforts were begun to bring the War to an end. The level of operational activity decreased and a more relaxed atmosphere prevailed. 'Though the cold was very severe and much snow fell in the early part of this year [1856], the Riflemen, having the protection of the huts and sufficient rations and fuel, were in far greater comfort than during the preceding winter.'[19]

The End of the War

By early February 1856 hostilities around Sebastopol ceased. On 25 February a peace conference was held in Paris resulting in the Treaty of Paris signed on 30 March which formally ended the War. On 4 June 1 RB embarked at Balaclava to return to England. On 8 June 2 RB did likewise. On arrival in July the Battalions were quartered at Aldershot where Queen Victoria reviewed them. Again quoting from the Regimental History:'The appearance of the Riflemen, all of whom wore the Crimean Medal, with three or four clasps, many the Kaffir Medal, and some the Sardinian and other decorations, specially attracted attention.'[20]

On 24 February 1857 the first list of VC recipients from the Crimean War was published as a *Supplement to The London Gazette*. The names of the eight officers and non-commissioned ranks whose deeds are described in this chapter were included. All eight subsequently attended the first VC Investiture in Hyde Park on 26 June 1857 (see pages 9–11). By then, the Indian Mutiny had been in progress for six weeks and others, whose deeds are described in the next chapter, were performing acts of gallantry which were soon to result in the award of many more VCs to members of the antecedent regiments of The Royal Green Jackets.

Chapter 3
The Indian Mutiny: Delhi, 1857

Origins

The outbreak of the Indian Mutiny in May 1857, or Sepoy Revolt as it should more accurately be termed, may be attributed to many causes, of which the heavy-handed annexation of Oudh in 1856 was one and the issue of new cartridges greased with animal fat was another. A sense of grievance and signs of unrest prevailed, although few can have anticipated the form, scale and the nature of the horrors that were to take place.

Regimental Involvement

When the Mutiny began, three out of the four antecedent regiments of The Royal Green Jackets were present in India. The 43rd Light Infantry (43rd LI) was in the south of the Country, the 52nd Light Infantry (52nd LI) was in the Punjab, and the 1st Battalion, 60th Rifles, KRRC (1st/60th) was at Meerut, 40 miles to the north-east of Delhi. It was not until the end of 1857, and after the recapture of Delhi in September, that reinforcements from England, including 3rd/60th, 2 RB and 3 RB, started to arrive in India, followed in mid-1858 by the 2nd/60th from South Africa.

The 43rd LI arrived at Madras in January 1854, following two years of campaigning in the South African (Kaffir) War. The Regiment was subsequently stationed at Bangalore and, because of the fear of the Mutiny spreading southwards from the Bengal to the Madras Presidency, did not march to the assistance of their colleagues in the north until 1858.

The 52nd LI arrived at Calcutta from Ireland at the end of 1853 and was stationed at Umballa (Ambala), 125 miles north of Delhi on the Grand Trunk Road that ran all the way from Calcutta, through Delhi and on to Lahore and Peshawar. In 1856 the Regiment joined the Oudh Field Force, participating in the controversial annexation of Oudh, occupying barracks at Lucknow and suffering severely from cholera. At the end of 1856 the 52nd was ordered to the Punjab, in what is now Pakistan, where the Regiment was at Sialkot (Sealkote), 70 miles north of Lahore and 300 miles north-west of Delhi, when the Mutiny began.

The 1st/60th arrived in India in 1845 and had already taken part in the Second Sikh War (1848–9) and in a number of punitive expeditions on the North-West Frontier adjoining Afghanistan in 1849–50. The Battalion moved from the Punjab to Meerut in early 1856, where, despite being full of veterans hardened to life in India, it, too, suffered severely from cholera.

Chronology

The Mutiny began at Meerut where the 1st/60th was stationed. At 6 p.m. on 10 May members of the Battalion were parading for church when news arrived that the Sepoys in the native regiments in the garrison had revolted.[1] Europeans were murdered and the town was alight. Detachments from the Battalion were immediately despatched to prevent further atrocities and to secure key points. Meanwhile, the mutineers (rebels) set off for Delhi where they joined with others in seizing the city. Pursuit, however, was delayed while order in Meerut was restored, and it was not until 27 May that a relief force, under the overall command of Brigadier-General Archdale Wilson, including 16 officers and 450 men of the 1st/60th under the command of Lieutenant-Colonel John Jones, departed for Delhi.

On 30/31 May the force fought a sharp action with a group of rebels at a causeway over the Hindun River, some nine miles from Delhi. On 1 June the Sirmoor Battalion of Gurkhas joined the relief column and on 7 June the force from Meerut became part of a larger column, later to be called the Delhi Field Force, commanded by Major-General Sir Harry Barnard. On 8 June a substantial rebel force was defeated at Budlee-ka-Serai, seven miles north of Delhi. The rebels withdrew into Delhi, while the Delhi Field Force moved to occupy the ridge immediately north of the city, behind which the British encamped.

General Barnard had too few troops to besiege a city as large as Delhi with a rebel force of uncertain but growing strength congregating behind its walls. The British, therefore, were constrained to holding the ridge, which overlooked the city from a distance of 1,200 yards and more, while reinforcements were assembled. However, there were few reinforcements to hand as the Mutiny spread to Lucknow (30 May), Cawnpore (5 June) and other garrisons, with each uprising usually accompanied by further horrific murders of European men, women and children.

For two months the Delhi Field Force, whose total strength amounted to no more than 4,000 men, many of whom were loyal native soldiers, tenaciously held its positions in the face of frequent rebel attacks on the ridge and, in particular, the key point, Hindu Rao's House, around and forward of which a number of guns were sited in range of the city. Meanwhile, conditions in the British camp deteriorated and disease proliferated. General Barnard died to be replaced, first, by General Reed, and then by Major-General Archdale Wilson who had commanded the relief force from Meerut. On 14 August a column,

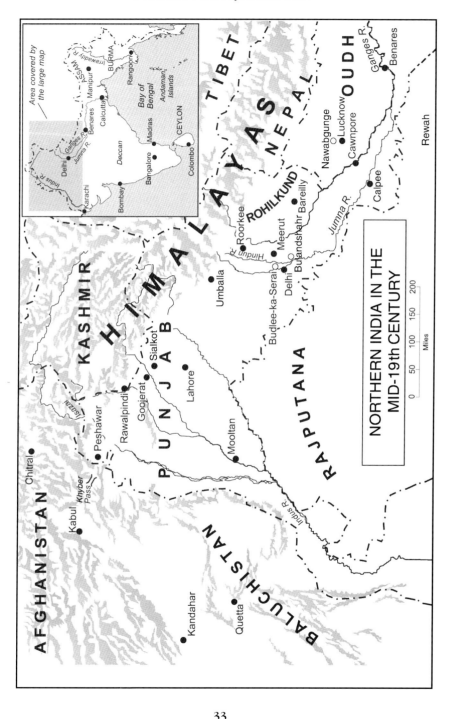

NORTHERN INDIA IN THE MID-19th CENTURY

0   50   100   150   200
Miles

under the command of Brigadier-General John Nicholson, arrived from the Punjab, including 680 men of the 52nd under command of Colonel George Campbell. This boosted the total strength of the Delhi Field Force to around 9,000 men, of whom a large number of the British contingent were unfit to fight. In early September a long-awaited siege train with big guns and howitzers arrived to start the bombardment and breaching of the city walls. During the night of 13 September reconnaissance revealed that sufficient damage had been inflicted for an assault to be ordered.

Assault and Recapture of Delhi, 14–20 September 1857

At 3 a.m. on Monday, 14 September 1857, five columns of assault troops, totalling around 5,500 men, awaited the signal to storm Delhi, defended by a rebel force variously estimated to number from 15–60,000. The first column was directed to carry the walls immediately east of the Kashmir Gate (see map opposite); the second column to storm the Water Bastion; the third column, under Colonel Campbell of the 52nd LI, including 200 men of his Regiment, to enter the Kashmir Gate; the fourth column to take the Kissen Gunge (a village settlement occupied by the rebels) and enter the Lahore Gate from the west; and the fifth column, the strongest of all, to act as a reserve. The 1st/60th, with 200 men, was tasked to cover in skirmishing lines the advance of the assaulting columns.

By the time the advance was ordered, it was daylight. With great élan and much heroism, the walls were breached and the assaulting troops entered the city. Six days of bitter street-fighting followed before the rebels fled and Delhi was restored to British rule. The rebels suffered severely, but so, too, did the Delhi Field Force losing 1,170 killed or wounded between 14 and 20 September.

Victoria Crosses

Out of the 182 VCs that were awarded for valour during the Indian Mutiny, forty-three were awarded for acts of gallantry in and around Delhi.[2] Of these, eight were awarded to members of the 1st/60th and two to members of the 52nd LI. Although the two awards to the 52nd were 'immediate' awards preceding the announcement of awards to the 1st/60th, all those relating to the 1st/60th, except the award to Ensign Lisle Phillipps, are covered first.

Rifleman S. TURNER VC

Rifleman Samuel Turner was born near Ipswich in Suffolk in February 1826. No other details are known prior to his appearance as a member of 1st/60th at Meerut, whence he marched to Delhi with the Battalion

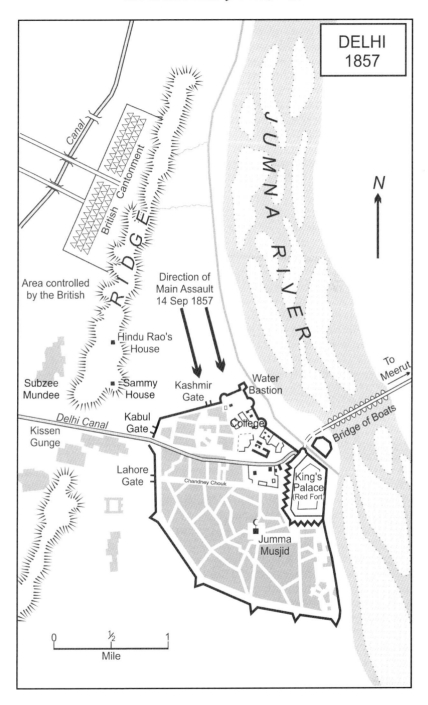

DELHI
1857

J U M N A   R I V E R

Canal

British Cantonment

R I D G E

N

Area controlled
by the British

Direction of
Main Assault
14 Sep 1857

Hindu Rao's
House

Subzee
Mundee

Sammy
House

Kashmir
Gate

Water
Bastion

To
Meerut

Delhi Canal

Kabul
Gate

College

Bridge of Boats

Kissen
Gunge

Lahore
Gate

Chandney Chouk

King's
Palace
(Red Fort)

Jumma
Musjid

0   ½   1

Mile

in May 1857. The act of bravery for which he was awarded a VC took place soon afterwards. The VC citation records the action:

> *For having, at Delhi, on the night of the 19th of June, 1857, during a severe conflict with the Enemy, who attacked the rear of the Camp, carried off on his shoulders, under a heavy fire, a mortally wounded Officer, Lieutenant Humphreys, of the Indian Service. During this service, Private Turner was wounded by a sabre cut in the right arm. His gallant conduct saved the above-named Officer from the fate of others, whose mangled remains were not recovered until the following day.*

There are no additional details in the Regimental History, although the fierce nature of the action was typical of the close-quarter fighting undertaken almost daily by members of the 1st/60th as the Delhi Field Force strove hard to prevent the rebels occupying Delhi Ridge. The unfortunate Lieutenant Humphreys of the 20th Bengal Native Infantry Regiment was attached to the 1st/60th, his Regiment having mutinied at Meerut on 10 May.

Although information about Turner is scarce, Roger Perkins in his book *The Kashmir Gate* states that 'after the Mutiny he [Turner] took his pension and retired to Meerut where he established himself in business as a "farrier and hotel keeper"'.[3] He certainly did not accompany 1st/60th when it left Calcutta to return to England in March 1860, as he was in India to receive his VC at an investiture at Umballa in December 1860. He subsequently died at Meerut on 13 June 1868, aged 42.

Colour-Sergeant S. GARVIN VC

(Later Colour-Sergeant S. Garvin VC DCM)

Colour-Sergeant Stephen Garvin was an Irishman born in County Tipperary in 1826. He enlisted in the 60th, KRRC, on 6 July 1842 and served in India with the 1st/60th from 24 November 1845. He took part in the Second Sikh War in 1848–9, including the recapture of Mooltan and the Battle of Goojerat, and in the punitive expeditions on the North-West Frontier in 1849–50. He was present at Meerut at the start of the Mutiny and marched with the 1st/60th to Delhi.

On 23 June 1857 it was anticipated that the rebels would mount a major attack to seize Delhi Ridge and avenge the decisive British victory at the Battle of Plassey exactly 100 years previously. When the attack was launched at 5 a.m., the defenders were prepared and for the next 12 hours the battle raged until eventually the rebels withdrew at sunset behind the city walls of Delhi. Quoting from the Regimental History:

> *During the course of the day Captain Fagan – a hero among heroes – commanding the right [artillery] battery in front of Hindoo Rao's house, asked Lieutenant Hare to drive the enemy from a temple –*

the Swansi (or idol), but corrupted by the British soldier into the 'Sammy House' [at the south-eastern extremity of Delhi ridge closest to the city] – *which the mutineers had occupied as a post of vantage, and whence a well-directed fire upon our embrasures was being maintained. This fire could not be returned; for, although the distance was only about 250 yards, the temple stood on ground so much below Fagan that he could not sufficiently depress his guns. The men of Hare's company were by this time lying on the ground utterly exhausted: the task appeared desperate; but at Hare's call for volunteers the whole Company at once rose and rushed down upon the Sammy House, which was soon in its possession. Sergeant Stephen Garvin set an example of distinguished valour, for which, in due course, he received the Victoria Cross. The Sammy House thus taken was never again occupied by the enemy.*[4]

Colour-Sergeant Garvin's VC citation later read: 'For daring and gallant conduct before Delhi on the 23rd June, 1857, in volunteering to lead a small party of men, under a heavy fire, to the "Sammy House" for the purpose of dislodging a number of the enemy in position there, who kept up a destructive fire on the advanced battery of heavy guns, in which, after a sharp contest, he succeeded. Also recommended for gallant conduct throughout the operations before Delhi.'

On 3 September, exemplifying the gallant conduct which Garvin showed 'throughout the operations before Delhi', he sustained a gunshot wound in the left side of his groin. He was later awarded a Distinguished Conduct Medal (DCM),[5] although the detail is not known, and a Long Service and Good Conduct Medal. In 1861 he transferred to the 64th (2nd Staffordshire) Regiment, before taking his discharge in 1865. In 1870 he was appointed a Yeoman of the Guard. He died at Chesterton in Cambridgeshire on 23 November 1874, aged 48. He was the only man to be awarded a VC and DCM during the Indian Mutiny.

Elected by Ballot

The award of a VC to Rifleman Turner and Colour-Sergeant Garvin was announced in *The London Gazette* on 20 January 1860. The same edition included the names of five other members of the 1st/60th who received VCs as a result of the ballot arrangements ordained under Clause 13 of the Royal Warrant of 29 January 1856 (see page 5).

The awards should have been made on a scale of one officer elected by the officers of the Battalion; one non-commissioned officer (NCO) elected by the NCOs; and two Private soldiers elected by the Privates. For some reason that M.J. Crook never established in his researches,[6] a third Private received an award. This was not the only occasion on which this happened.

Chapter 3

Ensign A.S. HEATHCOTE VC

(Later Captain A.S. Heathcote VC)

Ensign Alfred Heathcote was a Wykehamist, born in Winchester on 29 March 1832 and educated at Winchester College. After leaving school, he sailed for Australia during the Gold Rush of the 1850s. However, he stopped off at Christchurch, New Zealand, where he purchased 500 acres of land. He soon grew tired of farming and decided to continue on to Australia, where he mined for gold at Bendigo and purchased an allotment of land in Melbourne. He then went to sea and served on board an East Indiaman. Growing restless again, he travelled to the USA, Mexico, China and Singapore before returning to England and joining the 60th, KRRC, as an Ensign on 16 May 1856. He was sent to the Depot, which was then at Chatham, before being posted to the 1st/60th at Meerut, in time to be present at the outset of the Mutiny.

Heathcote's VC citation reads: 'For highly gallant and daring conduct at Delhi throughout the Siege, from June to September, 1857, during which he was wounded. He volunteered for services of extreme danger, especially during the six days of severe fighting in the streets after the assault. Elected by the Officers of his Regiment.'

A fuller description is provided by Lieutenant-Colonel F.R. Palmer, who was the senior Major in the 1st/60th in 1857/8 before transferring to command 2nd/60th, and who wrote on 14 March 1862: 'No one ever better deserved the Victoria Cross; he obtained it not only for one act, but for many acts during his active service, commencing with the march on Delhi. On one occasion an advanced post in Delhi was retained by his declaring to the officer in command, who wished to retire, that he could do so with his own men, but that he, Lieut. Heathcote, would endeavour to hold the post with six riflemen he had with him. On another occasion he made his way to the front with six men, supported by fourteen under my own command. He and his party killed eight or ten of the enemy. This was the first forward step taken after the Army had been three days in the portion of Delhi first occupied by it.'

Palmer's admiration for Heathcote's bravery was shared by Lieutenant-General Sir Edward Hutton, Colonel-Commandant of the 2nd Battalion, who knew Heathcote well and who wrote in a Memoriam in the 1912 KRRC Chronicle: 'There was scarcely an incident at this tragic time [Delhi, 1857] in which Heathcote did not bear a part, nor a dangerous enterprise for which he did not volunteer. Although more than once wounded, nothing seemed to daunt the young soldier's eagerness for fighting, nor damp the energy of his enthusiastic spirit. Heathcote, judging from the letters to the lady whom he afterwards made his wife, seems to have fairly revelled in the dangers and the glories of the personal element in the war. ... [He] seemed destitute of the element of fear.' The content of some of his letters are quoted later in this chapter.

After the recapture of Delhi, Heathcote took part with the 1st/60th in the Rohilkund and Oudh campaigns. He was promoted Lieutenant on 22 June 1858 and later became the Adjutant of the 1st/60th, before assuming command of a mixed force of police. When the 1st/60th returned to England in 1860, he transferred to the 2nd/60th, taking part in the same year in the Second China War, including in the assault on the Taku Forts and the capture of Peking. When the War was over, he returned to England and served at the Depot until retiring in 1863. Advised for the sake of his health to return to Australia, he did so, serving with the Volunteer forces in New South Wales, but he and his family fell upon hard times. In 1893 General Hutton found him in hospital in Sydney almost totally blind. At the Regimental Dinner in 1894 a subscription of over £200 was raised and sent to him. He died on 21 February 1912, aged 79, and was buried on the following day in the churchyard of St James's Anglican Church, Sydney.

Colour-Sergeant G. WALLER VC

Colour-Sergeant George Waller was born at West Horsley, Surrey, on 1 June 1827. He enlisted in the 39th (Dorsetshire) Regiment on 12 October 1843, transferring to the 60th, KRRC, on 30 June 1844. He sailed with the 1st/60th to India in 1845 and, like Colour-Sergeant Garvin, took part in the Second Sikh War in 1848–9, including the recapture of Mooltan and the Battle of Goojerat, and in the punitive expeditions on the North-West Frontier in 1849–50. He was present at Meerut at the start of the Mutiny and marched with the 1st/60th to Delhi.

Waller's VC citation reads: 'For conspicuous bravery at Delhi, on 14th September, 1857, in charging and capturing the Enemy's guns near the Cabul Gate; and again, on the 18th of September, 1857, in the repulse of a sudden attack made by the enemy on a gun near the Chandney Chouk.[7] Elected by the Non-Commissioned Officers of the Regiment.'

No additional account of Waller's actions figures in the Regimental histories. However, Roger Perkins records that Waller was severely wounded in the thigh by a gunshot on 19 June from which he may not have fully recovered by the time of the assault on 14 September.[8] The assault and fierce fighting within Delhi over the following six days also gave rise to many individual acts of gallantry and the fact that Colour-Sergeant Waller's fellow NCOs nominated him for a VC assuredly provides testimony that he was adjudged the bravest of them all and deserving of the award.

Waller was later awarded a Long Service and Good Conduct Medal and was discharged from the Army on 7 March 1865. According to Perkins, he became a Permanent Staff Instructor with the 13th Sussex Rifle Volunteers. He died at Cuckfield in Sussex on 10 January 1877, aged 49.

Rifleman W.J. THOMPSON VC

Rifleman James Thompson was born in 1829 at Hadley, near Yoxall in Staffordshire. As a young man he worked as a farm labourer before enlisting in the 1st/60th on 30 January 1852 and was with the Battalion at Meerut when the Mutiny began.

Thompson's VC citation reads: 'For gallant conduct in saving the life of his Captain (Captain Wilton), on the 9th of July, 1857, by dashing forward to his relief, when that Officer was surrounded by a party of Ghazees, who made a sudden rush on him from a Serai,[9] – and killing two of them before further assistance could reach. Also recommended for conspicuous conduct throughout the Siege. Wounded. Elected by the Privates of the Regiment.'

The Regimental History adds: 'On the 9th [July] another fight took place at Hindoo Rao's House, during which 15 men were lost. The 8th Irregular Cavalry [rebels] penetrated temporarily to the centre of the British camp. Wilmot's Company of the Rifles was sent down with four guns to clear the Subzee-Mundee [a suburb at the southern extremity of the ridge], which had been occupied by the enemy. A party of fanatics dashing out from a Serai surrounded Captain Wilmot. The day was wet and his pistol missed fire. Rifleman James Thompson rushed forward, bayoneted two of the assailants and saved his Captain's life.'[10]

Reference to Captain Wilmot in the above account has caused much confusion since, as Thompson's Captain was almost certainly, as the citation indicates, Captain F.R. Wilton who served with the 1st/60th at Delhi. Captain Wilmot was an officer in 2 RB, about whom more is written in the next chapter. Nevertheless, the absence of a place name in the citation has led some to think that Thompson's action may have taken place under Wilmot's command in an action with 2 RB and not at Delhi under Captain Wilton. This seems far-fetched as the reference in the citation to 9 July 1857, before 2 RB arrived in India, and to the ballot, make it clear that the action relates to the 1st/60th at Delhi and that the author of the Regimental History was mistaken.

Thompson was wounded at some point during his actions at Delhi and had his left arm amputated. He was subsequently invalided out of the Army and went to work in Scotland as a gamekeeper on Captain Wilton's family estate; thus giving further credence to the fact that it was Captain Wilton's life that he saved and not Captain Wilmot's. In 1865 he returned to the Midlands, working as a colliery watchman. In 1890 he was forced, due to poverty and ill health, to sell his VC. He died at Walsall on 5 February 1891, aged 61.

Rifleman J. DIVANE VC

Rifleman John Divane was an Irishman born near Loughrea, County Galway, in 1822. He is also sometimes referred to as Devine. Recently,

Richard Doherty, in his book *Irish Winners of the Victoria Cross*, presents a strong case that Divane's real name was Duane, and that it became corrupted to Divane when the 'u' was misread and copied as 'iv'.[11] However, in the VC Register and in public records he remains Divane.

Divane enlisted in the 60th, KRRC, in April 1854 and had an extremely chequered start to his military career. On joining the 1st/60th, he was awarded repeated periods of detention and forfeitures of pay for unspecified misdeeds. Concurrently, and extraordinarily, on 7 February 1857 he received his third good conduct badge. He was soon to prove, though, that, while he may not have been a model soldier in barracks, he was just the man for a fight and one of those chosen by his comrades as worthy of a VC.

His citation reads:'For distinguished gallantry in heading a successful charge made by the Beeloochee [Baluchi] and Sikh troops on one of the Enemy's trenches before Delhi, on the 10th of September, 1857. He leaped out of our trenches, closely followed by the Native Troops, and was shot down from the top of the Enemy's breastworks. Elected by the Privates of the Regiment.'

The Regimental History repeats the story but has nothing further to add. Divane's wounds, however, resulted in his right leg being amputated. In 1858 he was invalided out of the Army with a pension of 10 pence per day and the annuity of £10 awarded to VC recipients (see page 5). Unable to work, he became an In-Pensioner at the Royal Hospital, Chelsea. He then returned to Ireland before moving to Cornwall. He spent his last years as a fish hawker on the streets of Penzance, where he died in his mid-60s on 1 December 1888. He was buried in a pauper's grave.

Bugler W. SUTTON VC

Bugler Sutton was born at Ightham, Kent, in 1830. No other details are known prior to his appearance as a member of 1st/60th at Meerut, whence he marched to Delhi with the Battalion in May 1857.

Sutton's VC citation reads:'For gallant conduct at Delhi on the 13th of September, 1857, the night previous to the Assault, in volunteering to reconnoitre the breach. This Soldier's conduct was conspicuous throughout the operations, especially on the 2nd of August, 1857, on which occasion during an attack by the Enemy in force, he rushed forward over the trenches, and killed one of the Enemy's Buglers, who was in the act of sounding. Elected by the Privates of the Regiment.'

Ensign Heathcote described the first act in a letter dated 6 August 1857, which also exemplifies the nature of the actions in which he and many others were involved on an almost daily basis on Delhi Ridge:

At 10.30 p.m. [1 August], *when it was pitch dark, an order was sent me to take my section to the breastwork in front of our right heavy batteries. We had to cross over very rocky ground, and in crossing the ridge we came in for their grape, shrapnel, and musketry. ... The air was every minute lighted with the fuzes of the enemy's shells whizzing over our heads, then flashes right in front from their muskets, and the sharp ping of the bullets with the bursting of the shrapnel close among us and in our rear. At last we got safely down to the breastwork which the enemy was attacking. Volley after volley was poured in from the enemy. ... Then they would shout and charge, when up would jump our men and give them a volley that would fairly stagger 'John Sepoy'. This went on all night, their heavy guns and ours playing over our heads. The enemy occupied a breastwork about forty yards in front of us, and they were there in such numbers that we dare not charge them with our few. It was then a young bugler of ours, named Sutton, without any order from me, got upon the parapet of the breastwork and sounded our 'Regimental Call', the 'Retire' and the 'Double'. I was fearfully angry, and told him that I had a good mind to cut him down, and why did he do it, for, as he knew, the Rifles never retreat. His answer was, 'Never mind, sir, you'll see what will come of it'. Sure enough on they came out of their breastwork with their bayonets fixed, thinking we were on the go, when I gave the word 'fire', and the guns opened on them with canister and grape. Seeing that it was a dodge of ours to draw them on, they hastily retreated with heavy loss, ... and then with a cheer we charged them and drove them from their position.*[12]

Heathcote subsequently described his role in one of the two successful patrols launched to reconnoitre the breach on 13 September, although it is not certain whether Sutton accompanied him or was a member of the other patrol. In a letter dated 21 September 1857 Heathcote wrote:

We were all warned for the storming on the night of the 13th [September], *when I had command of twenty men to go with the engineer officer and see if the breach was practicable. I left all except four in rear of us, and then we managed cautiously to slip through their men in the advanced trenches of the enemy. We succeeded in getting into the ditch and some way up the breach, when we heard them talking, and had to retire. We were then between the enemy on the breach and their advanced picquets in the trenches, who were keeping up a fire on our batteries, which were quite close. We crawled along gradually on our hands and knees, and got quite safely back to our party. Had we been observed, it was, of course, certain death.*[13]

Clearly both Heathcote and Sutton were brave men; indeed, it needs little imagination to appreciate from accounts such as Heathcote's why both were chosen by their peers to be awarded VCs.

Not much is known about Sutton's subsequent career, although M.J. Crook records that on 20 January 1872 Sutton, who was then a member of the permanent staff of the Antrim Militia, was authorised to receive a replacement VC for the original, which he had declared to be lost. He was charged one pound four shillings for the privilege.[14] Roger Perkins also states that Sutton became a Sergeant, presumably while a permanent staff member of the Antrim Militia, but Regimental records lack corroborative evidence.[15] Sutton later retired to Ightham, his birthplace, where he died in the Union workhouse on 16 February 1888, aged 57/58.

The Arrival of the 52nd – Storming the Kashmir Gate

When, on 14 August 1857, the 52nd LI marched into the British lines at Delhi with the rest of Nicholson's column from the Punjab, the morale of those who had been resolutely defending the ridge since June was greatly boosted; the prospects of having enough troops to carry out an assault on the city were improved and there were more men among whom to share hazardous duties on and forward of the ridge. However, within days the 52nd, which arrived 680 strong on 14 August, with only 16 sick, was decimated by cholera. By 14 September, the day of the assault, the Regiment's effective strength had fallen to 240 all ranks.[16] It was these men who formed a part of Colonel Campbell's column that stormed the Kashmir Gate in one of the most heroic actions of the campaign, with Lieutenants Home and Salkeld, Sergeant Smith and Bugler Hawthorne[17] being among the best remembered of them all.

Lieutenant Home commanded the 'explosion party' consisting of a mix of European and native Bengal Sappers and Miners, among them, Lieutenant Salkeld, Sergeants Carmichael and Smith, and Corporal Burgess. Their task was to blow in the heavy wooden doors of the Kashmir Gate. Bugler Hawthorne of the 52nd accompanied the 'explosion party' ready to sound the regimental call as the signal to Colonel Campbell for the column to advance and storm the gateway.

There are many accounts of the action. Lieutenant (later Field Marshal Lord) Roberts VC, who was present at Delhi, wrote one of the more succinct.

No. 3 Column had advanced towards the Kashmir Gate and halted. Lieuts. Home and Salkeld, with eight Sappers and Miners, and a Bugler of the 52nd Foot, went forward to blow the gate open. The enemy were apparently so astounded at the audacity of this proceeding that for a minute or two they offered but slight resistance. They soon, however, discovered how small the party was and the object for which it had come, and forthwith opened a deadly fire upon the gallant little band from the top of the gateway, from the city wall and through the open wicket. The bridge over the gateway had been destroyed, and it was with some difficulty that

Artist's impression of Bugler Hawthorne sounding the advance
during the storming of the Kashmir Gate, Delhi,
14 September 1857

the single beam which remained could be crossed. Home, with the men carrying the powder-bags, got over first. As the first bags were being attached to the gate, Sergt. Carmichael was killed, and Havildar Madhoo wounded; the rest then slipped into the ditch to allow the firing party which had come up under Salkeld to carry out its share of the duty. While endeavouring to fire the charge, Salkeld, being shot through the leg and arm, handed the slow match to Corpl. Burgess, who fell mortally wounded, but not till he had successfully performed his task. As soon as the explosion had taken place, Bugler Hawthorne sounded the regimental call of the 52nd. Meeting with no response, he sounded it twice again. The noise of the firing and the shouting was so great that neither the sound of the bugle nor that of the explosion reached the column, but Campbell, after allowing the firing party what he thought was a sufficient time, gave the order to advance. Capt. Crosse, of the 52nd, was the first to reach the gate, followed closely by Corpl. Taylor of his own company, and Capt. Synge of the same regiment, who was Campbell's Brigade Major.[18]

Captain Crosse and his company from the 52nd very quickly forced their entry through the Kashmir Gate and brushing aside rebel resistance were soon inside the city, joining with other assaulting columns in the bitter street-fighting that lasted a further six days before the battle was won.

Bugler R. HAWTHORNE VC

Bugler Robert Hawthorne was an Irishman born at Maghera, County Londonderry, in 1822. After a basic education he began work as a labourer, aged 10. He subsequently enlisted for boy service in the 52nd on 15 February 1836, aged 14. He served with the Regiment in the West Indies, Canada, England and Ireland, before accompanying the 52nd to India at the end of 1853. He became a bugler in 1844 and in 1850 was sentenced at a regimental court-martial to 48 days' detention and to forfeit one penny a day from his pay for six months for taking part in a brawl in Liverpool.

His VC citation reads: 'Bugler Hawthorne, who accompanied the explosion party, not only performed the dangerous duty on which he was employed, but previously attached himself to Lieutenant Salkeld, of the Engineers, when dangerously wounded, bound up his wounds under a heavy musketry fire, and had him removed without further injury. (General Order of Major-General Sir Archdale Wilson, Bart., K.C.B., dated Head Quarters, Delhi City, September 21, 1857.)'

Various accounts record that Lieutenant Salkeld, when he was wounded, fell into the ditch below the bridge in front of the Kashmir Gate where Hawthorne, who was one of the first to arrive at the Gate, had taken refuge from the defenders' bullets and from the anticipated explosion once the charges had been laid and fired. It was there under the shelter of the front face of the ditch that he tended to Salkeld's wounds, although the officer was so badly hurt that he died on 10 October 1857. Lieutenant Home was in the ditch alongside Hawthorne and therefore well placed to order him to sound the regimental call of the 52nd the moment he saw that the explosives had blown in the Gate. In his own account of the action, Home wrote: 'As I was afraid that the bugle might not be heard, I caused the bugler to sound the call three times, after which the column advanced to the storm, and the gate was taken possession of by our troops.'[19]

Major-General Archdale Wilson watched the actions of the 'explosion party' from a vantage point 800 yards to the north of the city walls. As a result he felt empowered by the second proviso of Clause 7 of the Royal Warrant to award VCs 'on the spot', albeit subject to confirmation by the Monarch (see Appendix B). Clearly he considered the actions of the 'explosion party' to be so gallant and critical to the success of the whole assault that he may have wanted to award the whole group VCs. However, native troops were debarred from the award and posthumous awards had been ruled inadmissible (see page 6). He was thus constrained to granting 'immediate' awards, subject to confirmation, to the only members of the 'explosion party' who were eligible, namely, the four surviving Europeans, Home, Salkeld, Smith and Hawthorne. This he duly did seven days later with the issue of the General Order referred to in Hawthorne's VC citation. Subsequently Royal Assent was given and Hawthorne's award was published in *The London Gazette* on 27 April 1858.[20]

Hawthorne, meanwhile, after remaining with the 52nd for a further two years, returned to England in 1859 serving at Chatham before being discharged at his own request on 20 April 1861. He received four good conduct badges during his service but was denied a Long Service and Good Conduct Medal because of his earlier court-martial. He subsequently went to live and work in Manchester, where he died on 2 February 1879, aged 57.

Lance-Corporal H. SMITH VC

(Later Sergeant H. Smith VC)

The Kashmir Gate 'explosion party' were not the only members of the Delhi Field Force to receive 'immediate' awards. Lance-Corporal Henry Smith of the 52nd was another.

Lance-Corporal Smith was born at Thames Ditton, Surrey, in 1825. He enlisted in the 52nd LI on 9 February 1853, accompanying the Regiment to India later in the year. During the assault at Delhi on 14 September he received a mention for distinguished conduct in Colonel Campbell's despatch dated 16 September. The words used are almost identical to those in Smith's VC citation: 'Lance Corporal Smith most gallantly carried away a wounded comrade under a heavy fire of grape and musketry on the Chaundee Chouck, in the city of Delhi, on the morning of the assault on the 14th September 1857. (General Order of Major-General Sir Archdale Wilson, Bart., K.C.B., dated Head Quarters, Delhi City, September 21, 1857.)'

The Chaundee Chouck is the same street referred to in Colour-Sergeant Waller's VC citation, albeit differently spelt (see map on page 34). It runs east to west from the King's Palace (Red Fort) to the Lahore Gate and was close to marking the limit of British exploitation into the city on the day of the assault. The rebels resisted the British advance particularly strongly in the narrow streets in this area and around Delhi's main mosque, the Jumma Musjid.

No other account of Lance-Corporal Smith's action appears in the Regimental History. However, he was later promoted to the rank of Sergeant, but died of cholera at Gwalior in India on 18 August 1862, aged 36/37, being buried in a mass grave on the same day.

In his despatch Colonel Campbell singled out a number of other members of the Regiment for distinguished conduct during the assault at Delhi, among them Captain Crosse, Captain Synge and Corporal Taylor, all of whom were mentioned in Lieutenant Roberts's account of the storming of the Kashmir Gate. He also mentioned Sergeant-Major James Street, the senior non-commissioned officer in the 52nd, equivalent to the Regimental Sergeant-Major today. He was 39 years' old and, leading by example, was one of the first through the Kashmir Gate and up along the city wall to seize the ramparts of the Water Bastion. His bravery inspired the younger soldiers and made him an obvious candidate for a VC. At this point, however, he was shot, the ball passing through his stomach and emerging from the other side of his body. Miraculously he survived and after three months in hospital rejoined the 52nd. Although he did not receive a VC, he was rewarded with a commission in the 75th (Stirlingshire) Regiment. Sadly, he was increasingly affected by poor health caused by his wound and, having retired on half-pay and become depressed by his condition, he committed suicide by slashing his throat with a kitchen knife – a forgotten hero of the Kashmir Gate and another of its victims.[21]

Ensign E.A. LISLE PHILLIPPS VC†

Ensign Everard Lisle Phillipps is the last of the Delhi VCs to figure in this chapter because he did not receive a VC at the time of others, his descendants having to wait 50 years before King Edward VII consented to a posthumous award (see page 6). The story is complicated.

Lisle Phillipps was born at Gracedieu Manor, Leicestershire, on 28 May 1835, the second child in a respected Catholic family of 16 children. His father, Ambrose Lisle March Phillipps Esq, was a JP and

Deputy Lieutenant of Leicestershire, changing his name to Ambrose Lisle March Phillipps de Lisle in 1862. His mother, Laura Mary, was a daughter of the Hon. Thomas Clifford, fourth son of the fourth Lord Clifford. Thus, Lisle Phillipps and Lieutenant the Hon. Henry Clifford of The Rifle Brigade, who was awarded a VC for his gallantry at the Battle of Inkerman in the Crimea (see pages 19–22), were cousins.

Lisle Phillipps was privately educated, travelling to Paris in 1852 to learn Hindustani. His father, unable to afford the purchase of a commission for his son in a British regiment, used his influence to secure a cadetship for him in the service of the Honourable East India Company. In 1854 Lisle Phillipps attended Addiscombe, the East India Company's military seminary near Croydon, and was granted a commission in the 11th Regiment of Bengal Native Infantry. On 10 May 1857 he was serving with the Regiment at Meerut when the Sepoys mutinied. After a brave attempt to quell the rebellion, with his commanding officer being killed by his side, he managed to escape. In a letter home dated 15 May, he wrote: 'For the first three days [after the mutiny] I served with the Carabineers, now I am attached to the [60th] Rifles as orderly officer to Colonel Jones. As soon as ever this row is over I shall retire from the Company's service. ... Try and get me a commission in The Queen's service. ... Now perhaps I may fulfil your idea about distinguishing myself!'[22]

Four days later, on 19 May, he wrote to his father: 'Being orderly officer to Colonel Jones may give me the opportunity to have a commission given to me, so much the better, but I may need to purchase as I want you at once to get me in the Regiment. If I am not granted a commission without purchase, I want you to use what I shall get out of the legacy which is settled on the younger children.'

On 30 May during the 1st/60th's march on Delhi, Lisle Phillipps greatly distinguished himself in a fierce skirmish with the mutineers at the causeway over the Hindun River. In a letter to his mother on 1 June, he wrote: 'Mind you get me a commission in [the] 60th Rifles. I've now seen service with them. I wrote to Papa about it by the last mail. I shall try to get Colonel Jones to recommend me ... he has mentioned me in the official report of the affair on the 30th May. ... I will never serve with the native army again.' Following the battle at the Hindun River, Ensign William Napier died of his wounds on 5 June, a key date in the subsequent story.

During the months that followed Ensign Lisle Phillipps continued to distinguish himself at every opportunity, including during the assault on Delhi. Alas, he was killed after Major-General Wilson had already determined that he should be recommended for a VC. General Wilson, however, was not able to apply Clause 7 of the Royal Warrant and hence the procedure described on page 6 was adopted. On 21 October 1859 the following Memorandum appeared in *The London Gazette*: 'Ensign Everard Aloysius Lisle Phillipps, of the 11th Regiment of Bengal Native Infantry, would have been recommended to Her Majesty for the

48

decoration of the Victoria Cross, had he survived, for many gallant deeds which he performed during the siege of Delhi, during which he was wounded three times. At the assault of that city he captured the Water Bastion with a small party of men and was finally killed in the streets of Delhi on the 18th of September.'

Fifty years later, in *The London* Gazette on 15 January 1907, it was announced that: 'The King [Edward VII] has been graciously pleased to approve of the Decoration of the Victoria Cross being delivered to the representatives of the undermentioned Officers and men who fell in the performance of acts of valour, and with reference to whom it was notified in the London Gazette that they would have been recommended to Her late Majesty for the Victoria Cross had they survived.' Ensign Lisle Phillipps's name was among the six listed. On 6 February the VC was forwarded by registered mail to Edwin de Lisle, the elder of Lisle Phillipps's two surviving brothers.

The Memorandum of 21 October 1859 refers to Ensign Lisle Phillipps's 'many gallant deeds', during which he was wounded three times, on 30 May when his horse was killed under him, and twice on Delhi Ridge on 12 and 19 June. Sergeant P.J. O'Shaughnessy, 1st/60th, who was the equivalent today of Lisle Phillipps's platoon sergeant, wrote to Lisle Phillipps's brother on 24 November 1859, recording three actions, on 30/31 May, on 12 July and during the storming of the Water Bastion on 14 September. The following are extracts:[23]

Ensign Lisle Phillipps leading a party of 1st/60th storming the Water Bastion, Delhi, 14 September 1857. Painting by L.W. Des Anges.

Chapter 3

*On the memorable morning of the storming of Delhi the 14th
September 1857, your brother and myself entered the 'Breach' at
the Water Bastion together; after securing the battery and leaving
some men to guard it, he called me and said, 'Take all the rifle
men you can get, and follow me towards the College Compound'.
I did so; and on coming up I found him at the head of a
company of Sikhs and preparing to charge. The Sepoys were at
this time advancing in a strong body from the College, evidently
with the intention of turning our left flank, which they certainly
would have done if it was not for your brother, who seeing the
danger, collected a few scattered Sikhs, and put himself at their
head to resist them; ...We charged – and partly drove the enemy
back to the College, but they were more than ten to one of us,
and charged us back, and completely drove us out of the College
Compound. However, with your brother's orders we took up a
position behind the compound wall, determined to keep it or die.
... At this time the Sepoys seeing that I was alone, came rushing
at me. I turned round to your brother and said 'is there any relief
sir, I'll be cut down in a few moments'; but the answer he made
me was 'Don't retire, O'Shaughnessy'. I replied back and said,
'Then here I'll die, Sir'. I was just on the point of being cut to
pieces when I heard your brother's well known word of
command – 'Charge'. In a moment he was by my side and saved
my life.*

*Not only in that instance did he deserve the Victoria Cross, but
in several others, two of which I shall mention. 1st Every man who
is now living in my regiment, and who fought with it on the
Hindon on the 30th and 31st of May 1857, knows what lives he
saved when he rode with a sheepskin full of water on his back,
through shell and shot, in many parts of the field, where he served
many a poor fellow lying speechless for the want of a drop of
water. 2nd ly On the night of the 12th of July (as far as I can think)
before Delhi he had command of a party of men to take the
enemy's breastworks, and cover a working party, who were
ordered to cut down some trees in front of our position, which
afforded great shelter to the enemy. On getting near the enemy's
breastworks there was a slight panic caused by two or three
redcoats that were sent to reinforce us, which nearly caused the
whole to run away, when your brother shouted, 'Men recollect
what Regiment you belong to – recollect you belong to the 60th
Rifles'. – That was enough. The men required no more, but rallied
around him, and jumped into the enemy's breastwork, and took
it at the point of the bayonet. – I never yet knew a man more
reckless of his own life or more careful of others than he was; and
I am sure there never was an officer in the regiment more
regretted than he was.*

The Memorandum that appeared in *The London Gazette* was wrong in two important respects. First, Ensign Lisle Phillipps was killed on the 17th and not 18 September, and, although he did not know it at the time, his wish had been granted and he held a commission in the 60th, KRRC, and not the 11th Bengal Native Infantry.

There are a number of primary sources available to confirm Lisle Phillipps's date of death as 17 September 1857, of which the most telling is a letter written to his father by his Commanding Officer, Lieutenant-Colonel John Jones of the 1st/60th, on 25 September.[24]

Palace Delhi
September 25th 1857

My dear Sir,

Your son Lisle Phillipps having been mentioned to me in a letter from my Sister Mrs D.R. Jones I had great pleasure in having him attached to my Regt from the commencement of the outbreak at Meerut but the painful duty has fallen to me to announce to you his death on the 17th of this month by a gun shot wound in the head while bravely performing his duty with his men. It occurred in Street fighting. After having stormed and taken part of the City we had to work our way up to the Palace and while erecting a small breastwork to protect his men he received his mortal wound. He did not survive ten minutes after he was hit. In communicating to you this melancholy intelligence it may be some consolation to you to know that during the time he has done duty with my Regt he has always behaved in the most gallant manner. He was a thoro soldier and fond of his profession and had it pleased God to have spared him he would have been delighted to have obtained a commission in the Corps and I should have been proud to have had him as an Officer of the Regt. He was a universal favourite with the Officers of the Regt and they all hoped and trusted he would have succeeded in obtaining what he wished but the will of the Almighty thought fit to call him away to I hope a better world – It is the wish of the Officers of the Battalion to have placed in any place you choose to select a tablet in his memory in testimony of the esteem in which your son was held by them all – Capt Travers who now commands the Depot will be willing to provide the slab and have the inscription put on it that the Officers wish and will communicate with you in regard to your wishes on the subject – I had hoped that I should have had the pleasure of making your [acquaintance] under happier circumstances than by communicating to you your sad loss but we must all bow to the Divine will and submit as true Xtians to whatever he may see fit to order. Believe me My dear Sir

Yours most truly
John Jones Lt Col
Comdg 1st Bt K.R. Rifles

Lisle Phillipps was buried at Delhi under a gravestone erected by his brother officers. It records that he was an Ensign in the 60th Rifles and that his date of death was 17 September 1857. Clearly, though, Colonel Jones did not know of Lisle Phillipps's commission in the 60th at the time he wrote his letter. However, on 18 September 1857, seven days previously, the following entry had appeared in *The London Gazette*: '60th Foot, Everard Lisle Phillipps, Gent., to be Ensign, without purchase, vice W. H. Napier, died of wounds. Dated 5 June 1857.'

Not much notice seems to have been taken of *The London Gazette* entry of 18 September 1857 in subsequent official records. Hence, the Memorandum of 21 October 1859 and *The London Gazette* of 15 January 1907 repeated the error that Ensign Lisle Phillipps was an officer in the 11th Regiment of Bengal Native Infantry at the time of his actions. Five years ago the authors of this book sought to have the official record corrected, resulting in the Ministry of Defence appending a Memorandum to the VC Register dated 31 May 2001 stating that: 'It would be appropriate and honourable for The Royal Green Jackets to regard Ensign Phillipps as having held a commission in their forebears, the 60th Rifles, at the time of his death in the action for which he was subsequently awarded the Victoria Cross.'

Lisle Phillipps's untimely but glorious death created a great sensation in Leicestershire. To perpetuate his memory, a fine Gothic tower of rough-hewn granite, designed by Pugin, built in 1863 and paid for by public subscription, was erected overlooking his birthplace at Gracedieu Manor. This was later vandalised and demolished circa 1940. His name also figures among the names of others killed at Delhi on the wall of the Memorial, which still stands at the southern end of Delhi Ridge. In 1861, L.W. Des Anges painted a posthumous portrait of him, for which his sister, Freda, acted as sitter.

The Aftermath

Ensign Lisle Phillipps was the tenth member of the antecedent regiments of The Royal Green Jackets to be awarded a VC for their many acts of valour during the relief of Delhi in 1857. However, the recapture of the city cost the British dearly. Out of a force that was never more than 10,000 strong, the British lost 992 men killed and 2,845 wounded. Many hundreds more died of disease and exposure.[25] The 1st/60th's losses between 30 May and 20 September were 137 killed and 252 wounded out of a strength that, after reinforcement, reached 640. The 52nd's losses between 14 August and 20 September were 28 killed and 78 wounded out of a total of 680, while a further 98 died of cholera and other diseases.

As soon as the capture of the City was complete on 20 September 1857, the pursuit of the fleeing rebels began, resulting in the award of a VC to a former officer in The Rifle Brigade.

Captain (later Lieutenant-Colonel) the Hon. A.H.A. Anson VC

Captain the Honourable Augustus Henry Archibald Anson was born at Slebech Hall, Pembroke, in Wales, on 5 March 1835, a son of the 1st Earl of Lichfield. After attending RMC Sandhurst, he was commissioned into The Rifle Brigade on 27 March 1853, serving in the Crimea with 1 RB before transferring to the 84th (York and Lancaster) Regiment on 8 January 1856. After being sent to India he served as an ADC to his uncle, General the Hon. George Anson, Commander-in-Chief. During the operations following the recapture of Delhi he was ADC to Brigadier-General Sir James Hope Grant and was attached to the 9th Light Dragoons at the Battle of Bulandshahr, where a force of rebels fleeing from Delhi sought to defend the town against the pursuing British.

Quoting from Anson's VC citation, which covers two actions, the second during the Second Relief of Lucknow: 'The 9th Light Dragoons had charged through the town [of Bulandshahr on 28 September 1857] and were reforming on the Serai; the enemy attempted to close the entrance by drawing their carts across it, so as to shut in the cavalry and form a cover from which to fire upon them. Captain Anson, taking a lance, dashed out of the gateway, and knocked the drivers off their carts. Owing to a wound in his left hand received at Delhi, he could not stop his horse and rode into the middle of the enemy, who fired a volley at him, one ball passing through his coat. At Lucknow, at the assault of the Secundra Bagh, on 16th November, 1857, he entered with the storming part on the gates being burst open. He had his horse killed, and was himself slightly wounded. He has shown the greatest gallantry on every occasion, and has slain many enemies in fight.'

Anson transferred to the 7th Hussars in 1858 and after the Mutiny served during the Second China War. He became a Lieutenant-Colonel in 1870 and retired from the Army in 1873. During his military career he was mentioned in despatches 14 times in India and 17 times in total. He was MP for Lichfield from 1859–68 and MP for Bewdley from 1869–74. He died in the South of France on 17 December 1877, aged 42.

Chapter 4

The Indian Mutiny: 1858–9

The recapture of Delhi described in the previous chapter marked the turning point in the campaign to counter and suppress the Indian Mutiny. A key centre of critical strategic importance at the heart of Bengal and on the lines of communication to the Punjab had been recovered; the morale and unity of the rebel force had taken a severe knock; and British troops committed to the relief of Delhi were freed for other tasks. However, most of the regiments involved were exhausted and their numbers depleted. The 52nd LI, despite the Regiment's wish to remain engaged, no longer had the strength and, in October 1857, was ordered back to the Punjab, where it remained in relatively quiet circumstances during the remaining period of the Mutiny. The 1st/60th, too, needed time to recuperate and was ordered to stay at Delhi to garrison the city, while others were directed to pursue the fleeing mutineers.

Meanwhile, as soon as word of the Mutiny reached England, the 3rd/60th and 2 RB stationed in Ireland and 3 RB at Aldershot were ordered to India as reinforcements. The 3rd/60th, which had re-formed only two years earlier, was sent to Madras, arriving in December 1857. Subsequently the Battalion took no part in quelling the Mutiny in Bengal. 2 and 3 RB, on the other hand, arrived at Calcutta in November 1857 and within three weeks, with no time for acclimatisation, were in action at Cawnpore. 3 RB, like 3rd/60th, had re-formed only two years earlier and was full of relatively young and inexperienced Riflemen.

The 2nd/60th was the last of the battalions from the antecedent regiments of The Royal Green Jackets to arrive in India during the Mutiny. Throughout 1857 it was stationed on garrison duties in the Cape Colony of South Africa, where the authorities declined to release it for service in India. Eventually they relented, with the Battalion arriving at Calcutta in May 1858. Meanwhile, the 43rd LI which had remained in the Madras Presidency to prevent the spread of the Mutiny to the south of India, was ordered to Bengal, marching 1,300 miles to the north to take part in the punitive expeditions being mounted to hunt down the last of the rebels.

The arrival of the 2nd/60th in May 1858 increased the presence of the antecedent regiments of The Royal Green Jackets in India to the equivalent of seven battalions, three of which were present at the outset of the Mutiny and four of which were despatched as reinforcements.

Lucknow, March 1858

As soon as 2 and 3 RB arrived at Calcutta, they were immediately despatched to join a British force engaged in fighting the rebels at Cawnpore, where, on 6 December 1857, the rebels were routed and the city secured in British hands. Both battalions then took part in counter-insurgency operations in the surrounding countryside before being directed by Sir Colin Campbell, the Commander-in-Chief, to march on Lucknow, which was held by the rebels. The battalions set off on 3 March and by the 6th had arrived at the outskirts of the city, where, in company with others, they sought to penetrate the rebels' outer defences and force their way into the city. It was during one of these operations, near the Iron Bridge that spanned the River Goomtee immediately north of the Residency and city centre, that three members of 2 RB – Captain Wilmot, Corporal Nash and Rifleman Hawkes – engaged in an action on 11 March 1858 that was to result in each being awarded a VC.

Captain H. WILMOT VC
(Later Colonel Sir Henry Wilmot, Bt., VC KCB)

Corporal W. NASH VC
(Later Sergeant W. Nash VC)

Rifleman D. HAWKES VC

Captain Henry Wilmot was born the second son of Sir Henry Sacheverel Wilmot, Bt., of Chaddesden, Derbyshire, on 3 February 1831. He was educated at Rugby School before joining the 43rd LI in 1849. He transferred to The Rifle Brigade in August 1855, joining 2RB at the end of the Crimean War, accompanying the Battalion to India in 1857.

Corporal William Nash was an Irishman born in County Limerick on 23 April 1824. He subsequently enlisted as a boy, aged 14, on 2 June 1838. Rifleman David Hawkes was also an old soldier, being born at Witham, Essex, in 1822. His date of enlistment is not known.

The VC citation for each man is the same: 'For conspicuous gallantry at Lucknow on the 11th March, 1858. Captain Wilmot's Company was engaged with a large body of the enemy, near the Iron Bridge. That officer found himself at the end of a street with only four of his men, opposed to a considerable body. One of the four was shot through both legs and became utterly helpless: the two men lifted him up, and although Private Hawkes was severely wounded, he carried him for a considerable distance, exposed to the fire of the enemy, Captain Wilmot firing with the men's rifles, and covering the retreat of the party. Despatch of Brigadier-General Walpole, C.B., dated 20th of March, 1858.'[1]

Artist's impression of Captain Wilmot, Corporal Nash and Rifleman Hawkes rescuing a wounded comrade at the Iron Bridge, Lucknow, 11 March 1858

The Regimental History adds some detail:

> *On the 11th the two Battalions* [2 and 3 RB] *paraded on the Fyzabad road a little before six, in order to make a reconnaissance in force to ascertain the possibility of crossing by a bridge to Lucknow. The Riflemen, leading in skirmishing order, were distributed among orchards, buildings of various kinds, and narrow streets. They skirmished through these as well as they could, each captain acting in a measure independently, and handling his company as he thought best. The streets were so intricate and the continuity of the Battalions so broken that no other system was possible. The Riflemen worked their way through these obstructions, and reached the mosque on the Old Cantonment road, which commands the approach to the Iron bridge. This bridge they were ordered not to cross.... * [Subsequently] *On approaching the Iron bridge Captain Wilmot, 2nd Battalion, found himself with only four of his company at the end of a street opposed to a large force of the enemy* [resulting in acts of gallantry recorded in the VC citations].... *Eventually the Riflemen cleared the whole of the suburbs near the Old Cantonment road as far as the Iron bridge.* [2]

The final action at Lucknow took place on 21 March and the city cleared of rebels. Captain Wilmot was later appointed Deputy Judge-Advocate General in Oudh and, in 1860, Judge-Advocate General to the Forces during the Second China War. On returning to England he was the MP for South Derbyshire from 1869-85, becoming the 5th Baronet of Chaddesden in 1872. He was Honorary Colonel of the North Midland Volunteer Brigade from 1888-95 and was knighted in 1897. He died at Bournemouth on 7 April 1901, aged 70, and was buried at Chaddesden.

Corporal Nash reached the rank of Sergeant before being discharged in 1863.[3] He went to live in London and died on 6 April 1875, aged 48.

Rifleman Hawkes did not survive to receive his VC, publication of which in *The London Gazette* on 24 December 1858 occurred four months after his death at Fyzabad, India, on 14 August 1858, aged 35/36. The medal was sent to his father at Witham in Essex. Sadly, and despite his award, Hawkes has no known grave.

Re-conquest of Oudh, 1858

The 1st/60th ceased to garrison Delhi at the end of January 1858 and returned to Meerut. However, as soon as Lucknow was recaptured, Sir Colin Campbell decided to extend the re-conquest of Oudh into the countryside east of Delhi where many mutineers were taking refuge. Three columns were formed to march into and clear the area, including the Roorkee Field Force with the 1st/60th, and the Lucknow Field Force with 2 and 3 RB. On 6 May 1858 the Roorkee Field Force converged upon Bareilly, the capital of the province of Rohilkund, where Rifleman Bambrick performed the act of valour for which he was awarded a VC. In the following month 2 and 3 RB hastily marched out of Lucknow to engage and defeat a rebel force at Nawabgunge where, on 13 June 1858, Rifleman Shaw performed the act of valour for which he was awarded a VC.

Rifleman V. BAMBRICK VC

Rifleman Valentine Bambrick was born into a military family at Cawnpore, India, on 13 April 1837; his father and uncle were both troop sergeant-majors in the 11th Light Dragoons.[4] After working as a clerk, he enlisted in the 60th, KRRC, on 12 April 1853, joining the 1st/60th on 10 April 1854, but remaining at Meerut while the rest of the Battalion fought at Delhi.

Bambrick's VC citation reads: 'For conspicuous bravery at Bareilly, on the 6th of May, 1858, when in a Serai, he was attacked by three Ghazees, one of whom he cut down. He was wounded twice on this occasion.'

The Regimental History is a trifle more enlightening:

On the north side Bareilly is covered by the Dhuranea River, the bridge over which was commanded by some of the enemy's guns. Upon these our heavy guns, escorted by the Riflemen who were thrown into the gardens through which the road led, opened fire with great effect. The enemy's artillery being silenced, the Riflemen advanced. … In the street fighting which followed D Company under Lieutenant Cromer Ashburnham once more distinguished itself. A party posted on the roof of a house were warned of the approach of a body of Ghazis or desperadoes. The men dropped from the roof; Colour-Sergeant Henry Baily fell, covered with sword cuts, and Lieutenant Ashburnham barely escaped the same fate. A stroke from a tulwar [curved Indian sword] *hardly missed his head, and his own sword was too blunt to cut. A point therewith, however, finished the career of his assailant.*[5]

By nightfall Bareilly had been cleared of rebels. Although the Regimental History is not explicit, the VC citation and other reports indicate that the incident involving Lieutenant Ashburnham is the same as that in which Rifleman Bambrick took part, and that Bambrick's intervention was instrumental in helping to save Ashburnham's life.

Bambrick's service record reveals that he was frequently in trouble. He received three separate periods of detention in 1859 and when the 1st/60th left India in 1860, he decided to stay and transferred to the 87th (Royal Irish Fusiliers). However, by 1862 the 87th was in Ireland, with Bambrick once more in trouble, being sentenced to detention in July 1862, and in 1863 to 160 days imprisonment for being absent without leave. He was discharged at Aldershot on 16 November 1863.

Within a few hours of his discharge, Bambrick visited a hostelry where he witnessed a partially dressed soldier beating a woman. He intervened and a fight ensued. Bambrick's opponent had removed his medals from his tunic before the fight and afterwards they were gone. Bambrick was charged with assault and robbery. He was tried at Windsor Assizes on 3 December 1863, pleading guilty to assault but denying the charge of robbery. He was found guilty on both counts and, after abusing the judge, was sentenced to three years' penal servitude in Winchester and Pentonville prisons where he sought to clear his name. Both prison governors considered him to be an innocent man and petitioned for his release.[6]

Under the terms of Clause 15 of the Royal Warrant of 29 January 1856 (see Appendix B), Bambrick's name was erased from the VC Register 'for assault and theft of a comrade's medals'[7] and he forfeited his annuity (then £10). He was also required to return his VC. On 1 April 1864 he hanged himself in Pentonville, aged 26, leaving behind a letter that made it quite clear that his suicide was in remorse at the loss of his VC.

Rifleman Bambrick, although not a member of the Regiment at the time, has the dubious distinction of being one of only eight VC recipients to have had his name erased from the Register, another being Rifleman Corbett – see page 75. Although their names have never been formally reinstated, King George V's views (see page 5) effectively annulled the entries.

Rifleman S. SHAW VC

Rifleman Same (John) Shaw[8] was a Scot born on an unknown date at Prestonpans, East Lothian. Nothing is known about his early life except that he enlisted in the Army on 6 April 1849, with his employment shown as a labourer. Nothing, too, is known about his military service from 1849–54, as his name only appears for the first time in The Rifle Brigade in the re-formed 3 RB muster rolls of 1855. In July 1857 he left Aldershot with the Battalion, landing in India on 29 November. At Nawabgunge, more properly known as Nawabgunge-Burrabunkee, on 13 June 1858, he was a pioneer armed with a short, serrated pioneer's sword.

Shaw's VC citation reads:

'For the Act of Bravery recorded in a despatch from Major-General James Hope-Grant, K.C.B., Commanding the Lucknow Field Force, to the Deputy Adjutant-General of the army, of which the following is an extract: Nowabgunge [sic], 17th June, 1958."I have to bring to notice the conduct of Private Same Shaw, of the 3rd Battalion, Rifle Brigade, who is recommended by his Commanding Officer for the Victoria Cross. An armed rebel had been seen to enter a tope [clump] of trees. Some officers and men ran into the tope in pursuit. This man was a Ghazee. Private Shaw drew his short sword, and with that weapon rushed single-handed on the Ghazee. Shaw received a severe tulwar wound, but after a desperate struggle, he killed the man. I trust his Excellency will allow me to recommend this man for the Victoria Cross, and that he will approve of my having issued a Division Order, stating that I have done so.'

The Regimental history tells the same story more graphically:

One man, a Ghazee [a champion who fights against infidels], being cut off from his companions, seemed determined to make a desperate fight of it. Setting his back to a tree, he stood, sword in hand, glaring fiercely at his pursuers, for some officers and men had followed him into the tope. Some shots were taken at him, which he tried to avoid by dodging round the tree, but he was wounded and made more desperate. At last a Pioneer of the 3rd Battalion, Samuel Shaw, rushed at him and closed with him. The Ghazee wounded him on the head with his tulwar, but Shaw, drawing his Pioneer's sword, sawed at him with the serrated back and despatched him. Shaw rose from the ground covered with blood, but his opponent was slain. Many who witnessed it declared that this combat with a fanatic determined to sell his life to slay his foe, was the greatest instance of cool courage they ever saw.[9]

Examination of Shaw's VC citation indicates that General Hope-Grant, by announcing the award four days after the act, was following the procedure permitted under the second proviso of Clause 7 of the Royal Warrant (see Appendix B) and that Shaw's VC was an 'immediate' award.

At the end of the Mutiny in 1859, Shaw left India to return to England, most probably on discharge. On 27 December 1859 he died at sea, Max Arthur stating that Shaw committed suicide by jumping overboard 'as he could not stand the constant jibes of his comrades over his award!'[10] Regimental records provide no corroboration for this rather unlikely story, although the head wound he received at Nawabgunge might have disturbed the balance of his mind.

Lieutenant Andrew Green

On 8 October 1858, four months after Shaw's act of gallantry, a similar act took place during another punitive expedition to hunt down the rapidly reducing number of rebels still at large in Oudh. On this occasion a party of 100 men from 3 RB under command of Lieutenant Andrew Green encountered a large force of rebels some 40 miles from Lucknow. What happened next is recorded in the Regimental History:

On approaching the enemy's position, which was a strong one, a village on high ground and surrounded with dense jungle, fire was opened on them [Lieutenant Green's party] *from guns posted in the village and from matchlocks in the jungle. The Riflemen were extended in skirmishing order on the right, and entered the jungle. Lieutenant Green had warned the men not to lose communication with their files; but in the thickness of the jungle three men got separated, and were surrounded and wounded by the enemy. Hearing firing, Lieutenant Green at once made for the place, and was immediately surrounded by six rebels. He shot two with his revolver. As he was in the act of dismounting to attack the others, he was cut down and hacked at while on the ground. Springing to his feet, however, he managed to knock down two more of his assailants with the butt of his revolver, and drawing his sword, he kept the others at bay. While he was about to fall back in search of some of his men, he was attacked by three more of the enemy and a second time cut down. Again getting to his feet, he contrived with his wounded right hand to shoot another man, who was in the act of cutting at him with his tulwar, and whose blow, descending as he fell dead, inflicted a deep wound on Green's head.[11]*

Help then arrived. Green was by this time lying on the ground bathed in blood. He had received 14 sabre cuts and one gunshot wound. Four of his wounds were sewn up on the spot and his left arm was later amputated. Miraculously he survived. His gallantry was drawn to the attention of every level of command including Lord Canning, the Governor-General of India, who, in a despatch to London, reported his 'great satisfaction' at the conduct of Lieutenant Green. But that was his only reward. Comparing Green's act with Rifleman Shaw's, it is surprising that Green was not awarded a VC for he was clearly instrumental in saving the lives of his men, three of whom were wounded but none of whom were killed. One may conclude, however, that it was probably because there was no more senior officer than Green himself to witness and corroborate his action that he did not receive a VC.

Although the two Rifle Brigade battalions had only been in India a year, their deeds were clearly impressing others. Commenting in his diary in December 1858, William Howard Russell of *The Times*, wrote: 'The Rifle Brigade who are with us are as hard as nails; faces tanned brown, and muscles hardened into whipcord; and to see them step over the ground with their officers marching beside them is a very fine sight for those who have an eye for real first-rate soldiers. Lord Clyde [the Commander-in-Chief] is greatly pleased with the officers because they do not ride on ponies, as many officers of other regiments are accustomed to do.'[12]

43rd Light Infantry

In early 1858 the 43rd LI left Bangalore in the Madras Presidency on a route that was to cover 1,300 miles through the Deccan and central provinces of India to Calpee (Kalpi), about 50 miles south-west of Cawnpore, where the Regiment was about to play its part in the re-conquest of Oudh. A number of subsidiary operations were mounted along the way, with the last part of the march undertaken at the height of the dry season with the thermometer reaching 120°F [49°C] in the hospital tents. Three officers and 44 men died, most from sunstroke, some expiring in a few minutes, others lingering on in a state of coma for hours. It was an undoubted feat of endurance, not far removed from, and four times the distance of, Roberts's epic march from Kabul to Kandahar with the 2nd/60th in 1880. Furthermore, when the Regiment reached Calpee in July 1858, it was only to find that: 'No more desolate place than Calpee could be found in the world, Aden not even excepted.'[13]

On arrival in Bengal the 43rd spent many months hunting the remaining mutineers, who, by the end of 1858, were becoming ever more isolated and desperate. On 1 January 1859 a force of 100 men, including Private Addison and 29 others from the 43rd LI, was ordered to intercept a rebel band that was threatening the small semi-independent state of Rewah, 180 miles south-west of Calpee, the Rajah of which had remained loyal to the British throughout the Mutiny. Lieutenant Willoughby Osborne, the Resident Political Agent, who had secured the Rajah's loyalty, accompanied the force. At 1 a.m. on 2 October, spies provided information that the rebels were about a mile away. After lying low until daybreak, the force descended a small hill and encountered the rebels. Hand-to-hand fighting ensued.

Private H. ADDISON VC

Private Henry Addison was born at Bardwell in Suffolk on 1 February 1821. He enlisted in the 94th Regiment (later 2nd Battalion, The Connaught Rangers) on 9 February 1841. After training at Chatham, he joined the Regiment at Madras and served during the Moplah Revolt in 1849. In 1854, when the 94th returned to England, Addison, who had married an Anglo-Indian wife, decided to stay in India and transferred to the 43rd LI.

Addison's VC citation reads: 'For gallant conduct on the 2nd of January, 1859, near Kurrereah, in defending, against a large force, and saving the life of Lieutenant Osborn [*sic*], Political Agent, who had fallen on the ground wounded. Private Addison received two dangerous wounds, and lost a leg, in this gallant service.'

During the fighting, Lieutenant Osborne was attacked and wounded in the hand by a sword cut, thus preventing him from shooting his assailant with his pistol. Addison immediately placed himself between Osborne and his attackers, resulting in two dangerous wounds, which required the amputation of a leg there and then and without any anaesthetic. Thirty rebels were killed and two captured, the two prisoners being immediately tried summarily for mutiny and hanged.

On 7 August 1860, after his wounds had healed, Private Addison, who had previously been awarded a Long Service and Good Conduct Medal, was discharged from the Army. In gratitude for saving his life, Lieutenant Osborne, who continued to live in India, gave him a pension of £20 a year for life. Osborne died in 1881. Addison died at Bardwell, Suffolk, his birthplace, on 18 June 1887, aged 66.

End of the Indian Mutiny

It took nearly two years, following the recapture of Delhi in September 1857, before Lord Canning, the Governor-General, finally declared a 'State of Peace' throughout India on 8 July 1859. During the early days the mutineers inflicted many atrocities on the British and other Europeans living in the garrison towns and cantonments of northern India. The British then reciprocated, dealing mercilessly with captured rebels. British imperialism had triumphed, but at a cost of many lives. Bitterness amongst some Indians at the way that they had been treated lingered.The desire for independence, achieved less than 100 years later in 1947, never receded far below the surface.[14]

After the Mutiny the 43rd LI remained in India until moving to New Zealand in 1863.The 52nd LI returned to England in June 1859 and the 1st/60th a year later. In 1860 the 2nd/60th went to China to take part in the Second China War.The 3rd/60th moved to Burma at the end of 1861. Meanwhile, 2 RB remained in India until returning to England in 1867. 3 RB remained even longer before leaving India in 1870 and arriving in England at the end of 1871 after a year at Aden en route.

The Indian Mutiny resulted in the award of 182 VCs, sixteen of them to members of the antecedent regiments of The Royal Green Jackets, more than in any other war or campaign except the First World War.The 43rd LI received one, the 52nd LI two, the 60th, KRRC, nine, and The Rifle Brigade four. A VC was also awarded to a former officer in The Rifle Brigade.

Many have since argued that VCs were easier to come by during the Indian Mutiny than at any later date because the British authorities in India interpreted and applied the rules for awards more freely than those far distant in London would, by choice, have wanted. On the other hand, the fighting was at times extremely fierce, with no quarter given by either side. Roger Perkins, in referring to the citations of those awarded VCs at Delhi, wrote:'While reading those citations, it is as well to remember that the acts of valour which they describe were performed by men who had been marching and fighting for many weeks previously, who were already debilitated by chronic dysentery and heat exhaustion, and who found themselves part of a very small force isolated in a hostile land. Many were already at the end of their tether when they grimly fixed bayonets and went forward to the final assault.'[15] It is as well, too, to remember that the preamble to the Royal Warrant of 29 January 1856, published only 18 months previously, stressed Queen Victoria's wish that the VC should be an award 'which We are desirous should be highly prized and eagerly sought after'.While scarcity has a value, to be mean would have missed the point.

Chapter 5
Imperial Wars: 1864–84

This chapter covers the award of five VCs over a span of 20 years and a spread of three continents and five countries. The only common thread that unites them is the bravery displayed by the men who performed the acts of gallantry that resulted in these awards.

New Zealand, 1864

The arrival of settlers in New Zealand seeking land inevitably led to clashes with the indigenous Maoris, for example, in the Maori Wars between 1845–7 and 1860–6. After the British had quelled the Maoris in 1861, a truce followed, but this was broken in 1863 when the Maoris again rebelled. British troop reinforcements were immediately sent to New Zealand, including the 43rd LI who arrived in Auckland from Calcutta on 11 December 1863 on the screw-steamer *Lady Jocelyn* which had 'proved in such crank condition as to excite serious apprehensions' during the voyage![1]

On 29 April 1864 the 43rd, part of a combined force, assaulted a Maori stronghold at Puke-hina-hina (Gate Pa), about 5 miles from Tauranga (Te Ranga) on the North Island of New Zealand, where a fierce battle ensued during which the Commanding Officer of the 43rd, Lieutenant-Colonel Booth, was mortally wounded. The British withdrew, but were able to take possession of the position on the following day after the Maoris had slipped away during the night. Subsequently, in June 1864, about 600 Maoris occupied another stronghold, this time at Tauranga. On 21 June the position was assaulted and another fierce but brief battle ensued before the Maoris retired. It was during this battle that Captain Smith's gallant conduct led to the award of a VC.

The War was finally brought to a close in early 1866. The 43rd almost immediately left New Zealand for England in March. In 1913 the courage and humanity shown by the Maoris during the conflict was reflected in the establishment of an alliance between the 43rd and the New Zealand Hauraki Regiment.

Captain F.A. SMITH VC
(Later Lieutenant-Colonel F.A. Smith VC)

Captain Frederick Augustus Smith was born on 18 November 1826 in Dublin, Ireland. On 1 January 1849 he was commissioned as an Ensign

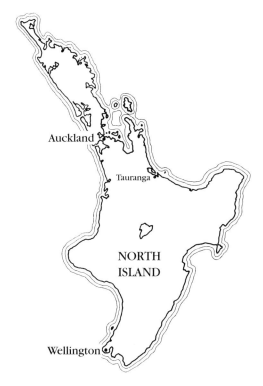

North Island, New Zealand

in the 1st Regiment of Foot (The Royal Scots). He served with the Regiment in the Crimean War at Alma, Inkerman and Sebastopol, before exchanging to the 43rd LI as a Captain on 9 April 1861.

His VC citation reads: 'For his distinguished conduct during the engagement at Tauranga, on the 21st of June [1864]. He is stated to have led on his Company in the most gallant manner at the attack on the Maories' position, and, although wounded previously to reaching the Rifle Pits, to have jumped down into them, where he commenced a hand to hand encounter with the Enemy, thereby giving his men great encouragement, and setting them a fine example.'

Quoting from the Regiment's Historical Records: 'Colonel Greer [who was commanding the British forces at Tauranga], in his report of the action, says that the enemy made a gallant stand at their rifle-pits; "they stood the charge without flinching, and did not retire until forced out at the point of the bayonet, which everywhere did its work." This defeat was a most stinging blow to the enemy, and doubtless influenced the large number who during the following month surrendered themselves and their arms.'[2]

Captain Smith, who was first into the rifle pits at the head of his company, was severely wounded at Tauranga and returned home to recuperate. After the announcement of his VC in *The London Gazette* on 4 November 1864 he appears to have been either unfit or no investiture was arranged as, on 31 January 1865, the War Office despatched his VC by post to him at an address in Scotland. On 21 March 1865, *The London Gazette* announced his promotion to Brevet Major and in 1866 he was in command of the 43rd's depot companies at Winchester, whence they joined the Regiment on its return from New Zealand in July 1866.

Smith was granted the rank of Brevet Lieutenant-Colonel in 1874, followed by substantive promotion in 1875, before retiring from the Army in 1878. He died at his home at Duleek, County Meath, Ireland, on 22 July 1887, aged 60.

Canada, 1866

After returning from the Crimean War 1 RB was stationed in England and Ireland before being warned at Dublin on 4 December 1861 to hold itself in readiness for active service in Canada should war break out with the United States following the 'outrageous' American seizure from a British ship of two Commissioners from the Southern Confederate States en route to London.

By February 1862, after a tortuous journey by sea and overland through ice and snow, 1 RB occupied requisitioned quarters at Hamilton, Ontario, only a few miles from the border with the United States. War, however, between Britain and the United States did not materialise and in 1864 the Battalion transferred to Montreal and in 1865 to Quebec, before returning to England in 1870.

Meanwhile, the American Civil War ended in the spring of 1865, after which a large number of discharged men of Irish descent established Fenian bands intent on causing trouble on the Canadian border. Their hope was that by capturing parts of Canada they could force the British Government in a trade-off to grant independence to Ireland. Heightened security was ordered and ammunition in transit guarded. It was while carrying out this duty that Rifleman O'Hea performed the act of gallantry that resulted in the award of a VC.

Rifleman T. O'HEA VC

Rifleman O'Hea was born at Schull, County Cork in Ireland on 11 June 1843. He enlisted in The Rifle Brigade on 6 November 1863, aged 20, and was sent to join the 1st Battalion in Canada.

O'Hea's VC citation reads: 'For his courageous conduct on the occasion of a Fire which occurred in a Railway Car containing ammunition, between Quebec and Montreal, on the 9th of June last. The

Serjeant in charge of the Escort states that, when at Danville Station, on the Grand Trunk Railway, the alarm was given that the Car was on fire; it was immediately disconnected, and, whilst considering what was best to be done, Private O'Hea took the keys from his hand, rushed to the Car, opened it, and called out for water and a ladder. It is stated that it was due to his example that the fire was suppressed.'

The following is a more detailed account:

> *During the Fenian troubles in Canada, it became necessary to forward a large supply of ammunition - including 95 barrels of gunpowder - from Quebec to Lake Erie, under such precautions that only some of the highest railway officials were aware of the nature of the consignment: This was placed in charge of T. O'Hea, and three other picked men of the Rifle Brigade - and the trucks were attached to a passenger train, conveying some 800 German immigrants westward.*
>
> *On the 19ᵗʰ June 1866, as the train drew into a by-station - Danville, not far from Quebec - O'Hea noticed that one of the trucks was on fire, and gave the alarm, telling the contents of the trucks, and calling for assistance, in the Queen's name: According to his statement, the railway officials, and a company of* [Canadian] *Infantry, which was drawn up in the station yard - as well as his three comrades - withdrew to a safe distance - O'Hea, having found a bucket, and a short ladder, and water not far off, mounted the burning truck, 19 times, single handed, and entirely without assistance, and succeeded in extinguishing the fire - a task which occupied him almost an hour, while his comrades, and the others, were shouting to him to come back: the immigrants were locked into their carriages; and, in total ignorance of the dire peril that awaited them, were enjoying the scene from the windows.*[3]

A Board of Inquiry was convened to examine the circumstances of the fire and recommended that O'Hea should be awarded the VC, which, after publication in *The London Gazette* on 1 January 1867, was presented to him in Canada, in the presence of several regiments, by Colonel T.H. Pakenham of the 30th (Cambridgeshire) Regiment.

Rifleman O'Hea is one of only six men ever to have been awarded a VC for an act of gallantry not performed 'in the presence of the enemy',[4] and the only man to have been awarded a VC for valour in Canada.

Under Clause 5 of the Royal Warrant of 29 January 1856 (see Appendix B) a VC could only be awarded for acts of gallantry performed 'in the presence of the enemy'. However, by Royal Warrant of 10 August 1858, eligibility was extended to permit award to individuals 'under circumstances of extreme danger, such as the occurrence of a fire on board Ship, or of the foundering of a vessel at Sea, or under any other circumstances in which through the courage and devotion displayed, life or public property may be saved'. These circumstances were applied in Rifleman O'Hea's case. Indeed, and as if to emphasise the point, the Permanent Secretary at the War Office, Sir Edward Lugard, when writing to O'Hea to advise him that he had been awarded a VC and would receive an annuity of £10, crossed out the words 'for your conspicuous bravery in the presence of the enemy' and substituted 'for your conspicuous courage under circumstances of great danger'.[5]

The extension of eligibility under Clause 5 was considered by many to be inappropriate. Unusually, the terms of the Royal Warrant of 10 August 1858 were never published in *The London Gazette* and, when a new VC Warrant was signed on 24 April 1881, eligibility reverted to cover only those whose acts of gallantry were performed 'in the presence of the enemy'.

On 17 March 1868 Rifleman O'Hea was discharged from Netley Hospital and from the Army having been diagnosed with tuberculosis and declared unfit for further service. He subsequently made his way to New Zealand and spent five months in the Otago Police (1872-3) and a year in the New Zealand Armed Constabulary (1873-4) before moving to Australia in June 1874.[6] On arrival in Sydney he managed to persuade the organisers to allow him to join an expedition into the outback of Queensland seeking traces of an earlier exploration. After trekking roughly 1,300 kilometres through the bush, the expedition ran out of water and, in November 1874, the expedition leader and O'Hea, aged 31, died of thirst near Nocatunga Station in Sturt Stony Desert, 1,140 kilometres west of Brisbane. One man survived to tell the tale of their ordeal, which lack of space does not permit to be told in full here.

Just before he left Sydney in July 1874, O'Hea entrusted his VC to a friend, Major H.S.W. Crummer, who, unable to trace O'Hea's representatives, kept it for 30 years before presenting it on 28 April 1905 to the National Art Gallery of New South Wales, of which his brother-in-law was President. Meanwhile, in 1900, another medal purporting to be the VC awarded to O'Hea was sold for £57 at Debenham's Auction Room, London, to Messrs Spink & Son, acting on commission for an American collector, Mr Sanford Saltus, who later donated it to the American Numismatic Society. Doubt was raised as to which was the original medal – the one in Australia or the one sold at auction.

Major Crummer, in an affidavit dated 2 June 1905, swore that the medal he had received from O'Hea had never been absent from his possession 'for an hour' since he had been given it almost 31 years earlier.[7] Nevertheless, to be sure, the Art Gallery's medal was returned via the War Office to Messrs Hancock, the manufacturers, who, in 1907, declared that, in their opinion, it was the original. However, the War Office was sufficiently concerned about counterfeiting to write to Hancocks on 14 September 1906 recommending that all VCs cast thereafter should be marked 'so that genuine Crosses may be distinguished from spurious imitations', which Hancocks have dutifully done ever since.

Over 40 years elapsed before, in February 1950, a researcher 'came upon' O'Hea's VC in the Art Gallery of New South Wales. Unsure what to do with it, the Gallery offered it to the Canadian Government. On hearing this, Field Marshal Lord Wilson of Libya, Colonel-Commandant of The Rifle Brigade, intervened, persuading Canada's Minister for External Affairs, Mr Lester Pearson, that 'as O'Hea was not a Canadian and that as the Rifle Brigade was not permanently associated with Canada although it was serving there when the cross was awarded, it would be a gracious act for the Canadian Government to waive its right and to allow the cross to come to the museum of the Rifle Brigade at Winchester.'[8] This was agreed and the medal presented to the Regiment on 29 May 1951.

In 1953 the American Numismatic Society again questioned the authenticity of the medal. This time Hancocks examined both medals, declaring the medal in The Rifle Brigade's possession to be the original. In particular, and apart from differences in the engraving, the VC held by the American Numismatic Society incorrectly showed the date of O'Hea's action to be '19th June 1866' and not '9th June', a mistake appearing in D.H. Parry's book, *Britain's Roll of Glory*, published in 1895, from which the counterfeiter most probably sourced the wrong date.[9] Since 1953, the matter has been allowed to rest.

Counterfeit   Original

The reverse of Rifleman O'Hea's counterfeit and original VC

Chapter 5

Great Fire, Quebec

On 14 October 1866, four months after Rifleman O'Hea's action at Danville station, a great fire occurred at Quebec during which the Riflemen of 1 RB took a very active part in endeavouring to suppress it, to save life and to rescue property. Rifleman William Berry particularly distinguished himself by rescuing a child from a house, which the engineers were about to blow up to prevent the extension of the fire. The fuse was already burning when Berry rushed into the house and rescued the child. Like O'Hea, Berry's act was not conducted 'in the presence of the enemy' but did conform to the circumstances described in the Royal Warrant of 10 August 1858. His name was put forward for a VC, but on this occasion Sir Edward Lugard at the War Office did not support the recommendation, commenting: 'although praiseworthy, [this act] was scarcely one which should be rewarded by the bestowal of this high Distinction.'[10]

Zululand, 1879 (*see map on page 80*)

In 1852, Transvaal in South Africa became an independent Boer Republic, but one whose existence was always threatened by the warlike tendencies of the Zulus. By 1877 the Boer Republic was almost bankrupt and considered by the British to be no longer capable of self-government or self-defence. The British, fearing Zulu intentions and the implications for the security of Britain's possessions in South Africa, annexed Transvaal in April 1877. The Zulus responded by committing several acts of violence on the border with Natal. In December 1878 the British issued an ultimatum demanding, inter alia, that the Zulu army should be disbanded. When the ultimatum was ignored, Lord Chelmsford, commanding the British forces, immediately launched an offensive against the Zulus. The result was the disastrous defeat of the British at the Battle of Isandhlwana on 22 January 1879. A British column was also blockaded but not attacked at Etshowe.

It was during the subsequent operations to restore British authority that Brevet Lieutenant-Colonel Redvers Buller of the 60th, KRRC, commanding the Frontier Light Horse, performed the acts of gallantry that resulted in the award of a VC.

Brevet Lieutenant-Colonel R.H. BULLER VC CB
(Later General Sir Redvers Buller VC GCB GCMG)

Lieutenant-Colonel Redvers Buller was born on 7 December 1839 at Downes, the family home near Crediton in Devon. He was educated at Harrow School, briefly, and then Eton College. He became an Ensign in the 60th on 23 May 1858, purchasing his commission for £450. After attending The Rifle Depot at Winchester, he joined the 2nd/60th in India in 1859, taking part with the Battalion in the Second China War (1860), including the capture of the Taku Forts and the advance on Peking. Returning to England with the 2nd/60th in early 1862, he purchased his promotion to Lieutenant on 9 December 1862 and was posted to 4th/60th in Canada, whence he returned to England with the Battalion in the summer of 1869. On 28 May 1870 he purchased his promotion to Captain but because there was no vacancy in the 4th/60th he returned to Canada to join the 1st/60th just in time to excel during Colonel Garnet Wolseley's Red River Expedition to Fort Garry (now Winnipeg) in 1870. In 1872 he attended the Staff College at Camberley, but did not complete the course as he was chosen by Wolseley, whose protégé he had become, to be a staff officer on Wolseley's expedition to Ashanti on the Gold Coast of West Africa (now Ghana). Again he excelled, being awarded a CB and brevet promotion to Major on 1 April 1874. In the same year he inherited the family estates, covering 5,000 acres in Devon and Cornwall with an annual value in excess of £14,000.

Buller never served at regimental duty with the 60th after leaving the 1st Battalion to attend the Staff College in 1872. Instead, on return from the Ashanti Expedition, he became Deputy Assistant Adjutant General at the War Office leaving, in 1878, to join the Commander-in-Chief's staff during what was known as the Ninth Kaffir War in South Africa. On 22 April 1878 he was appointed to command the 250-strong Frontier Light Horse, 'a mixed bunch of often disreputable characters, Boers, British and others, its Regimental Sergeant Major a deserter from the 80th Foot [Staffordshire Volunteers]. They were "in terribly bad order", as he told his sister …, "and I fear there is not much credit to be got out of being associated with them, but I will do my best".'[11]

Buller flourished in command soon earning an enviable reputation for fearlessness before the Ninth Kaffir War ended. On 11 November 1878 he was promoted to Brevet Lieutenant-Colonel. The action, though, for which he was awarded the VC, did not take place until March 1879, after the start of the Zulu War and the defeat at Isandhlwana, when Lord Chelmsford decided to launch a diversionary 'reconnaissance in force' on a mountain stronghold held by 4,000 Zulus at Hlobane (Inhlobana), while he attempted to relieve the column blockaded at Etshowe.

On 28 March 1879 Buller commanded the main 'assault' at Hlobane, ascending the eastern face of the mountain before dawn. However, his small force of 400 colonial horsemen and 300 native auxiliaries ran into trouble, being surprised by the arrival of a very much larger Zulu force. Buller and his men were forced to beat a hasty retreat down the almost sheer sides of Hlobane. The British suffered nearly 100 men killed. Some only escaped death thanks to the bravery of Buller and others. Five VCs were awarded following the action at Hlobane. This setback, however, and the possible impact on Buller's reputation of being associated with failure, was quickly forgotten when the Zulus were soundly defeated on the following day at Kambula, in a battle in which Buller and the remnants of his Frontier Light Horse bravely charged and harried the fleeing Zulus.

Buller's VC citation is explicit: 'For his gallant conduct at the retreat at Inhlobana, on the 28th March, 1879, in having assisted, whilst hotly pursued by Zulus, in rescuing Captain C. D'Arcy, of the Frontier Light Horse, who was retiring on foot, and carrying him on his horse until he overtook the rearguard. Also for having on the same date and under the same circumstances, conveyed Lieutenant C. Everitt, of the Frontier Light Horse, whose horse had been killed under him, to a place of safety. Later on, Colonel Buller, in the same manner, saved a trooper of the Frontier Light Horse, whose horse was completely exhausted, and who otherwise would have been killed by the Zulus, who were within 80 yards of him.'

Colonel Evelyn Wood,[12] a column commander at the time, is later alleged to have said that he had recommended Buller for the VC 'for having saved three lives, but he had really won it a dozen times'.

On 4 July 1879 Buller was present at the British victory at Ulundi before returning to England, physically exhausted, in August. His subsequent career, well documented in a number of books and in the *Dictionary of National Biography*, embraced further service in South Africa in 1881 during the First South African (Boer) War; in Egypt, including at the Battle of Tel-el-Kebir on 13 September 1882; and in Sudan at the battles of El Teb on 29 February and Tamaai on 13 March 1884. After taking part in the failed expedition to relieve Gordon at Khartoum, he returned to England at the end of 1885 and, after a short spell in Ireland, became Quartermaster General on 15 October 1887 and Adjutant General on 1 October 1890, a post he held until 30 September 1897. He was then on half-pay for 12 months before being appointed to command at Aldershot on 9 October 1898 and then, a year later, reluctantly, to be Commander-in-Chief in South Africa at the start of the Second South African (Boer) War.

Buller's time in command in South Africa was marked by failure followed by success, but the latter only after Field Marshal Lord Roberts had superseded him as Commander-in-Chief. In November 1900 he returned to England and resumed his post at Aldershot. However, in October 1901, he was dismissed from his command for commenting injudiciously about the conduct of the South African War at a public luncheon in London. Thereafter he retired to Devon, much loved and respected by those whom he had commanded and a stalwart supporter of the 60th of which he was Colonel-Commandant for 13 years prior to his death from cancer at Downes on 2 June 1908, aged 68. To quote from the Regiment's Annals:

Redvers Henry Buller was a remarkable personality, of independent opinion and habit of thought. Endued with unusual physical strength and clever with his hands, he had in a high degree three qualities – an astonishing capacity for work, whether of mind or body; great love of argument; and a personal

General Sir Redvers Buller VC GCB GCMG

magnetism which gained for him the love, confidence and devotion of every N.C.O. and private soldier with whom he came in contact. Buller was the last man to curry favour with them; but that an electric current flowed incessantly between them and him is undeniable. Such a power is given to few English soldiers.[13]

Egypt, 1882 (*see map on page 80*)

In 1881/2 the ascendance of Colonel Ahmed Arabi was threatening the security of British and French citizens in Egypt. There was concern, too, that the Egyptians might interrupt free passage through the Suez Canal. In May 1882 a British and French fleet entered Alexandria harbour, prompting a Moslem massacre of Christians. The despatch of a British expeditionary force under the command of Sir Garnet Wolseley was immediately initiated. On 11 July the British Mediterranean Fleet returned to bombard Alexandria and on 13 July landing parties found Alexandria unoccupied by Egyptian forces. The city was secured and a Mounted Infantry company formed, including a troop of 30 officers and men from 3 KRRC, who arrived at Alexandria from Malta on 17 July.

In early August the British conducted a reconnaissance in force to locate and engage the Egyptians, which they did on 5 August 1882 at Kafr Dowar, 15 miles south-east of Alexandria. It was during this action, which was little more than a skirmish, that Rifleman Corbett performed the act of gallantry for which he was awarded a VC.

Kafr Dowar was followed, on 13 September 1882, by the Battle of Tel-el-Kebir where the Egyptians were comprehensively defeated. Two days later Cairo surrendered and the campaign successfully concluded.

Rifleman F. CORBETT VC

Rifleman Frederick Corbett's real name was David Embleton, born, according to family records, on 17 September 1853 in Maldon, Essex.[14] As a young man he served as a Volunteer Rifleman with G Company, 2nd Essex Rifle Volunteers, at Maldon. At some point prior to the Cardwell Reforms and the removal on 1 July 1881 of '60th' from the Regiment's title, he joined the 3rd/60th in South Africa, accompanying the Battalion, officially re-titled 3 KRRC, to Malta in February 1882 and then to Egypt in July. Family oral history suggests that he may have arrived in South Africa as early as 1879 and taken part in the latter stages of the Zulu War and in the actions fought by the 3rd/60th in early 1881 during the First South African (Boer) War, but confirmation is lacking. On arrival at Alexandria in July 1882 Corbett, presumably having had some experience with horses, possibly with the Essex Rifle Volunteers, joined the Mounted Infantry.

Corbett's VC citation reads: 'During the reconnaissance upon Kafr Dowar, on 5th August, 1882, the Mounted Infantry, with which Private Corbett was serving, came under a hot fire from the enemy and suffered some loss, including Lieutenant Howard-Vyse,[15] mortally wounded. This officer fell in the open, and there being then no time to move him, Private Corbett asked and obtained permission to remain by him, and though under a constant fire, he sat down and endeavoured to stop the bleeding of this officer's wounds, until the Mounted Infantry received orders to retire, when he rendered valuable assistance in carrying him off the field.'

At the time of Kafr Dowar Corbett was acting as orderly to the Commander of the Mounted Infantry, Major H.H. Parr of the Somerset Light Infantry. He recommended Corbett for the DCM, but Sir Garnet Wolseley thought a VC to be more appropriate.

Corbett was present at the Battle of Tel-el-Kebir on 13 September before being encouraged by Major Parr to join the Military Foot Police, which Parr was appointed to command on 7 October 1882. Corbett dutifully transferred on 14 November and was later promoted Corporal. He was discharged from the Army as medically unfit with varicose veins on 18 June 1883.

On return to England Corbett sold his VC for 15 guineas. In October 1883 he applied to rejoin the Army and on 15 December re-enlisted as a driver in the Royal Horse Artillery. He was sent back to Egypt in February 1884 returning to England in June. He then went absent without leave from 12–23 July. On 30 July he appeared before a district court martial at Aldershot charged with absence without leave and theft and embezzlement from an officer. He was convicted and imprisoned for 28 days with hard labour. Under the terms of Clause 15 of the Royal Warrant of 29 January 1856 (see Appendix B), his name was erased from the VC Register and he forfeited his annuity (then £10). He was also required to return his VC, which he had sold, but would appear to have been in possession of a copy, which was confiscated together with his other medals.

On leaving prison Corbett was sent to India with the Artillery and imprisoned twice more, in 1887 for losing kit and replacing it with a comrade's, and in 1889 for striking a NCO. He had numerous other disciplinary entries on his conduct sheet. In 1890 he was sent back from India and was medically discharged from the Army, for the second time, on 16 January 1891. His medical records refer to periods of treatment for alcoholism and for sexually transmitted diseases. He received no pension and, after leaving the Army, was frequently in trouble in the courts. He died destitute in Maldon Workhouse Infirmary on 25 September 1912, aged 59, and was buried in a pauper's grave.

Various copies of Corbett's VC surfaced during his later life and subsequently. Both the Royal Artillery and the KRRC at one time thought they had the original, but both were declared to be fakes. However, in 1962, the original came up for sale and was purchased by the Regiment.

M.J. Crook comments on 'the curious history of the VC of Frederick Corbett ... [whose] Cross had, apparently, come in 1903 into the possession of a Mr Mansfield, Clerk of Kingsbury Urban District Council, who approached the WO [War Office] apparently with a view to restoring it to the recipient or his family. He was, however, informed that "... as the name of Frederick Corbett was erased from the VCR [Victoria Cross Register] ... the cross should not be delivered to him or his representatives". This reply seems to have worried Mr Mansfield as to whether he was in order in retaining the decoration himself, but a further letter from the WO confirmed that, in view of Corbett's having sold his Cross at a time when he was not subject to the Army Act, Mr Mansfield was entitled to retain it.'[16]

Rifleman Corbett, although not a member of the Regiment at the time, is one of only eight VC recipients to have had his name erased from the VC Register, another being Rifleman Bambrick (KRRC) – see page 58.Although their names have never been formally reinstated, King George V's views (see page 5) effectively annulled the entries.

Sudan, 1884 (*see map on page 80*)

In February 1884 a large British expeditionary force landed at Trinkitat on the Sudanese coast to suppress a rebellion incited by the self-proclaimed Mahdi and his supporters, who, for some while, had been besieging various Egyptian garrisons in the Sudan and then annihilating

The Rifles Company of the Mounted Infantry Camel Corps
in the Sudan, 1884/5 (R. Simkin)

the relief columns. The force included 3 KRRC and a Mounted Infantry company with a troop of Rifles. Marching inland, a 3,000-strong body of Arabs was defeated at the Battle of El-Teb on 29 February 1884. The British then re-embarked at Trinkitat, landed at Suakin and attacked the main Arab force of 12,000 fierce-looking dervishes at Tamaai. As they did so, they encountered the enemy in a ravine to their front. Disaster nearly followed before the British recovered the situation and the battle was won. By May 1884 the expeditionary force had fulfilled its purpose and returned to Egypt.

Lieutenant P.S. MARLING VC

(Later Colonel Sir Percival Marling, Bt., VC CB)

Lieutenant Percival Scrope Marling was born on 6 March 1861 at Stanley House, King's Stanley, Gloucestershire, three miles from the family's ancestral home at Stanley Park. After attending Harrow School, he entered RMC Sandhurst in September 1879, commenting in his memoirs published in 1931, that it was 'in those days a very different place from what it is now. I mercifully had a room to myself, which was a great comfort, and I thoroughly enjoyed my time there. We were allowed leave every Saturday after morning parade till 10 p.m. on Sunday night.' He later reported that: 'In July 1880 I passed seventy-sixth out of Sandhurst. There was an awful row the last night of the term, as we took an unpopular under-officer and threw him into the lake.'[17]

On 11 August 1880 Marling was commissioned as a Second Lieutenant in 3 KRRC. He served with the Battalion during the First South African (Boer) War, including at Laing's Nek on 28 January and Ingogo on 8 February 1881. He accompanied 3 KRRC to Malta and on 1 July 1882 was promoted Lieutenant shortly before deploying with the Battalion to Egypt, where he was present at the Battle of Tel-el-Kebir. At the end of December 1883 he joined the Mounted Infantry, with whom he served in Sudan at El-Teb and at Tamaai, where, on 13 March 1884, he performed the act of gallantry recorded in his VC citation:

> *For his conspicuous bravery at the battle of Tamai* [sic], *on the 13th March last, in risking his life to save that of Private Morley, Royal Sussex Regiment, who, having been shot, was lifted and placed in front of Lieutenant Marling on his horse. He fell off almost immediately, when Lieutenant Marling dismounted, and gave up his horse for the purpose of carrying off Private Morley, the enemy pressing close on to them until they succeeded in carrying him about 80 yards to a place of comparative safety.*

Marling adds nothing substantive in his memoirs to the bald facts in the VC citation, except that Private Morley died from his wounds on the following day. It is clear, though, from a despatch written after the earlier battle of El-Teb by the officer commanding the Mounted Infantry, that Marling was considered 'a very dashing young officer, who, although he has been but a short time in the Mounted Infantry, handled his men very ably, and carried out the orders given him with great coolness and dash'.[18]

On returning to Egypt in mid-1884, the Mounted Infantry was expanded into a Camel Corps (see picture on page 76), Marling taking part with the Corps in the failed Nile Expedition to relieve General Gordon at Khartoum in 1884–5. In October 1885 he assumed command of a Mounted Infantry company, remaining in Egypt until February 1887 before transferring to the 18th Hussars. He subsequently served with the Hussars in India and during the Second South African (Boer) War, and was present at Talana Hill on 20 October 1899 and was part of the garrison at Ladysmith during the siege. He commanded the 18th Hussars during the later stages of the War and was awarded a CB on 17 July 1902. He was promoted Brevet Colonel in command of York Garrison and District in 1905, serving as a temporary brigadier in South Africa in 1909, before retiring in 1910 after being injured by his horse falling on him.

Marling re-joined the Army at the start of the First World War, serving in France with the Headquarters Staff, Indian Army Corps, until being invalided home in 1915. He inherited the baronetcy and Stanley Park in 1919, where he died on 29 May 1936, aged 75.

Chapter 6
Imperial Wars: 1899–1903

This chapter covers the award of four VCs during the Second South African (Boer) War and one for actions during the campaign in Somaliland in 1903.

South Africa, 1899–1902

By the middle of 1899 relations between Great Britain and the Boer Republics of Transvaal and the Orange Free State were close to breaking point. British imperialism and access to the mineral wealth of Transvaal were in conflict with Boer nationalism and their intention not to be dictated to or dispossessed by the British. Conflict became unavoidable and on 11 October 1899 the Second South African (Boer) War began.

Battalions from all the antecedent regiments of The Royal Green Jackets participated in the War, with the major battles being fought between October 1899 and August 1900, after which the Boers resorted to hit and run commando raids ranging over 150,000 square miles of open country. The British, faced with this change of tactics, endeavoured ruthlessly to hunt down the Boers while, at the same time, being obliged to tie down large numbers of troops protecting their lines of communication and key points. Eventually the conditions for a cessation of hostilities were achieved and the War ended with the signing of the Treaty of Vereeniging on 31 May 1902.

During the War two members of the KRRC and two members of the RB were awarded VCs, the first two awards resulting from acts of gallantry during the Battle of Colenso on 15 December 1899.

Captain W.N. CONGREVE VC
(Later General Sir Walter Congreve VC KCB MVO)
Lieutenant the Hon. F.H.S. ROBERTS VC†

Captain Walter Congreve, known in the Regiment as 'Squibs' because of his ancestral connection to Sir William Congreve (1772-1828) of Congreve Rocket fame, was born at Chatham on 20 November 1862. After attending Harrow School, he spent two years at Pembroke College, Oxford, matriculating in 1881, and was in the North

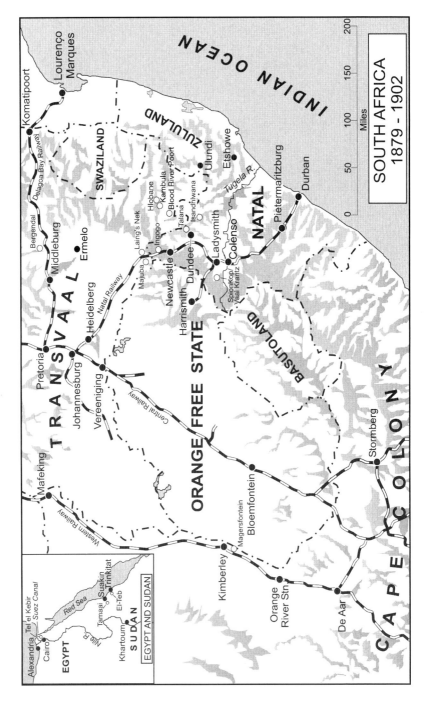

SOUTH AFRICA 1879 - 1902

Staffordshire Militia before joining the Regular Army. On entering RMC Sandhurst, he shared rooms with Douglas (later Field Marshal Earl) Haig, and on leaving was commissioned as a Second Lieutenant in The Rifle Brigade on 7 February 1885. He was posted to the 1st Battalion in India, applying a few months later to transfer to 4 RB at Meerut. In 1889 he returned to England with 4 RB but, on promotion to Captain on 6 December 1893, he was sent back to India to join 3 RB. In 1896 he was in England, first, at The Rifle Depot and then, two years later, as District Inspector of Musketry at Aldershot. As soon as War broke out in South Africa he hastened to join 2 RB. However, by the time of his arrival at Durban on 23 November 1899, 2 RB was already besieged as a part of General White's force at Ladysmith. Being at a loose end, he was attached to the staff of 4 Infantry Brigade, and then to General Buller's Headquarters as press censor.

Lieutenant Frederick (Freddie) Roberts was born at Umballa, India, on 8 January 1872, a son of Lieutenant-Colonel F.S. (later Field Marshal Lord) Roberts VC. He attended Eton College and RMC Sandhurst before being commissioned in The King's Royal Rifle Corps on 10 June 1891. He was immediately sent to join the 1st Battalion in India, taking part in the Isazai Expedition on the North-West Frontier in 1892, in Waziristan in 1894, and in the Chitral Expedition in 1895. He served as Kitchener's ADC during the re-conquest of Sudan from 1897–8 and was mentioned in despatches for his services at the climactic Battle of Omdurman on 2 September 1898. At the outset of the South African War, Roberts immediately sought to rejoin 1 KRRC, which was in South Africa before the War began. However, like Congreve, he arrived after the Battalion was besieged at Ladysmith. Instead, he was attached to the staff of Major-General Clery, commanding the 2nd Division.

General Redvers Buller, the Commander-in-Chief, who arrived at Cape Town on 31 October and at Durban on 25 November, decided by early December 1899 that he had sufficient forces in Natal to break through the Boer positions on the Tugela River at Colenso and relieve General White's force at Ladysmith. Battle was joined on 15 December and to quote from the KRRC Regimental Annals: 'Everything went wrong from the start.'[1] It was in trying to save the situation and, in particular, the guns, that Captain Congreve, Lieutenant Roberts and five others became involved in the actions that were to result in all of them being awarded VCs.[2]

The VC citation for Congreve reads: 'At Colenso on the 15th December, 1899, the detachments serving the guns of the 14th and 66th Batteries, Royal Field Artillery, had all been either killed, wounded, or driven from their guns by Infantry fire at close range, and the guns were deserted. About 500 yards behind the guns was a donga [gully] in which some of the few horses and drivers left alive were sheltered. The intervening space was swept with shell and rifle fire. Captain Congreve, Rifle Brigade, who was in the donga, assisted to hook a team into a limber, went out, and assisted to limber up a gun. Being wounded, he took shelter; but, seeing Lieutenant Roberts fall, badly wounded, he went out again and brought him in. Captain Congreve was shot through the leg, through the toe of his boot, grazed on the elbow and the shoulder, and his horse shot in three places.'

The VC citation for Roberts is exactly the same as Congreve's with two additional sentences at the end: 'Lieutenant Roberts assisted Captain Congreve. He was wounded in three places.'

Due to a misunderstanding of Buller's orders, the 1st Field Artillery Brigade came into action little more than 1,000 yards from the nearest enemy entrenchments and were subjected to a storm of bullets and shells. Faced with the loss of a significant number of his guns, Buller immediately decided that it would no longer be possible to force the passage of the Tugela River and that the priority was to save the 12 guns of the 14th and 66th Batteries. Buller, who was by now personally involved, turned to some of the staff officers around him and directed them to go and help. Congreve and Roberts were among those who responded, galloping forward with two limbers over half a mile of open plain. Describing the scene, Congreve later wrote:

I have never seen, even at field firing, bullets fly thicker. All one could see was little tufts of dust all over the ground, and one heard a whistling noise and a phut where they hit and an unceasing rattle of musketry somewhere in front. My first bullet went through my left sleeve and just made the point of my elbow bleed; next a clod of earth caught me no end of a smack on the other arm; then my horse got one; then my right leg one; my horse another and that settled us, for he plunged and I fell off about a hundred yards short of the gun we were going to. A little nullah [hollow] was close by, and into that I hobbled and sat down.[3]

Two guns were recovered, but ten were left to their fate. Roberts, meanwhile, had fallen mortally wounded. After about an hour the enemy's fire abated and Congreve, looking out from his position, saw Roberts lying on the ground about 20–30 yards behind the 66th Battery. He immediately set off as fast his wounds would permit and, with the help of others, brought Roberts back into the shelter of the donga. Again, describing the scene, Congreve wrote:

We lay in the donga from eleven to four-thirty, no water, not a breath of air, no particle of shade, and a sun which I have never felt hotter even in India; a knife could not be held in a bare hand. It was the most beastly day I ever spent, and seemed interminable, and what it must have been for the badly wounded I hardly like to think.[4]

At about 4.30 p.m. the Boers overwhelmed the party in the donga, treating the wounded very well and giving them water before releasing them without their equipment to be removed in an ambulance. Roberts

Recovering the guns at Colenso, 15 December 1899 (John Charlton)

did not survive, dying two days later, on 17 December 1899, aged 27. Congreve was repatriated to Cape Town, where he recovered quickly, being appointed Adjutant of Kitchener's Horse, a corps of irregular cavalry, on 2 January 1900.

Lieutenant Roberts's premature death and subsequent award of a VC created something of a precedent at a time when posthumous awards were still not permitted. M.J. Crook, in his book *The Evolution of the Victoria Cross*, wrote:'With the outbreak of the South African War, cases soon arose to test the rules relating to the award of the VC to the dead. Indeed, the first list of VCs conferred for that war contained the name of one "since deceased" recipient, Lt F.H.S, Roberts, only son of the CinC South Africa, Lord Roberts. As no official papers appear to survive regarding this award it is impossible to say whether the case received any treatment not strictly in accord with the existing rules though one can understand why, in view of who his father was, the WO [War Office] might have desired to stretch a point in this instance. It was certainly at Queen Victoria's request that his Cross was forwarded to her for personal presentation to Lord Roberts, instead of being sent by letter as had been done in all similar cases. In any event, as Lt Roberts did not die until two days after his act of gallantry at the battle of Colenso, the criterion for an actual award instead of a memorandum, that the man should have been alive at the time he was recommended, could conceivably have been met.'[5] Indeed, this was almost certainly the case, as, although no official record survives, it is popularly believed that

General Buller wrote on 16 December 1899, the day after the battle and the day before Lieutenant Roberts died, recommending him for the award of a VC.

The award of Lieutenant Roberts's VC was announced in *The London Gazette* on 2 February 1900. Queen Victoria subsequently despatched the VC to Lady Roberts, as her husband was in South Africa, with a note stating 'here is something that I have tied up with my own hands'.[6] No doubt Lord Roberts, who had received his VC after an act of gallantry while serving with the Bengal Artillery during the Indian Mutiny, was extremely proud that he and his son should both have been awarded VCs, the first father and son pair to do so. Later, one of the guns that Lieutenant Roberts died trying to save was presented by the War Office to Lord Roberts and was used for the carriage of his coffin at his funeral in 1914.

Meanwhile, Captain Congreve, after spending less than three months as Adjutant of Kitchener's Horse, became Brigade Major of 18 Infantry Brigade and in November 1900 joined the staff of Lord Kitchener, Lord Roberts's successor. On 21 December 1901 he was promoted to Brevet Lieutenant-Colonel and in November 1902 he became Assistant Military Secretary and ADC to HRH The Duke of Connaught in Ireland. In 1903 he was awarded a MVO. He continued to progress thereafter in a series of appointments in UK, including as Second-in-Command of 3 RB in 1906 and as Commandant of the School of Musketry at Hythe in 1909. In 1911 he received a CB and assumed command of 18 Infantry Brigade at Lichfield, proceeding with his brigade to France at the start of the First World War. During the following four years he commanded 6 Division, 13 Corps, 7 Corps and 10 Corps. In 1917 he received a KCB. Matters, however, did not go well for him during the German offensive in March 1918 and on 15 May, following a reorganisation of the armies in France, he was ordered home, Field Marshal Haig, with whom he had shared rooms at Sandhurst, refusing to see him.

After remaining on half-pay until August 1919, Congreve was appointed to command the British forces in Syria and Palestine and in 1920 the British troops in Egypt. In 1921 he became Colonel-Commandant of 1 RB. In April 1923 he assumed command of Southern Command at Salisbury. He became Governor of Malta in June 1924 and died in post at Valletta on 28 February 1927, aged 64. He was buried at sea between Malta and Gozo in what is now called the Congreve Strait. It had been intended to give him a baronetcy, which was awarded instead to the second of his three sons, Geoffrey. His eldest son, Billy, was killed on the Somme in 1916 performing the acts of gallantry that led to his posthumous VC (see pages 115–21). Both Billy and Walter Congreve's third son, Christopher, served in The Rifle Brigade.

In the *Dictionary of National Biography*, from which some of the above information is sourced and more may be found, Congreve is described as 'a man of great physical and moral courage' and 'supremely a fighting general, incurring great risks in visiting the front line' during the First World War. Quoting a subordinate, Congreve 'infinitely preferred walking out in full view and quite close to the enemy than anything else. He simply asked for trouble.' Indeed, he was the only corps commander wounded during the First World War, having his left hand shattered by a shell while visiting his artillery near Vimy Ridge in June 1917. The hand was amputated, requiring a period of recuperation in UK.

Bergendal, 27 August 1900

A series of battles followed Colenso before Ladysmith was relieved on 28 February 1900. Buller then advanced into the Transvaal, reaching Bergendal, a feature just north of the railway line from Pretoria to Lourenço Marques, in August. Here 2 RB excelled in a successful attack in which Rifleman Durrant was a participant.

Rifleman A.E. DURRANT VC

(Later Acting Corporal A.E. Durrant VC)

Rifleman Alfred Durrant was born at Kentish Town in London on 4 November 1864, enlisting in The Rifle Brigade on 31 July 1883. He saw service overseas, including with 2 RB at the Battle of Omdurman, before proceeding with the Battalion to South Africa in 1899, arriving just in time to join the garrison in the defence of Ladysmith. He later took part with 2 RB at an action at Laing's Nek on 12 June prior to the battle at Bergendal on 27 August 1900.[7]

2 RB at Bergendal, 27 August 1900. Painting by J.P. Beadle.

Durrant's VC citation reads: 'At Bergendal, on the 27th August, 1900, Acting-Corporal Weller having been wounded, and being somewhat dazed, got up from his prone position in the firing line, exposing himself still more to the enemy's fire, and commenced to run towards them. Private Durrant rose, and, pulling him down endeavoured to keep him quiet, but finding this impossible he took him up and carried him back for 200 yards under heavy fire to shelter, returning immediately to his place in the firing line.'

The special correspondent of *The Standard* described the scene as follows:

> *The final action began at ten a.m. … About noon, seeing that the kopje [where the Boers were positioned] had to be carried at all costs, General Buller directed Colonel Metcalfe to extend his Rifle Brigade in front, and take it by assault, the Inniskilling Fusiliers acting in support.*
>
> *The Rifles deployed, company after company, like a machine. They found themselves at once under a hot fire … The crucial moment came when the leading line got to within four hundred yards of the kopje. The way was then over ground as flat as a billiard table, and at the other end of the four hundred yards rose the hill, more commanding than ever. The firing became deafening … Then came the final rush of the Rifles. Their Colonel, moving about as coolly as if on parade, led the charge, and was bowled over in the act – a bullet, going through his right arm, and passing over his stomach, seared as if a hot iron had been placed there. But the word had been given, and on went the men … the Boers broke. The Rifles had done magnificently.*[8]

One officer and 13 men from 2 RB were killed and seven officers and 57 men wounded at Bergendal. Rifleman Durrant was unhurt and promoted to Acting Corporal[9] soon afterwards. In 1903 he was awarded the Long Service and Good Conduct Medal and in 1904 was discharged after 21 years' service. He then worked for the Post Office for 25 years, at the end of which, in 1930, he was awarded the Imperial Service Medal. He died in Tottenham, London, on 29 March 1933, aged 68.

Blood River Poort, 17 September 1901

During the course of the War the Mounted Infantry was greatly expanded with Mounted Infantry companies in most battalions, and with battalions from across the Army contributing volunteers to man 25 independent Mounted Infantry regiments. One of these, 24 Mounted Infantry, was commanded by Lieutenant-Colonel Hubert Gough of the 16th Lancers, the older brother of Brevet Major Johnnie Gough of The Rifle Brigade, about whom more is written later in this chapter. 24 Mounted Infantry included a company from 2 KRRC and troops from 3 KRRC and 1 RB. Lieutenant L.A.E. Price-Davies was the Adjutant.

In August 1901, Louis Botha, a Boer commander, who had been hiding in the remote border areas of eastern Transvaal, decided to launch a major raid with 1,000 commandos across the Buffalo River into Natal, with his first target, the British camp at Dundee, which lay 10 miles inside Natal. On hearing of this, Lord Kitchener, the British Commander-in-Chief, ordered 24 Mounted Infantry with two field guns to travel 500 miles by rail and hunt down Botha's force. Botha, meanwhile, had his own difficulties with exhausted animals and little fodder. By 17 September he had reached no further than Blood River Poort, 25 miles north-east of Dundee and still in Transvaal. It was here that Gough's 24 Mounted Infantry spotted some 250 of Botha's men. Gough, however, despite intelligence reports to the contrary and without ordering adequate reconnaissance, decided that the 250 Boers constituted the main force and, in attacking them, was lured into an ambush, where a much larger number of Boers surrounded and overwhelmed the British.

Lieutenant L.A.E. PRICE-DAVIES VC DSO
(Later Major-General L.A.E. Price-Davies VC CB CMG DSO)

Lieutenant Llewellyn Alberic Emilius Price-Davies was born in London on 30 June 1878, but in the light of his unusual Christian names was always known to his friends as 'Mary'. He attended Marlborough College from 1892–4 and RMC Sandhurst in 1896–7 before being commissioned in The King's Royal Rifle Corps on 23 February 1898. He joined 2 KRRC in India and accompanied the Battalion to South Africa, where, after promotion to Lieutenant on 21 October 1899 and as a member of the Mounted Infantry, he avoided being besieged at Ladysmith. Instead, he took part in Buller's relief operations, being present between December 1899 and February 1900 at the battles at Colenso, Spion Kop, Vaal Krantz and the Tugela Heights. He later took part in Buller's advance from Natal into the Transvaal and was present at Laing's Nek on 12 June 1900. Thereafter he remained with the Mounted Infantry, being awarded a DSO on 1 April 1901 'for services in South Africa'.

Lieutenant Price-Davies's VC citation reads: 'At Blood River Poort, on the 17th September, 1901, when the Boers had overwhelmed the right of the British column, and some 400 of them were galloping round the flank and rear of the guns, riding up to the drivers (who were trying to get the guns away) and calling upon them to surrender, Lieutenant Price-Davies, hearing an order to fire upon the charging Boers, at once drew his revolver and dashed in among them, firing at them in a most gallant and desperate attempt to rescue the guns. He was immediately shot and knocked off his horse, but was not mortally wounded, although he had ridden to what seemed to be almost certain death without a moment's hesitation.'

The orders, decorations and medals of
Major-General L.A.E. Price-Davies VC CB CMG DSO (RGJ Museum)

Price-Davies, who was shot in the shoulder, soon recovered and was promoted Captain on 2 January 1902. Hubert Gough's reputation, however, suffered a temporary jolt with his impetuosity at Blood River Poort resulting in the most humiliating reverse suffered by the British against the Boers in the first nine months of 1901. Six officers and 38 men were killed or wounded, with the rest, six officers and 235 men, taken prisoner. Gough escaped during the course of the following night, while Price-Davies and all the remaining prisoners were stripped of their weapons, ammunition and equipment, before being released to their own lines. Botha subsequently suffered a series of reverses and retired whence he had come. Gough later commanded the Fifth Army during the First World War.

Shortly after his promotion to Captain, Price-Davies was severely wounded in a clash with the Boers at Ermelo, Transvaal, on 26 January 1902. He took no further part in the War, but remained with the Mounted Infantry until attending the Staff College in 1908–9. He then filled a number of different staff appointments before and after the outset of the First World War. On 1 September 1915 he became a substantive Major and on 25 November a temporary Brigadier-General in command, successively, of 113, 214 and 8 Infantry Brigade. Between April and November 1918 he served as a Special Liaison Officer in Italy with the temporary rank of Major-General.

After the War, Price-Davies commanded 145 (South Midland) Infantry Brigade (TA). He retired from the Army as an Honorary Major-General on 15 April 1930. During the Second World War he commanded a battalion of the Home Guard. He died at his home at Sonning, Berkshire, on 26 December 1965, aged 87, a much respected and highly decorated officer (see the picture of his orders, decorations and medals opposite).

Somaliland, 1903

In 1901 a local force was raised in Somaliland to protect tribes loyal to the British from warring factions led by Mahommed-bin-Abdullah Hassan, the Mad Mullah. After two years of inconclusive campaigning the Somaliland Field Force, including three battalions of the King's African Rifles and troops from India, arrived in early February 1903 at two ports, Berbera in British Somaliland and Obbia in Italian Somaliland. Each formed a column with the main advance from Obbia. On 17 April the 500-strong advance guard of the Obbia Column was heavily defeated at Gumburu. On 22 April the Berbera Column, under

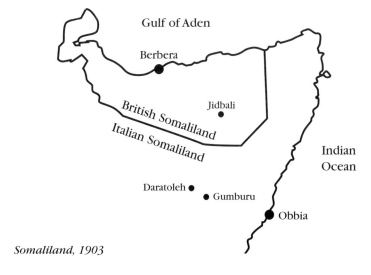

Somaliland, 1903

89

command of Major Gough, encountered the victors of Gumburu at Daratoleh, where, in a fight lasting several hours, the Column was forced to form a square only 30 yards by 30 yards in thick bush. As the ammunition ran low, Major Gough ordered his men to retire.

Brevet Major J.E. GOUGH VC
(Later Brigadier-General Sir John Gough VC KCB CMG)

Brevet Major John (Johnnie) Gough was born on 25 October 1871 at Murree in India, although the family home was in Tipperary, Ireland. After attending Eton College, he was a Second Lieutenant in the Westmeath Militia[10] for a year before, following in the footsteps of his older brother, Hubert, he entered RMC Sandhurst in 1891. He was commissioned in The Rifle Brigade on 12 March 1892 and joined 2 RB, taking part with a detachment from the Battalion in suppressing a rebellion in Mashonaland, Central Africa, in 1896-7. He accompanied 2 RB to Sudan and was present at the Battle of Omdurman in 1898. He remained with the Battalion while it was in South Africa, greatly distinguishing himself in command of A Company during the defence of Ladysmith. He was mentioned in despatches three times and received the brevet rank of Major.

Gough's VC citation reads: 'During the action of Daratoleh, on 22nd April last, Major Gough assisted Captains Walker and Rolland in carrying back the late Captain Bruce (who had been mortally wounded) and preventing that Officer from falling into the hands of the enemy. Captains Walker and Rolland have already been awarded the Victoria Cross for their gallantry on this occasion, but Major Gough (who was in command of the column) made no mention of his own conduct, which has only recently been brought to notice.' Below the citation in the same *London Gazette* dated 15 January 1904 his promotion to Brevet Lieutenant-Colonel is announced 'in recognition of his services in command of the Troops during the action at Daratoleh', back-dated to the date of the action on 22 April 1903.

In amplification of the citation, after Gough's order to retire, the Column was pursued for several hours, during which the rearguard became separated from the rest of column due to the thick bush and the need to cover the evacuation of the wounded by camel. At this point Captain Bruce, Gough's staff officer, was shot through the body from a distance of 20 yards and fell, unable to move. Captain Rolland and Captain Walker tried to help Bruce but he was too heavy to lift. While Walker held off the enemy with his carbine, Rolland went in search of assistance. Gough then arrived on the scene and after Rolland had returned with a camel they hoisted Bruce on to its back, but not before Bruce was wounded again and almost immediately died.

The Berbera Column lost two officers and 13 men killed at Daratoleh and 29 all ranks wounded out of a total strength of 213. Around 200 of the Mad Mullah's dervishes were killed. Gough recommended Rolland and Walker for VCs, but omitted to mention his own part. His skilful handling of the force and his gallantry under fire only came to light when his comrades informed the authorities; thus, his award was announced five months after the other two. Meanwhile, the Somaliland Field Force was reinforced and, on 10 January 1904, defeated the Mullah's army at Jidbali. The Mullah, although alive and free, fled south into neighbouring Italian Somaliland and nothing more was heard of him for a while.

After the 1903-4 Somali campaign, Gough attended the Staff College, after which he was appointed Inspector-General of the King's African Rifles (1907-9). In 1909 he commanded another expedition to quell the rebellious Somalis, but was invalided home in mid-year with hepatitis. In 1910 he was awarded the CMG for his services in East Africa. He then spent four years as a Colonel on the staff at the Staff College. In October 1913 he was appointed a Brigadier-General on the General Staff of Sir Douglas Haig's Headquarters at Aldershot. In March 1914, with Home Rule for Ireland high on the Asquith Government's agenda, he and his brother, Hubert, who was commanding the 3rd Cavalry Brigade at the Curragh, threatened resignation if the Government were to order the British Army to undertake military operations against the Unionists in Ulster. Their action was widely supported by others and the Government relented, without any apparent effect on their careers.[11]

At the outbreak of the First World War, the Headquarters at Aldershot moved immediately to France as HQ 1 Corps, with Gough assuming the role of Haig's Chief of Staff. He was still holding the appointment when, while visiting his old Battalion, 2 RB, in the front line on 20 February 1915, he was hit in the stomach at a range of over 1,100 yards by a German sniper located on the Aubers Ridge, in the vicinity of Neuve Chapelle. Lieutenant-Colonel Stephens, the Commanding Officer of 2 RB, later told General Haig that it was a chance shot which had ricocheted off the road nearby. Gough was immediately moved to a field ambulance station and there was some hope that he would survive, but two days later his heart failed and he died on 22 February 1915, aged 43. On 22 April 1915 he was awarded a posthumous KCB, a rare occurrence but richly deserved.

When considering the history of the VC and those who have been awarded it, the Gough family record is remarkable. Gough's father, General Sir Charles Gough, when a Major in the 5th Bengal Cavalry, received a VC for, inter alia, saving the life of his brother, Lieutenant H.H. Gough, at Delhi on 15 August 1857. Gough's uncle, later General Sir Hugh Gough, whose life his father had saved, was also awarded the VC for charging the enemy's guns on two separate occasions during the Indian Mutiny while serving with the 1st Bengal Cavalry.

The Goughs, whose actions were in 1857 and 1903, were the second pair of fathers and sons to be awarded VCs, the actions of the first, the Roberts's, occurring in 1857 and 1899.

Chapter 7
The First World War: 1914–16

The origins of the First World War, and certainly the nature and scale of it, will be familiar to most, if not all, who read this book. It was a titanic struggle and a war of attrition of epic proportions involving millions of soldiers and affecting the lives of tens of millions of civilians. From a British perspective the battles fought on the Western Front in Belgium and France had the greatest impact and were of the greatest importance since German victory in France would have opened the way for invasion of Great Britain.

When German entry into neutral Belgium prompted Great Britain to declare war on Germany on 4 August 1914, the general consensus in Britain was that the War would be over by Christmas and that it was the patriotic duty of every able-bodied citizen to serve the Country by enlisting in the Armed Forces. Rapid expansion of the Army followed, with Lord Kitchener's appeal for volunteers resulting in the creation of many hundreds of Service battalions in Kitchener's 'New Army'.

During the War the antecedent regiments of The Royal Green Jackets deployed a total of 58 front-line Regular, Service and Territorial battalions overseas, mostly to the Western Front.

Number of Battalions Overseas

Regiment	Regular	Service	Territorial	Total
Oxf & Bucks LI	2	3	4	9
KRRC	4	11	12	27
RB	4	8	10	22
Total	10	22	26	58

Note: These figures exclude over 30 Pioneer, Garrison, Reserve, Special Reserve and Young Soldiers' battalions, some of which served overseas, while others remained in UK responsible for training and drafting reinforcements to the front-line battalions.

1914

Immediately war was declared, battalions from the Regular Army were despatched as part of the British Expeditionary Force (BEF) to France and Belgium, where they were soon engaged in fighting the Germans near the Belgian town of Mons - 70,000 British troops with 300 guns faced 160,000 Germans with 600 guns. It was here that the actions giving rise to the award of the first VCs of the War took place on 23 August 1914.[1] However, the unexpected withdrawal of the French on the BEF's right flank, and the possibility of being outflanked by the Germans on the left, necessitated a British retreat to the River Aisne and then the Marne.

Captain F.O. Grenfell VC

On 24 August a former member of The King's Royal Rifle Corps, Captain Francis Grenfell of the 9th Lancers, greatly distinguished himself during the first day of the British retreat in an action that was to result in his name appearing in the opening list of First World War VC recipients published in *The London Gazette* on 16 November 1914. While still in Belgium, Captain Grenfell took part in a cavalry charge against a large body of German infantry at Audregnies. The casualties among the men and horses were very heavy and he was left as the senior officer. While rallying part of the Regiment behind a railway embankment, he was twice hit in the hand and thigh and seriously wounded. In spite of his injuries, when asked for help in saving a battery of guns, he and several volunteers, under a hail of bullets, manhandled the guns out of range of the German fire.

Francis Grenfell was a nephew of Field Marshal Lord Grenfell (KRRC).[2] He was educated at Eton College and became an internationally renowned polo player and a leading steeplechase rider. He initially joined The Seaforth Highlanders, accompanying them to Cairo, before transferring to The King's Royal Rifle Corps in May 1901. He served with the Regiment in the Second South African (Boer) War and in India with 2 KRRC, before transferring to the 9th Lancers in May 1905. He was killed at Hooge, near Ypres, on 24 May 1915, aged 34. His twin brother, Riversdale (Rivy) Grenfell, a Royal Buckinghamshire Hussar (Territorial) attached to the 9th Lancers, was killed a few months earlier.

Captain H.R. Ranken VC†, Royal Army Medical Corps, attached 1 KRRC

In early September the Allied retreat was halted on the Marne and on 6 September the French counter-attacked. On 13 September the British re-crossed the River Aisne. Fierce fighting followed during which the Regimental Medical Officer of 1 KRRC, Captain Harry Ranken, a Scotsman, was mortally wounded in an action for which he was subsequently awarded a posthumous VC. His citation reads: 'For tending wounded in the trenches under rifle and shrapnel fire at Hautvesnes, on 19th September, and on 20th September continuing to attend to wounded after his thigh and leg had been shattered. (He has since died

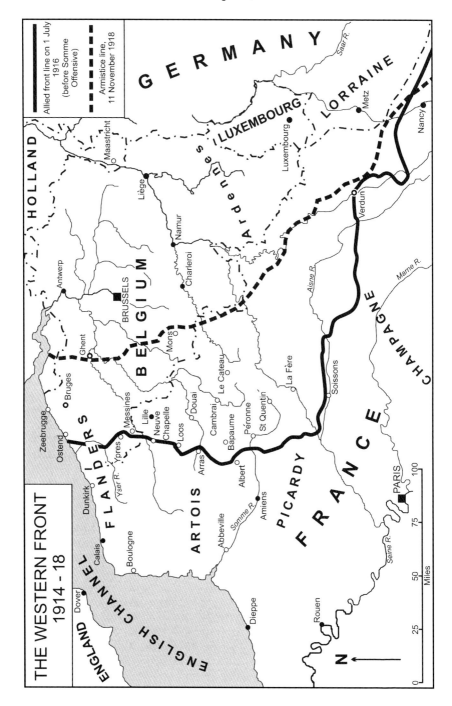

of his wounds.)'[3] When Captain Ranken was finally carried to the rear, having bound up his own wounds in the meantime, it was too late. His leg was amputated but to no avail. He died on 25 September 1914, aged 31.

Considering the nature of Captain Ranken's selflessness and the number of Riflemen's lives that he saved, it is surprising that his bravery received no mention or word of thanks in the Regimental Annals. They were certainly due. Although the BEF had been in action for less than a month, his gallant conduct from 21–30 August during the retreat from Mons had already attracted the attention of others with a mention in despatches and the award of the French Legion of Honour.

First Battle of Ypres, 19 October to 22 November 1914

At the beginning of October 1914 the BEF moved to the left flank of the Allied armies to cover a 35-mile frontage around the Belgian town of Ypres in Flanders. By now the front-line was close to extending to the sea and with out-flanking manoeuvres no longer possible, it became a matter of whether one side was strong enough to break through and overwhelm the other.

The First Battle of Ypres, an encounter battle between the opposing armies, began on 19 October. 2 KRRC, of which Lieutenant Dimmer was a member, was one of the battalions involved.

Lieutenant J.H.S. Dimmer VC

(Later Lieutenant-Colonel J.H.S. Dimmer VC MC)

Lieutenant John Dimmer was born on 9 October 1883 at Wimbledon in Surrey. He enlisted as a Rifleman in The King's Royal Rifle Corps in 1902 and was posted to South Africa. In the following year he was promoted to Corporal for reconnaissance work in Orange River Colony and in 1905 to Lance-Sergeant[4] for scouting and signalling in the Mounted Infantry. In 1906 he was sent, with remarkable prescience, to study the military systems of Germany and Belgium, and in 1907 he worked overseas on intelligence duties, receiving a special letter of thanks from the Army Council. In January 1908 he was commissioned. From 1908–14 he served in West Africa, returning to UK just in time to accompany 2 KRRC to France in August 1914.

During the First Battle of Ypres, on 10 November 1914, 2 KRRC entered the line at Klein Zillebeke in Belgium. Lieutenant Dimmer commanded a Vickers machine-gun section of two guns. Heavy fighting had taken place in the sector in October and the No Man's Land between the British and German trenches was littered with shell holes and unburied bodies.

Quoting from *Deeds that Thrilled the Empire*,[5] a publication intended to inspire the British public with rather over-dramatised

1 RB in Ploegsteert Wood, eight miles south of Ypres, November/December 1914

accounts of derring-do: 'On the 12th [November], on which day the enemy began a series of attacks on the Klein Zillebeke positions, and along the whole of our line towards Messines, all was quiet until noon, when the German artillery started a violent bombardment of the Green Jackets' trenches. This continued for about half an hour, when it slackened, and the enemy's machine-guns began to pour a torrent of bullets through the gaps in the British parapet made by their artillery fire. Then, at 1 p.m., the Prussian Guard, in mass formation, advanced from the wood, the men marching shoulder to shoulder, in perfect order, as though they were on parade. At once the British machine-guns began to spit death amongst them, Lieut. Dimmer firing one of the guns himself, and the storm of bullets tore through their serried ranks, mowing them down as corn falls before the sickle. But still they came on, and presently the Lieutenant's gun jammed, owing to the belt getting wet. In a moment he had climbed on to the emplacement, a large adjustable spanner in his hand, and got the deadly weapon again in working order: but, as he did so, a rifle bullet struck him in the right jaw. Heedless of the pain, he began to pour a fresh stream of lead into the advancing masses, but he had not fired many rounds when the gun stuck when traversing. Reaching up to remedy the stoppage, he was again hit by a rifle bullet, this time in the right shoulder. But he got his gun going again for all that, and before the blast of death the Huns fell in swathes. Then a shrapnel shell burst above him, and he was hit for the third time, three bullets lodging in his injured shoulder. But, with the blood streaming from his wounds, the heroic officer went on firing his gun, until, when within fifty yards of our trenches, the Germans suddenly broke and ran for cover. Their artillery covered their retreat with a rain of shrapnel, and Lieut. Dimmer's gun was hit and destroyed, and his face spattered with splinters of broken metal. Exhausted with pain and loss of blood, he lost consciousness for a time, but on coming to, insisted on proceeding to Brigade Headquarters to report in person to the Earl of Cavan, commanding the 4th (Guards) Brigade. Scarcely, however, had he made his report then his strength gave out, and he collapsed and was taken to the dressing-station.'

Dimmer's VC citation was much briefer and a lot less enlightening: 'This officer served his Machine Gun during the attack on the 12th November at Klein Zillebeke until he had been shot five times – three times by shrapnel and twice by bullets, and continued at his post until his gun was destroyed.' 2 KRRC subsequently held their positions until relieved on 16 November.

Dimmer was evacuated to England to convalesce from his wounds. With amazing speed, on 19 November 1914, only a week after the action, the award of his VC was published in *The London Gazette*. On 1 January 1915 he was awarded a MC, presumably for another action which is not described in *The London Gazette* but must have occurred before 12 November 1914. On 7 April 1915, at a meeting of Wimbledon

Borough Council, it was suggested that, as Dimmer was the recipient of a VC, he should be presented with the Freedom of the Borough. Dimmer replied, however, that while he would appreciate the honour, he had to decline it as too much publicity had already been given to his name and had caused him great concern.

After recovering from his wounds, Dimmer remained in England until being sent to Salonika in 1916 where he qualified as an observer attached to a front-line squadron of the Royal Flying Corps. In October 1917 he was given command of the 2nd/4th Battalion, The Royal Berkshire Regiment, serving on the Western Front. On 21 March 1918 he was killed, aged 34, leading his battalion rather unwisely on horseback in an unsuccessful counter-attack against the Germans near St Quentin. He had been married two months.

West Africa, 1914

While the trenches were being dug on the Western Front and the barbed wire was being uncoiled, an Anglo-French invasion was launched to evict the Germans from their colony in the Cameroons, West Africa. Lieutenant Butler of The King's Royal Rifle Corps, serving with the Gold Coast Regiment, was one of those involved.

Lieutenant J.F.P. Butler VC

(Later Captain J.F.P. Butler VC DSO)

Lieutenant John (Jack) Butler was born on 20 December 1888 at Berkeley in Gloucestershire. He attended Wellington College and RMC Sandhurst before being commissioned into The King's Royal Rifle Corps on 13 February 1907. He initially served in India until being seconded to the Gold Coast Regiment in 1913. His uncle, Lieutenant (later Major) Lord Gifford of the 24th (2nd Warwickshire) Regiment, was awarded a VC for gallantry during the Ashanti campaign in 1873–4.

The actions, which resulted in Lord Gifford's nephew, Lieutenant Butler, receiving a VC, are described in his citation: 'For most conspicuous bravery in the Cameroons, West Africa. On 17th November, 1914, with a party of 13 men, he went into the thick bush and at once attacked the enemy, in strength about 100, including several Europeans, defeated them, and captured their machine-gun and many loads of ammunition. On 27th December, 1914, when on patrol duty, with a few men, he swam the Ekam River, which was held by the enemy, alone and in the face of brisk fire, completed his reconnaissance on the further bank, and returned in safety. Two of his men were wounded while he was actually in the water.' No other account has come to light to supplement the information in the citation.

In March 1915 Butler was promoted to Captain and on 5 June 1916 was awarded a DSO for his further service with the Gold Coast

Regiment in West Africa. In July 1916 he accompanied the Regiment to East Africa where the Allies were seeking to drive the Germans out of German East Africa (now Tanzania). On 4 September his company was advancing along a road to the east of Matombo Mission Station when it came under heavy German machine-gun fire. In seeking to dislodge the enemy, Butler was mortally wounded, dying on the following day, 5 September 1916, aged 27. Apart from the VC and the DSO, he was mentioned in despatches three times while serving with the Gold Coast Regiment.

1915

The Battle of Neuve Chapelle, 10–12 March 1915

The First Battle of Ypres ended in stalemate on 22 November 1914. Winter set in, with both sides adjusting to the unpleasantness of trench warfare and with each mounting small-scale attacks against the other. It was not until March 1915 that the first major offensive of the year was launched by the British at Neuve Chapelle, where Sir John French, the British Commander-in-Chief, intended to overwhelm the Germans using 48 battalions against nine. Neuve Chapelle, a small village occupied by the Germans, was part of the initial objective, which was quickly captured during the opening hours of the battle on 10 March 1915. Thereafter the British failed to exploit success, giving the Germans time to counter-attack in force, which they duly did. Nine VCs were awarded for gallantry at Neuve Chapelle, two to members of 2 RB.

2 RB at Neuve Chapelle, March 1915. Painting by J.P. Beadle.

Company Sergeant-Major H. Daniels VC

(Later Lieutenant-Colonel H. Daniels VC MC)

Acting Corporal C.R. Noble VC[†]

Company Sergeant-Major (CSM) Harry Daniels was born on 13 December 1884 at Wymondham in Norfolk, the 13th child in a family of 16 children. His mother died when he was four years' old and his father died shortly afterwards, leaving six children under the age of 14. Harry was placed in a Boy's Home in Norwich, but ran away, living on turnips for two days on the first occasion and being absent for two months on the second while working as a cabin boy on a fishing smack. He was then apprenticed as a carpenter but, on hearing of the death of his eldest brother at Magersfontein while serving with the 2nd Battalion, Coldstream Guards during the Second South African (Boer) War, he decided, without telling anyone, that he would join the Army. On 31 January 1903 he enlisted in The Rifle Brigade and accompanied 2 RB to India in 1905, where he earned a fine reputation as a boxer and participant in amateur dramatics. He was promoted to the rank of Sergeant in 1910 and to Company Quartermaster Sergeant on 10 October 1914. In November he accompanied 2 RB, who had just returned from India, to France and became a CSM on 12 December.

Acting Corporal Noble was born at Bournemouth on 4 June 1891, but so disliked his Christian name, Cecil, that when he enlisted in The Rifle Brigade in 1910, he used his second name, Reginald. To compound the complexity, his family called him 'Tommy'.

CSM Daniels and Corporal Noble were both in D Company 2 RB. After successfully participating with the Battalion in the capture of the village of Neuve Chapelle on 10 March, the Company's progress was halted until, on 12 March, the Battalion was ordered to resume the advance. By then the Germans were repeatedly subjecting the British front line to counter-attack. At 12.30 p.m. A and B Company moved forward to be met by a hail of machine-gun fire and were unable to continue. At 5.15 p.m. the Commanding Officer was ordered, against his better judgement, to try again with C and D Company. However, D Company's front was blocked by wire. 'The wire had to be cut and instead of picking a number of men for the "suicidal task", No. 9665 CSM Harry Daniels asked his friend, No. 3697 A/Cpl Reginald "Tom" Noble, to accompany him as he had on many dangerous night patrols in the past. The two friends, now armed with wirecutters, shook hands before setting out; they managed to cover the few yards to the wire unhurt and, lying on their backs, began to cut the lower strands; this done they raised themselves to sever the higher wires and finally to a kneeling position to reach the highest of the wire. It was then that Daniels was hit in the left thigh and dropped to the ground; after a few minutes he heard Noble gasp. Daniels asked, "What's up, Tom?" to which Noble

100

replied, "I am hit in the chest, old man" [which seems a rather unlikely form of address for a Corporal to use in speaking to his Company Sergeant-Major, even if they were old friends in the middle of No Man's Land and both wounded! Be that as it may,] Daniels managed to roll into a shell hole and apply rudimentary first-aid to his wound; he remained there for four hours before trying to return to the battalion's trenches after dark when he was seen and picked up by his comrades. The attack, meanwhile, had been stopped.'[6]

The VC citations for both men were identical:'For most conspicuous bravery on the 12th March, 1915, at Neuve Chapelle. When their Battalion was impeded in the advance to the attack by wire entanglements, and subjected to a very severe machine-gun fire, CSM Daniels and Corporal Noble voluntarily rushed in front and succeeded in cutting the wires. They were both wounded at once, and Corporal Noble has since died of his wounds.'

Corporal Noble died on the following day, 13 March 1915, aged 23. Daniels subsequently read the news of his VC in a newspaper, while recovering from his wounds in Hammersmith Infirmary. He later described Noble as 'the best chum I have ever had, the bravest man I've ever known'.[7] During the Battle of Neuve Chapelle lasting only 48 hours, 2 RB lost 12 officers and 365 other ranks killed, wounded or captured.

After recovering from his wounds, CSM Daniels was fêted in Norwich and presented with a purse of gold by the Sheriff. On 21 July 1915 he was granted a commission in The Rifle Brigade. In September 1915 the Lord Mayor of Norwich received a telegram stating that Daniels had been killed in action. Regulation field postcards received by Daniels' relatives in Norwich disproved this information and on 1 October 1915 a contradiction of his reported death was issued by the Press Association.

On 30 March 1916 Daniels was awarded a MC for an act of bravery on 2 March 1916 at Fromelles. The citation reads: 'When a man of his patrol was wounded on the edge of the enemy's wire, he carried him in some 300 yards under very heavy fire. On another occasion, when two successive patrols had failed to find a wounded corporal, Second Lieutenant Daniels volunteered to take out a third patrol, and brought in the corporal's body.' He was twice mentioned in despatches.

In 1917 Lieutenant Daniels returned to England and in 1918 he became a member of the British Military Mission to the USA. In 1920 he boxed for Great Britain in the Olympic Games at Antwerp. On 9 April 1921 he transferred to the Loyal North Lancashire Regiment as a Captain, retiring as a Brevet Major in 1930. He then became a hotel manager before rejoining the Army as a recruiting officer in December 1933. He was promoted to Lieutenant-Colonel in 1934, remaining a recruiting officer in the North of England until retiring from the Army for a second time in 1942. He then took up the post of resident manager of the Leeds Grand Theatre, where he was very popular with artistes, the staff and public alike. Invited to attend the Coronation of Queen Elizabeth II in 1953, Daniels suffered a heart attack in London shortly before the event. He died later that year in a Leeds hospital on 13 December 1953, his 69th birthday. His wife, whom he had married at Calcutta in January 1914, predeceased him in 1949.

Hill 60, Belgium, April/May 1915

Hill 60 (three miles south-east of Ypres) was little more than an earth-heap, 60 metres high, created from the spoil from a nearby cutting for the Ypres-Lille railway line. Its importance was that it afforded the Germans an artillery observation post overlooking the northern extremity of the British front. On 17 April 1915 the British exploded seven mines under the hill, blowing up a trench line and 150 Germans, after which, under cover of heavy artillery fire, the position was taken. The Germans fought fiercely to recapture the position. Each attack was repulsed, but the hill formed a salient which exposed the British to fire from three sides. The 1st/9th (County of London) Battalion, The London Regiment (Queen Victoria's Rifles), a Territorial battalion, which deployed to France in November 1914, was one of the British battalions engaged in what became an heroic struggle to hold Hill 60, which was later described in *The Official History* as 'a medley of confluent mine and shell craters, strewn with broken timber and wire: and in this rubbish heap it was impossible to dig without disturbing the body of some British or German soldier'.[8]

Second Lieutenant G.H. Woolley VC

(Later The Revd. G.H. Woolley VC OBE MC)

Second Lieutenant Harold Woolley was born at St Peter's Vicarage, Bethnal Green, London, on 14 May 1892, one of the 10 children of Reverend George Herbert Woolley and his wife, Sarah. He was educated at St John's School, Leatherhead, and Queen's College, Oxford. He joined the 5th Battalion, The Essex Regiment, on the day war was declared, transferring to Queen Victoria's Rifles (QVR) on 26 August 1914. He was a platoon commander during the battle for Hill 60 and was awarded a VC for his gallantry.

Woolley's citation reads: 'For most conspicuous bravery on "Hill 60" during the night of 20th-21st April, 1915. Although the only Officer on the hill at the time, and with very few men, he successfully resisted all attacks on his trench, and continued throwing bombs and encouraging his men until relieved. His trench during all this time was being heavily shelled and bombed and was subjected to heavy machine gun fire by the enemy.'

To expand, at 9.30 p.m. on 20 April A and C Company 1 QVR received orders to advance from their trenches in the salient around Hill 60 and take up a position close to the top. The German bombardment was so intense that it took them two hours to traverse 200 yards to their objective, before digging in among the craters on the hill. During the night the fighting was fierce and at close quarters. Soon there were only 30 men left unharmed. At this critical moment Second Lieutenant Woolley was spotted making his way towards them, sometimes running, sometimes crawling forward through the deluge of fire. On reaching them, he immediately took command. Seeing a supply of 'jam-pot bombs' and borrowing a box of matches from Second Lieutenant Summerhayes to light the fuses, he proceeded to lob them over the brow of their position, with some of his men acting as observers to direct his throws. Summerhayes was killed immediately after handing over his matchbox. Woolley was now the only surviving officer on this part of the hill. At intervals various runners brought up boxes of Hales [stick] grenades which Woolley employed to keep the enemy at bay. Two NCOs, Pulleyn and Peabody, who assisted Woolley, each earned a DCM for their bravery. An officer arrived from Battalion Headquarters with a verbal order and later written instructions to Woolley to bring back all the men of his regiment. He refused to comply until he was properly relieved, as there were so few surviving men of other regiments left on Hill 60. At dawn he descended the hill to fetch a group of 60 bombers from The Northumberland Fusiliers, after which the 14 survivors from the original 150 men returned to their lines. Woolley recounts in his autobiography, *Sometimes a Soldier*, that he was near to becoming a casualty himself on Hill 60 when a small German egg-type hand-grenade struck him on the head; fortunately the blast went upwards and outwards, stunning him momentarily and tearing two large rents in his cap, but otherwise leaving him unscathed.

On 22 April 1915, the day after Woolley's gallantry on Hill 60, the Germans began the Second Battle of Ypres, using poison gas for the first time during the War. On 5 May the British were forced to abandon Hill 60, partly because of repeated gas attacks. Woolley, meanwhile, was promoted to Captain on 26 April and appointed to command A Company 1 QVR, but he had been badly affected by the gas. In June he was sent to convalesce at Osborne on the Isle of Wight. In September 1915 he returned to his Battalion, assuming command of B Company. In February 1916 he left the Battalion to become, at various times, an instructor at Third Army's Infantry School and a staff officer at HQ Third Army, where he served until the end of the War. He was twice mentioned in despatches on 31 May 1915 and 20 December 1918, and was awarded a MC on 3 June 1919 for his services with Third Army.

During the First World War, Woolley started to write poetry, including *The Hilltop and Other Poems*, which was published by Toc H. In 1916 one of his brothers, Bertie, was killed on the Somme while serving with the London Rifle Brigade. In March 1919 he was demobilised and

Captain G.H. Woolley VC MC in 1919

returned to Oxford to read for a MA in Theology. He was ordained into the Church of England at Coventry Cathedral in December 1920 and appointed an Assistant Master at Rugby School. From 1923-6 he was Vicar of Monk Sherborne in Hampshire. In 1927 he became a Master at Harrow School and, in 1932, the School Chaplain, remaining at Harrow until 1939. During the Second World War he joined the Army as a chaplain (1 February 1940), serving at Chatham and Hounslow before accompanying the Second Echelon of First Army to North Africa in November 1942. A month later his son, Rollo, a Spitfire pilot, was killed in a dogfight over Tunis.

In North Africa, Woolley was Senior Chaplain, Algiers Area, where he founded 20 clubs for allied troops and published *A Pocket Book of Prayers*, which was in much demand amongst the troops. He was later awarded an OBE 'in recognition of gallant and distinguished services in North Africa' where he was known as the 'Woodbine Willie of Algiers'.[9] In 1944 he moved to Italy expecting to become Senior Chaplain, Rome Area, but in April, before the US Fifth Army reached Rome in June, his car was in collision with a US lorry and he suffered a spinal injury necessitating his evacuation to England. He was granted indefinite release from the Army on 16 June 1944, finally relinquishing his commission on 14 May 1952.

Woolley was Vicar of St Mary's Church, Harrow, from 1944-52 and Vicar of West Grinstead in Kent from 1952-8, before retiring to live at West Chiltington in Sussex. In 1956 he became Vice Chairman (UK) of the VC & GC Association, holding the appointment until his death at West Chiltington on 10 December 1968, aged 76. His first wife, Janet, whom he married in June 1918, was the widow of Captain George Culme-Seymour of The King's Royal Rifle Corps, and Adjutant of 1 QVR, who died on 7 May 1915 from wounds received during the fighting at Hill 60. She died in 1943 and he married again in 1945. His second wife died in 1979. A son by his second marriage, Nicholas, was born in 1946.

On 9 September 1923 the Reverend Harold Woolley officiated at the dedication of a Memorial on Hill 60 to all those in 1 QVR who died there in 1915. In 1940 the Germans destroyed the Memorial. In 1952 he officiated again when a second Memorial was dedicated.

Second Lieutenant Woolley was the first Territorial to be awarded a VC during the First World War.

Second Battle of Ypres, 22 April to 25 May 1915

The Second Battle of Ypres was one of the more testing battles of the First World War during which the Allies were fully stretched to prevent the German offensive succeeding. The use of poison gas invoked panic among the French and Algerian troops most affected. The Canadians, however, stood fast, resulting in the award of four VCs during the opening few days of the battle, 22-25 April, the first VCs to be awarded to the Canadians during the First World War. Among them was

Lieutenant E.D. Bellew of the British Columbia Regiment, a regiment with which The Royal Green Jackets retains an alliance. During the battle, another Green Jacket Territorial distinguished himself.

Lance-Sergeant D.W. Belcher VC

(Later Captain D.W. Belcher VC)

Lance-Sergeant Douglas Belcher was born on 15 July 1889 at Surbiton in Surrey. He was educated at Tiffin's School, Kingston-upon-Thames, and before the First World War was employed in the antiques department of Messrs Waring & Gillow. In 1906 he joined the 26th Middlesex (Cyclist) Volunteer Corps, transferring to the 9th (County of London) Battalion, The London Regiment (Queen Victoria's Rifles) when the Territorial Force was created in 1908. In 1914 he transferred to the 1st/5th (City of London) Battalion (London Rifle Brigade) (LRB), moving with the Battalion to France in November 1914.

Belcher was a very fit young man, regularly swimming across the River Thames and back on summer mornings. He enjoyed rowing, cycling, cricket and tennis, and was a boy chorister at his local church. Being a Territorial was his principal passion. He was a particularly good rifle shot.

On 13 May 1915, Lance-Sergeant Belcher was a section commander in one of two 1 LRB companies in the front line when the British were subjected to the heaviest bombardment to date during the Second Battle of Ypres, with shells falling at a rate of over a hundred a minute. It was a gloomy, wet day and many of the trenches were soon flattened, turning the area into a muddy quagmire. Two platoons of 1 LRB, occupying what was rather too aptly known as Shell Trap Farm, were effectively wiped out. Belcher and the remnants of his section, together with other members of 1 LRB, 18 men in all, held one small section of trench, less than 40 yards long, just south of the Wieltje-St Julien Road. Gradually the incessant bombardment took its toll of Belcher's small group, who continued to pour volleys into any Germans who approached nearer than 200 yards to the battered trench. Rifles jammed with mud or became too hot to hold but still Belcher's men stayed put while other troops holding another short section of trench on their right retired. As the breastwork to their trench became almost non-existent, Belcher decided to occupy the vacant trench to his right which appeared to be less damaged than the position he held. His party, now reduced to only five men, quickly moved to the other position. Within minutes further shelling demolished the trench which they had just abandoned. For over nine hours they remained in position, firing at any enemy infantry who appeared until they were finally relieved. Belcher escaped with just a graze on his chin and a shrapnel rent in his cap.

Belcher's citation later read: 'On the early morning of 13th May, 1915, when in charge of a portion of an advanced breastwork south of the

Wieltje-St. Julien Road during a very fierce and continuous bombardment by the enemy, which frequently blew in the breastwork, Lance-Serjeant Belcher, with a mere handful of men elected to remain and endeavour to hold his position after the troops near him had been withdrawn. By his skill and great gallantry he maintained his position during the day, opening rapid fire on the enemy, who were only 150 to 200 yards distant, whenever he saw them collecting for an attack. There is little doubt that the bold front shown by Lance-Serjeant Belcher prevented the enemy breaking through on the Wieltje road, and averted an attack on the flank of one of our Divisions.'

On 23 June 1915 Belcher received a mention in despatches. In July he was in England for his investiture and was later presented with a silver rose bowl by his former employers, Messrs Waring & Gillow, with over 3,000 employees attending a ceremony in his honour at the firm's business premises at White City, where tents and aeroplane parts were manufactured. His mother also told a *Daily Express* reporter: 'Although we knew that he had distinguished himself, and that he had been recommended for a medal of some sort, we had no idea it was to be the VC. My son was unwilling to discuss the affair at all, saying, I remember, when someone present at his first meal home tried to get him to talk about it, "Oh, let's get on with the tea, shall we?"'[10]

On 10 November 1916 Belcher was commissioned as a Second Lieutenant in his former regiment, Queen Victoria's Rifles. He was promoted to Lieutenant a year later and on 2 November 1918 transferred to the 1st/6th Gurkha Rifles. He became a Captain and company commander in Mesopotamia during the Arab rising in 1921 and later saw service in Burma with the 5th/70th Burma Rifles. He retired from the Army on 19 July 1922. Thereafter he suffered problems with his health and found it difficult to hold down a job and make ends meet. His wife abandoned him for another man and a divorce followed.

Immediately prior to the Second World War, Belcher rejoined the LRB as a Rifleman, aged 50, and was quickly promoted to Sergeant, but he suffered a bad fall and was medically discharged in May 1940 with the rank of Captain. He remarried in 1941 and died at Claygate, Surrey, on 3 June 1953, aged 63.

Lance-Sergeant Belcher was the first Territorial soldier holding non-commissioned rank to be awarded a VC during the First World War.

Battle of Festubert, May 1915

On 9 May 1915, while the Second Battle of Ypres was still in progress, the Allies launched a counter-offensive to the south, in Artois, towards the Aubers Ridge not far from Neuve Chapelle. The attack failed but, on 15 May, a fresh assault was launched at Festubert, two miles to the south of the Aubers Ridge. 2 KRRC was not a part of the attacking force but was committed to holding a sector nearby.

Rifleman W. Mariner VC

Rifleman William Mariner, whose real surname was Wignall, was born on 29 May 1882 at Chorley in Lancashire. After moving to Salford and attending school, he worked as a collier before joining the Army in 1902. He was posted to 2 KRRC, spending the whole of his service in India where he was a lightweight wrestling champion. He left the Army in 1908 and found work as a brick-setter. He also found himself on the wrong side of the law, acquiring a criminal record for breaking and entering. Thus, when he re-enlisted in The King's Royal Rifle Corps on 26 August 1914, he chose to do so under the assumed surname of Mariner.

Mariner joined 2 KRRC in France in November 1914. On 22 May 1915 he was a member of B Company 2 KRRC in the forward trenches of a sector which had been the scene of much fighting during the preceding months. Having suffered many casualties from a German machine-gun post, Rifleman Mariner volunteered to silence the weapon and its crew, knowing full well that the chances of his return were slim. What happened is best described in the words of his VC citation:

> During a violent thunderstorm on the night of the 22nd May, 1915, he [Rifleman Mariner] left his trench near Cambrin, France, and crept out through the German wire entanglements till he reached the emplacement of a German machine gun which had been damaging our parapets and hindering our working parties. After climbing on the top of the German parapet he threw a bomb in under the roof of the gun emplacement and heard some groaning and the enemy running away. After about a quarter of an hour he heard some of them coming back again and climbed up on the other side of the emplacement and threw another bomb among them left-handed. He then lay still while the Germans opened a heavy fire on the wire entanglements behind him, and it was only after about an hour that he was able to crawl back to his own trench. Before starting out he had requested a sergeant to open fire on the enemy's trenches as soon as he had thrown his bombs. Rifleman Mariner was out alone for one and a half hours carrying out this gallant work.

In August 1915, Mariner returned to England on leave and 'on 12 August left his mother's house in Salford without informing her of his plans. She suspected that he was to receive his VC that day and with her daughter entrained for Windsor. At Windsor Mrs Wignall was informed that the award ceremony was at Buckingham Palace, so she joined the hundreds of people outside the Palace and was able to see her son after the investiture.'[11] Mariner was also treated to a civic reception in Salford and presented with an illuminated address and a gold watch. However, he was soon in France again where he was wounded and invalided back to England on 24 August. He returned to France on 12 October after appearing in court charged with two days' absence. At his court appearance he wore his VC only to be ticked off by the magistrate and warned 'not to bring that Cross into court again in such circumstances'.[12]

At 9.15 p.m. on 30 June 1916, on the day preceding the start of the Battle of the Somme and while still a member of B Company 2 KRRC, Rifleman Mariner took part in a diversionary attack near Loos. The German line was reached but, in the ensuing action lasting over four hours, Mariner was killed. A colleague later described him losing his senses and running in pursuit of the retreating enemy, but being caught by a shell while bayoneting a prone German and being blown to bits. Because the date of his death is recorded as 1 July 1916, it is often erroneously thought that he must have died on the Somme.

Mariner's story, however, does not end there. 'Because of his alias, the newspaper which reported the death and disappearance in action of a VC hero (the *Daily Sketch*) was unable to find any relatives for him back home – instead they fêted him as having a hero's grave on a famous battlefield, and cited the police as his only "friends".'[13]

Rifleman Mariner may well have been a villain, but not untypical of many Riflemen over the years whose conduct 'in barracks' has fallen short of the desirable but whose fighting qualities have been second to none. His VC action was an extraordinary act of individual, pre-meditated bravery different in context to those acts conducted in the heat of battle. He died unmarried, aged 32, his body never found, but with his name commemorated on the Thiepval Memorial to the Missing.

Hooge, 30 July 1915

The Allied offensive in Artois ended on 27 May 1915 with some small territorial gains achieved at a cost of 16,000 casualties. The next Allied offensive was launched at Loos in September. Meanwhile, the first of Kitchener's 'New Army' Service battalions had arrived in France and were cast into the trenches. The 14th (Light) Division, with 7, 8 and 9 KRRC, and 7, 8 and 9 RB, was among them, occupying a sector in the Ypres salient, near Hooge. During the night of 29/30 July, 8 RB relieved 7 RB in the front line. At dawn on the following morning the Germans attacked using flamethrowers for the first time during the War in what was literally a baptism of fire for these New Army battalions. Unsurprisingly the shock effect was considerable and just about all the British forward positions were overrun. Hastily contrived counter-attacks in the afternoon failed to recover lost ground and added to the casualty roll. During the course of the day 8 RB suffered 19 officers and 469 men killed, wounded or missing, among them Second Lieutenant Woodroffe.

2 Oxf & Bucks LI in the trenches, 1915

Viewing No Man's Land through a trench periscope, 2 Oxf & Bucks LI, 1915

Second Lieutenant S.C. Woodroffe VC†

Second Lieutenant Sidney Woodroffe was born on 17 December 1895 at Lewes in Sussex. He was educated at Marlborough College, excelling at his studies and on the sports field. He gained a scholarship to read Classics at Pembroke College, Cambridge, but before he could take advantage of it, the War intervened. On 23 December 1914 he was commissioned in The Rifle Brigade, accompanying 8 RB to France in May 1915, where he was a platoon commander in A Company.

His VC citation describes his act of gallantry: 'For most conspicuous bravery on the 30th July, 1915, at Hooge. The enemy having broken through the centre of our front trenches, consequent on the use of burning liquids, this Officer's position was heavily attacked with bombs from the flank and subsequently from the rear, but he managed to defend his post until all his bombs were exhausted, and then skilfully withdrew his remaining men. This very gallant Officer immediately led his party forward in a counter-attack under an intense rifle and machine-gun fire, and was killed while in the act of cutting the wire obstacles in the open.'

Lieutenant-Colonel R.C. Maclachlan, the Commanding Officer of 8 RB, later wrote to Woodroffe's father: 'Your younger boy [see below] was simply one of the bravest of the brave, and the work he did that day will stand out as a record hard to beat … When the line was attacked and broken on his right he still held his trench, and only when the Germans were discovered to be in the rear of him did he leave it. He then withdrew his remaining men very skilfully right away to a flank, and worked his way alone back to me to report. He finally brought his command back, and then took part in the counter-attack. He was killed out in front, in the open, cutting the wire to enable the attack to be continued. This is the bald statement of his part of that day's action. He risked his life for others right through the day and finally gave it for the sake of his men. He was a splendid type of young officer, always bold as a lion, confident and sure of himself too. The loss he is to me personally is very great, as I had learnt to appreciate what a sterling fine lad he was. His men would have followed him anywhere.'[14]

The Regimental History also observes that: 'Very unjust criticism was at the time directed against the battalions involved in the Hooge disaster. It is now generally recognised that all ranks put up a most heroic defence against completely overwhelming odds. Individual gallantry abounded. The Victoria Cross won by Lieutenant Woodroffe was gained by a splendid combination of initiative, skill and courage.'

Sidney Woodroffe had two older brothers who, like him, were educated at Marlborough and joined The Rifle Brigade. Kenneth, the eldest, was killed at Neuve Chapelle on 9 May 1915, while attached to the 2nd Battalion, The Welsh Regiment. Leslie, the middle brother, served with Sidney in 8 RB and was severely wounded at Hooge, receiving a

MC and a mention in despatches. He later recovered from his wounds, returning to the Front on 1 June 1916. On the day of his arrival he was wounded again and died in hospital on 4 June 1916. The pain to the parents of all three sons being killed in action in a little over a year can only be imagined and the grief too awful to contemplate. All three brothers, though, had served their Country with honour and Sidney, in particular, with exceptional valour.

Second Lieutenant Woodroffe died aged 19. He has no known grave, but is commemorated at the Menin Gate.

Battle of Loos, 25 September to 15 October 1915

After the failure of the first Allied offensive in Artois in May, a second offensive was ordered in the autumn. On 25 September 2 KRRC took part in the initial attack during which the British used gas for the first time during the War. With the wind varying in direction, the gas proved to be a double-edged weapon with 200 men in the Battalion being incapacitated before the assault began. Almost immediately Rifleman Peachment was involved in an act of gallantry for which he was later to receive a posthumous VC. Over the following weeks stalemate resulted, the Battle of Loos ending on 15 October with the British suffering 50,000 casualties for no appreciable gain.

Rifleman G.S. Peachment VC[†]

Rifleman George Peachment was born on 5 May 1897 at Bury in Lancashire. After attending school he worked as an apprentice fitter. Immediately the War started he tried to enlist but was rejected as too young. He eventually succeeded on 19 April 1915, three weeks before his 18th birthday, and was posted to 2 KRRC. Shortly before the Battle of Loos he was appointed orderly to Captain G.R. Dubs, commanding A Company.

At 5.50 a.m. on 25 September the British turned on the gas and smoke shells were fired from Stokes mortars. The wind then veered to the south and all the gas blew back. The gas was turned off. The wind then veered back towards the German lines and at 6.20 a.m. the gas was turned on again. The assault was ordered shortly thereafter. However, as the advancing troops moved forward into a pall of smoke and gas, they were quite unable to see their way and were choking on the poisonous fumes. Two enemy machine guns opened fire in enfilade and as the British line approached the German positions, it was discovered that the wire was not cut, compelling the British 'to retire in order to reorganise'. It was at this moment that Rifleman Peachment noticed his company commander lying wounded some 15 yards from the German lines. His VC citation describes what happened.

For most conspicuous bravery near Hulluch on the 25th September, 1915. During very heavy fighting, when our front line was compelled to retire in order to reorganize, Private Peachment, seeing his Company Commander, Captain Dubs, lying wounded, crawled to assist him. The enemy's fire was intense, but, though there was a shell hole quite close, in which a few men had taken cover, Private Peachment never thought of saving himself. He knelt in the open by his Officer and tried to help him, but while doing this he was first wounded by a bomb and a minute later mortally wounded by a rifle bullet. He was one of the youngest men in his battalion, and gave this splendid example of courage and self-sacrifice.

In early October Peachment's parents became concerned about the lack of news from their son and decide to enquire after him. They were told that he had been killed in action and were given the basic facts, which were confirmed in a long letter from Captain Dubs, who by then was convalescing from his wounds. He indicated that their son had been recommended for a posthumous VC, which was later announced in *The London Gazette* on 18 November 1915.

Rifleman Peachment's act of valour was truly, as his Citation indicates, an act of supreme courage and self-sacrifice and a splendid example to others for which he paid the ultimate price. One can only marvel, too, that a man so young, who had been in France for only a few months, should have acted so unhesitatingly to save the life of another at such great risk to himself.

He was one of eight 18-year olds to be awarded a VC during the First World War. Like so many others, he has no known grave, but is commemorated on the Loos Memorial.

Lieutenant G.A. Maling VC, Royal Army Medical Corps, attached 12 RB

While the main assault was being launched at Loos, 12 RB took part in a diversionary attack, which after initial success ended in the Battalion finishing up where it had begun, losing seven officers and 322 men killed, wounded or missing. During the course of the battle a heavy shell landed on Battalion Headquarters killing all except the Commanding Officer and the Adjutant. It also wrecked the Regimental Aid Post. Captain George Maling, the Regimental Medical Officer, was later awarded a VC for his actions on that day.

His VC citation reads: 'For most conspicuous bravery and devotion to duty during the heavy fighting near Fauquissart on 25th September, 1915. Lieutenant Maling worked incessantly with untiring energy from 6.15 a.m. on the 25th till 8.00 a.m. on the 26th, collecting and treating in the open under heavy shell fire more than 300 men. At about 11 a.m. on the 25th he was flung down and temporarily stunned by the bursting of a large high-explosive shell which wounded his only assistant and killed several of his patients. A second shell soon covered him and his instruments with debris, but his high courage and zeal never failed him, and he continued his gallant work single-handed.'

Lieutenant Maling was a graduate of Uppingham School, Exeter College, Oxford, and St Thomas's Hospital, London. He was the only member of the Royal Army Medical Corps to be awarded a VC on the Western Front in 1915. He died aged 40 in 1929.

Winter 1915

The Battle of Loos was the last major offensive initiated by either side on the Western Front in 1915. Its conclusion was followed by a winter of trench warfare, with Corporal Drake being the last Green Jacket to be awarded a VC for an act of gallantry during the year.

Corporal A.G. Drake VC†

Very little is known about Corporal Alfred Drake's early life, except that he was born in Stepney, East London, on 10 December 1893, enlisting in The Rifle Brigade after the start of the War in 1914. On 23 November 1915, 8 RB was in the line at La Brique, near Ypres, when Lieutenant Tryon was ordered to lead a four-man reconnaissance patrol into the No Man's Land between the British and German forward positions. Corporal Drake, aged 21, was a member of the patrol.

Drake's VC citation reads: 'For conspicuous bravery on the night of 23rd November, 1915, near La Brique, France. He was one of a patrol of four which was reconnoitring towards the German lines. The patrol was discovered when close to the enemy, who opened heavy fire with rifles and a machine gun, wounding the Officer and one man. The latter was carried back by the last remaining man. Corporal Drake remained with his Officer and was last seen kneeling beside him and bandaging his wounds regardless of the enemy's fire. Later, a rescue party crawling near the German lines found the Officer and Corporal, the former unconscious but alive and bandaged, Corporal Drake beside him dead and riddled with bullets. He had given his own life and saved his Officer.'[15]

The Regimental History tells much the same story in different words: 'The patrol had been surprised when quite close to the enemy's lines. Heavy fire was opened on it, wounding Lieutenant Tryon and one of the patrol. Corporal Drake, the N.C.O., detailed the one unwounded man to carry back the wounded rifleman and himself remained with the officer who was too badly hit to be moved. The enemy fire still continued but Corporal Drake, although hit repeatedly, succeeded in bandaging the wounds of his officer and thus saving his life.'[16]

Corporal Drake's act of absolute selflessness was very similar in form to that of Rifleman Peachment only two months previously. Each died in circumstances where the officers they were seeking to save survived and they did not. Theirs was the ultimate sacrifice. In the words so often found on the headstones of the fallen in war: 'Greater love hath no man than this, that a man lay down his life for his friends.'[17]

1916

The early part of 1916 was marked by a grand offensive launched by the Germans against the French at Verdun, which over the following nine months cost each side 350,000 casualties and which resulted in the Germans finishing up where they started. There were no grand offensives on the British front until the Battle of the Somme.

The Battle of the Somme, 1 July to 25 November 1916

On 1 July the British attacked the Germans on a 15-mile frontage just north of the River Somme. The French attacked on an eight-mile frontage on the right flank. Bitter fighting ensued over many weeks. By the middle of October the weather had completely broken and the battle became a struggle against the mud. By the time the offensive was abandoned on 25 November 1916, the British had suffered nearly 420,000 casualties. German losses were also considerable and in the wider context, the Battle of the Somme probably saved the French from defeat at Verdun. During the first month of the Battle, two Green Jackets performed exceptional acts of valour that resulted in the award of VCs, both posthumous.

Brevet Major W. La T. Congreve VC DSO MC[†]

Major William (Billy) La Touche Congreve was born on 22 March 1891 at Burton Hall, Cheshire. He was the eldest of General Sir Walter Congreve's three sons,[18] his father receiving a VC for gallantry at Colenso in 1899 (see pages 79–85). La Touche was his Mother's maiden name.

Billy was educated at Summer Fields School, Oxford, and at Eton College, before entering RMC Sandhurst in 1909, where he was runner-up for the Sword of Honour. He was commissioned into The Rifle Brigade, his father's Regiment, on 4 March 1911 and posted to 3 RB in Ireland. On 1 February 1913 he became a Lieutenant and accompanied 3 RB to France in September 1914. On 21 September he was appointed ADC to the GOC 3rd Division, Major-General Hamilton, who a month later was killed by a sniper's bullet. Congreve was retained as a General Staff Officer at Divisional Headquarters, where he remained until being appointed the Brigade Major of the 76th Infantry Brigade on 8 December 1915.

Despite his role as a staff officer, Billy Congreve was regularly in the front line. During the course of 1915 he took part in actions which were

Lieutenant W. La T. Congreve in 1913-14

to result in the award of a MC, the French Legion of Honour and two mentions in despatches. On 3 April 1916, during a night attack at St Eloi, south of Ypres, progress was halted by firing from an unknown number of Germans occupying a mine crater, which had been inadvertently bypassed in the thick fog that was prevailing at the time. Congreve arrived on the scene as dawn was breaking and realised that the German position, only 50 yards away, needed to be neutralised quickly before the situation deteriorated any further. Seizing the initiative and instructing an officer and four men to accompany him, he pulled out his revolver and boldly made straight for the crater. Halfway up the crater's side he was fired at, but not hit. On reaching the rim he looked in to find it full of Germans. Levelling his revolver, he ordered them to surrender and over 70 men did so. Congreve was recommended for a VC but awarded a DSO on the grounds, allegedly, that his father had already received a VC.

At the end of May 1916 Congreve returned to England on leave and on 1 June married Pamela Maude at St Martin-in-the-Fields, in a service at which the Bishop of London officiated. However, Congreve had to return to France quickly to prepare for the Battle of the Somme. In the same month that he married, he was promoted Brevet Major and on 15 June 1916 was mentioned in despatches for a third time.

The acts of gallantry that resulted in Major Billy Congreve being awarded a posthumous VC took place during the second and third weeks of the Battle of the Somme, at which point the 76th Brigade, still in the 3rd Division, formed a part of XIII Corps, commanded by his father. Initially the Division was held in reserve, but was committed to the battle on 6 July. Billy's subsequent acts are described in his VC citation.

For most conspicuous bravery during a period of fourteen days preceding his death in action. This officer constantly performed acts of gallantry and showed the greatest devotion to duty; and by his personal example inspired all those around him with confidence at critical periods of the operations. During preliminary preparations for the attack he carried out personal reconnaissances of the enemy lines, taking out parties of officers and non-commissioned officers for over 1,000 yards in front of our line, in order to acquaint them with the ground. All these preparations were made under fire. Later, by night, Major Congreve conducted a battalion to its position of employment, afterwards returning to it to ascertain the situation after assault. He established himself in an exposed forward position from whence he successfully observed the enemy, and gave orders necessary to drive them from their position. Two days later, when Brigade Headquarters was heavily shelled and many casualties resulted, he went out and assisted the medical officer to remove the wounded to places of safety, although he was himself suffering severely from gas and other shell effects. He again on a subsequent occasion showed supreme courage in tending wounded under heavy shell fire. He finally returned to the front line to ascertain the situation after an unsuccessful attack, and whilst in the act of writing his report, was shot and killed instantly.

Billy died at 10.55 a.m. on 20 July 1916 in an area to the north-west of Delville Wood, near Longueval. The fatal shot came from the direction of some standing corn. 'He stood for half a second and then collapsed. He never moved or spoke, and he was dead in a few seconds.' He was 25-years old. When his Father was told of his son's death, 'he was absolutely calm to all outward appearance and, after a few seconds of silence, said quite calmly, "He was a good soldier". That is all he allowed to appear.'[19] It was often said afterwards, though, and despite the stiff upper lip, that General Congreve was deeply affected by the loss of Billy, whom he sometimes referred to lovingly as 'Bildie', and never properly recovered from it. Two days later, on 22 July, with the Battle of the Somme still raging, he wrote in pencil to Christopher, his youngest son, aged 13, in terms so poignant that, on reading the letter, it is difficult not to be moved to tears.

July 22 [1916]

Very dear little son,

I laid our dear Bildie to rest in Corbie cemetery last night. He lies with many other gallant soldiers on a hill looking up the valley of the Somme over miles of many coloured crops, sheets of water & lines of poplar trees – a very beautiful view which he will love. The Horse Artillery carried him and the Oxfordshire Light Infantry supplied the firing party. Old Cameron [his orderly], *utterly broken down, walked with me and there were some officers of the Gordon Highlanders, of my staff and of the 3rd Division – all the rest were up in the battle. There were some beautiful flowers sent by his friends and mine, amongst them a great wreath tied with tricolor ribband from the French general beside me (so he lies under our united colours) but those he would most have appreciated were some bunches of wild flowers gathered on the battle field & sent by the men – I had those put in with him so as to be as close as possible. He was shot thru' the neck and killed instantly whilst helping the Suffolk Regiment to repel a fierce German attack on a trench in Longueval village. I went in to see him in the mortuary and tho' I had dreaded doing so I was so glad I had for he lay there looking splendid, such a strong, calm, happy face. I have never seen a finer one in my life and proud as I had been of his great achievements … I never felt as proud of him as I did then & do now. His face was an inspiration to us to go on & do our best and I feel, as he used to say, 'helping' us to know he will go on doing so all our lives until we meet him again. He could not have looked as he did if it were not so, and so little son remember all yr days that he is helping you to be like him, & make up your mind it shall be so, & Bildie will not have died in vain. I gave him a kiss from us all and pressed his hand which has given mine so many loving pleasures & so I left him, but I shall see that face all my life and am thankful for it. We can thank God to have had him. Goodbye, bless you little son, & much love to you.*

Yrs affectionately, WMC[20]

The letter written by General Sir Walter Congreve VC CB MVO to his youngest son, Christopher, on 22 July 1916, the day after the burial of his eldest son, Brevet Major W. La T. Congreve VC DSO MC, at Corbie

Following Congreve's death, Major-General J.A.L. Haldane, GOC 3rd Division, who had been Billy's Divisional Commander for 20 months, wrote: 'His loss to me is irreparable, and the Army in him loses one of its very best soldiers and by far the most promising officer I have ever known. Young, almost boyish in appearance, he possessed qualities which are generally found only in men of much riper years and of far greater experience. He was unsurpassed in bravery, and was distinguished by the highest standards of duty which guided him. Had he lived but a few months longer he must inevitably have attained command of a Brigade. Under his modesty and gentleness he possessed great strength of character. The whole Division mourns his loss, for he was beloved by all ranks, and the fine example he set of duty well done will for long keep him alive in their memories.' A member of The Rifle Brigade wrote: 'He was beloved by all…. Everyone grieved his loss, and none more so than his devoted orderly who broke down in tears on news of his master's death.'[21]

On 1 November 1916, Congreve's widow, Pamela, went to Buckingham Palace to receive the VC, DSO and MC which her husband had been awarded. He was also mentioned in despatches for a fourth time on 4 January 1917. On 21 March 1917 Pamela gave birth to a daughter, Gloria. On 22 December 1919 she married Major the Hon. William Fraser DSO MC of The Gordon Highlanders, who had been best man at Billy's wedding in 1916.[22]

Major William Congreve was the first person in the First World War to be awarded a VC, DSO and MC.[23] He and his father, General Sir Walter Congreve, are the last of only three pairs of fathers and sons to be awarded VCs and the only pair to have served in the same regiment.

Remarkably, Billy Congreve's VC, DSO and MC were all awarded for actions while he was serving as a staff officer, a feat probably not replicated by anyone else and difficult to imagine today, yet alone during the First World War. Bravery in the family, however, was not confined to the male line.

Lady Congreve

At the beginning of the War, Billy's mother, Sir Walter's wife, Cecilia, volunteered for service as a nurse and went to Antwerp in September 1914 with a unit called the Belgian Field Hospital. She described the experience in her unpublished memoirs:

> *We were a mixed lot, doctors, trained nurses, Red Cross VADs, one or two women with their own cars and three girls who wore breeches and acted as orderlies. The nurse's uniform was very becoming, blue linen dresses with small violet velvet bonnets and violet cloth cloaks. …*
>
> *We were quite near the front, or rather the front was quite close to Antwerp, but everything seemed to be in a good deal of muddle*

in more ways than one, and the wounded men were not brought in as quickly as they should have been. We often had to cut them out of their uniforms before they could get off the stretchers to which they were firmly glued by dried blood. ...

At Antwerp the end came very suddenly, one night's shelling and we were evacuated ... as we drove out of one gate the Germans came in the other.

Lady Congreve (she became Lady Congreve in 1917) served in two other hospitals between 1915–17 before arriving at Rosières-aux-Salines, a huge hospital of 1600 beds near Nancy in France, which was situated close to a factory. Inevitably, when the Germans bombarded the factory in 1918, some shells fell on the hospital. Ignoring orders to take cover, Lady Congreve and two other nurses rushed to take care of their patients and were awarded the Croix de Guerre for their bravery. She records: 'The day we were presented with our Croix de Guerre is a definite memory. There was a big camp with lots of people, ceremony and champagne. Our Medicine Chief pinned the order on to my apron – pricking me rather severely in the process! – and kissed me on both cheeks.'

Sergeant A. Gill VC†

Sergeant Gill was the second Green Jacket to be awarded a VC for gallantry during the Battle of the Somme. He was born on 8 September 1879 in Birmingham and worked for the Post Office for 17 years before enlisting in the Army at the start of the War. On the day of his act of gallantry, 27 July 1916, he was a member of 1 KRRC involved in an assault to clear the Germans from Delville Wood, an objective ultimately achieved 24 hours later.

His VC citation reads: 'For most conspicuous bravery. The enemy made a very strong counter-attack on the right flank of the battalion, and rushed the bombing post after killing all the company bombers. Sergeant Gill at once rallied the remnants of his platoon, none of whom were skilled bombers, and reorganized his defences, a most difficult and dangerous task, the trench being very shallow and much damaged. Soon afterwards the enemy nearly surrounded his men by creeping up through the thick undergrowth, and commenced sniping at about twenty yards range. Although it was almost certain death, Sergeant Gill stood boldly up in order to direct the fire of his men. He was killed almost at once, but not before he had shown his men where the enemy were, and thus enabled them to hold up their advance. By his supreme devotion to duty and self-sacrifice he saved a very dangerous situation.'

In a subsequent letter to his widow dated 16 August 1916, his Company Commander wrote: 'Your husband was one of the most valued men in my company and [a man] who anyone would be proud to call [a] friend. He was killed when rallying his men under terrible fire.... I was quite close to him, and he was quite cool, despite the very trying circumstances. The battalion had just taken a wood [Delville], and the Germans were counter-attacking heavily. I am glad to say we drove them back, and we have since received the thanks of everyone, from Sir Douglas Haig down. It was entirely owing to the heroic example and self-sacrifice of men like your husband that we did so well. He was loved by his platoon, of which I am sorry to say only four or five men remain. That day's work will always remain fixed in my memory as the one in which I lost so many gallant comrades. I lost all the officers and sergeants in my own company, and very many of the men. You should justly be proud of your husband in his life and death. He had one of the finest natures I have ever known. No words of mine can express my sympathy with you in your terrible sorrow. May the memory of his heroic end support you.'[24]

Sergeant Gill was aged 36 when he died, one of 51 men awarded VCs for acts of valour during the Battle of the Somme, of which one-third were posthumous. The War, however, was not yet ended, with many more demands still to be placed on the bravery and fortitude of the men fighting on the Western Front and in other theatres across Europe, Africa and the Middle East.

The First World War: 1917–18

1917

Although the opening years of the War in France and Belgium did not result in great tactical success or territorial gain for the Allies, Germany was gradually being worn down and forced on to the defensive at the strategic level by the cumulative effects of fighting on both the Western Front and in Russia. It would not be long, too, before the Americans entered the War (6 April 1917) tipping the military balance firmly in favour of the Allies once the Americans arrived in strength in Europe. At the start of the year, however, the British were still recovering from their losses on the Somme, while the French prepared to launch what they intended to be a decisive breakthrough of the German positions in Champagne. The role of the BEF was to take over more of the front line while the French concentrated their forces for the offensive, and to maintain sufficient pressure on the Germans to prevent them withdrawing troops to fight the French. The Germans, meanwhile, retired to heavily fortified positions on the newly constructed Hindenburg Line, reducing their frontage by 25 miles and freeing 14 divisions for operations elsewhere.

Second Lieutenant G.E. Cates VC[†]

Second Lieutenant George Cates was born in Wimbledon on 8 May 1892. He attended Rutlish School and King's College, Wimbledon. Following the start of the War he joined the 28th (County of London) Battalion, The London Regiment (Artists Rifles), for officer training. He was subsequently commissioned into The Rifle Brigade in 1915 and joined the 2nd Battalion in France.

On 4 March 1917, 2 RB was in reserve when the 8th Division successfully occupied the German first and second lines three miles to the north of Péronne. Four days letter, on 8 March, Cates was in charge of a working party engaged in deepening a captured German trench at Bouchavesnes, near Péronne, when he performed the act of gallantry for which he was subsequently awarded a posthumous VC. His citation reads: 'For most conspicuous gallantry and self-sacrifice. When engaged with some other men in deepening a captured trench this officer struck with his spade a buried bomb, which immediately started to burn. 2nd Lt. Cates, in order to save the lives of his comrades, placed his foot on the bomb, which immediately exploded. He showed the most conspicuous gallantry and devotion to duty in performing the act which cost his life, but saved the lives of others.'

Cates died of his wounds on the following day, 9 March 1917, aged 24. Amongst the personal effects returned to his family were a cigarette case, a pipe, a comb, a broken pen, a gold ring, a key chain, a whistle and strap, a collar stud, a pocket book, a tobacco pouch and some small coins[1] – seemingly incongruous items of no great monetary value but a potential source of huge comfort to the bereaved, indicating a care and concern for the loss of human life and its impact upon families which contrasts starkly, almost oddly, with the impression so often gained about officialdom during the First World War.

Whilst Cates's bravery is not in dispute, his action was similar to some eight or 10 others during the First World War – the protection of fellow soldiers from the effects of an explosion 'where the presence of the enemy was virtually irrelevant to the nature of the act of heroism for which the VC was awarded'.[2] Today, if an act of gallantry such as Cates's were to occur, a GC would almost certainly be considered a more appropriate award than a VC.

Second Lieutenant George Cates is commemorated on the war memorial of St Mary's Church, Wimbledon, alongside the names of his brothers, Geoffrey and William, who also died in the service of their Country during the Great War.

French Offensive, April/May 1917

The French grand offensive in Champagne began on the Aisne on 16 April, preceded on 9 April by a significant subsidiary attack by the British to preoccupy the Germans at Arras. By the middle of May, however, the French offensive ended in failure with General Pétain swiftly replacing General Nivelle as the French Commander-in-Chief.

Company Sergeant-Major E. Brooks VC

Company Sergeant-Major (CSM) Edward Brooks was born on 11 April 1883 at Oakley in Buckinghamshire. Prior to the War he worked for a building firm in Oxford. There is a suggestion, too, that he served at some point in the Grenadier Guards. In October 1914 he enlisted in the 2nd/4th Battalion, The Oxfordshire and Buckinghamshire Light Infantry, a Territorial battalion, which did not land in France until 24 May 1916, first experiencing action on the Somme on 19 July 1916. Meanwhile, and prior to moving to France, Brooks worked his way through the ranks, becoming a Sergeant in May 1915. He became a CSM in July 1916. He was well known to be an excellent rifle shot.

In April 1917 the 2nd/4th Battalion was occupying positions at the village of Fayet near the German-held town of St Quentin. Here a plan

Company Sergeant-Major E. Brooks VC

was made to raid the German lines in the belief that their forward trenches were unoccupied. The raid was timed to begin at 4.20 a.m. on 28 April. It was only discovered later that the Germans were contemplating a similar operation at the same time. Brooks was CSM C Company.

As the raiding party moved forward in pitch darkness, the Germans attacked from the flanks, causing the first wave to falter. At this point Brooks intervened in an act that was to result in the award of a VC. His citation reads:'For most conspicuous bravery. This Warrant Officer, while taking part in a raid on the enemy's trenches, saw that the front wave was checked by an enemy machine gun at close quarters. On his own initiative, and regardless of personal danger, he rushed forward from the second wave with the object of capturing the gun, killing one of the gunners with his revolver and bayoneting another. The remainder of the gun's crew then made off, leaving the gun in his possession. C. S./M. Brooks then turned the machine gun on to the retreating enemy, after which he carried it back into our lines. By his courage and initiative he undoubtedly prevented many casualties, and greatly added to the success of the operations.'

Brook's intervention – the brave act of a single man – was clearly instrumental in averting disaster and turning what threatened to be failure into success. He also gained a reputation for gallant deeds, since four months later, while the 2nd/4th was engaged in the Third Battle of Ypres, the Battalion History described him as 'the redoubtable Sgt-Maj. Brooks, who besides being a great fighter possessed high organising powers'.[3]

Brooks left the Army on discharge in 1919 and worked for 25 years at Morris Motors at Cowley, Oxford, where he was known to, and often featured in photographs alongside, Lord Nuffield. He died, after suffering a severe attack of thrombosis, at Oxford on 26 June 1944, aged 61. Prior to his death, he was a regular participant at veterans' events.

The Third Battle of Ypres, 31 July to 10 November 1917

The failure of the French offensive on the Aisne meant that the burden of maintaining the momentum of operations on the Western Front now fell to the BEF. This led Field Marshal Sir Douglas Haig, the British Commander-in-Chief, to decide that the moment had come to launch a long-planned offensive in Flanders aimed at capturing the high ground near Passchendaele, seven miles north-east of Ypres.

The Flanders offensive began on 31 July 1917, a day resulting in the award of 14 VCs, the highest number awarded for gallantry on a single day during the First World War.[4] Alas, after 12 days of heavy preliminary bombardment, rain set in, turning the ground into a bog. The well-constructed concrete pillboxes and wire defences of the German positions also presented a formidable obstacle to the assaulting troops.

In his book, *Passchendaele 1917*, Stephen Snelling describes the battle as 'a tragedy in eight parts, eight distinct battles fought in varying conditions with varying degrees of success'.[5] The second of these parts was fought at Langemarck from 16 to 18 August where Sergeant Cooper of 12 KRRC performed, as his citation states, 'a magnificent act of courage' resulting in the award of a VC.

Sergeant E. Cooper VC

(Later Major E. Cooper VC)

Sergeant Edward Cooper was born at Stockton-on-Tees in County Durham on 4 May 1896. He was the sixth of nine children. His father was a steelworker. At the age of 13 he left school to work as an errand boy for his uncle who ran a butcher's shop. A year later, at the age of 14, he worked for the local Co-operative Society as an assistant on a cart selling fruit. Two years later he took charge of his own cart. However, at the outbreak of the War, the Army commandeered most of the Co-op's horses and Cooper was without a job. Although 18 years old, he was initially declared too young to join the Army but, after 'advancing' his age by a year, he was enlisted into The King's Royal Rifle Corps, attracted by their green uniform and black buttons.

Cooper was posted to 12 KRRC and accompanied the Battalion to France in July 1915. He fought at Loos, on the Somme and in the Ypres salient, and became a Sergeant on 13 March 1917.

On 16 August 1917 Cooper was a platoon sergeant in A Company, which, after acting in reserve during the initial phase of the British attack on the German positions at Langemarck, was required to seize the final objectives. However, forward movement became extremely difficult as fire from German pillboxes held up the advance. Cooper's platoon commander was killed. What happened next is best described by quoting from Snelling's book:

> *The main enemy position was a concrete blockhouse about 250 yds away, set in a ruined farmhouse. Its two machine-guns appeared to cover the whole area but Cooper was not convinced. Picking up his officer's revolver and maps, he gathered a small party and set about putting his own plan into effect. More than fifty years later, he recounted:'I could see that he* [the Germans] *was firing at an angle; that if I were at a certain point he couldn't fire at me, and instead of going straight at him I went across his flank and got out of the range of the machine-gun. I then found myself on a road. I had set off with four men, but I finished up on my own … and I was making good progress. I ran forward and got behind the blockhouse and instead of doing what I should have done, put a couple of bombs in and then ask them to surrender, I called them to surrender first, and I was patiently waiting for the first man to come out …*

But Cooper had failed to notice there were two entrances, and while he covered one with a revolver he had never used before, the first German emerged from the other, behind him: 'When I turned round and saw this German I was that terrified … I pointed it [the revolver] *at him and the damned thing went off … The Germans rushed back in the blockhouse and I had to start all over. So I decided that I would put the revolver in my belt and rely on my rifle and belt. I called on them again to surrender and eventually the next man* [came] *out. I was just standing near the opening and as he passed I just cuffed him across the ears and kicked him up the pants. I didn't realise what I was doing at the time. But then all the others came out and, to my surprise, there was* [sic] *forty-five prisoners and seven machine-guns … Instead of taking them out of the front of the blockhouse, I kept them at the back where the Germans could see what was happening. That was a fatal mistake. I lined them up and waved my men forward … and before we could get them moving again the Germans had opened up on us and killed several of their own men and wounded two or three of my own men.'*

Cooper got his men under cover and ordered the prisoners to pick up the wounded and carry them to the rear. … His platoon by then reduced to 15–20 men, Cooper pushed on to the next enemy position, where two prisoners were taken and he was almost knocked out by one of his own men's grenades. They eventually reached the final objective and dug in. Later, a German counter-attack recaptured a nearby trench, but Cooper's party appeared to escape detection. They clung on until some signallers reached them with orders to support a renewed attack by 12th Rifle Brigade to retake the lost trench. In the ensuing struggle, Cooper was almost killed when a shell from the covering barrage landed nearby. Although half-buried, he managed to extricate himself and one other man, but a third was suffocated.[6]

Cooper's VC citation describes events equally impressively albeit a trifle differently: 'For most conspicuous bravery and initiative in attack. Enemy machine guns from a concrete blockhouse, 250 yards away, were holding up the advance of the battalion on his left, and were also causing heavy casualties to his own battalion. Sjt. Cooper, with four men, immediately rushed towards the blockhouse, though heavily fired on. About 100 yards distant he ordered his men to lie down and fire at the blockhouse. Finding this did not silence the machine guns, he immediately rushed forward straight at them and fired his revolver into an opening in the blockhouse. The machine guns ceased firing and the garrison surrendered. Seven machine guns and forty-five prisoners were captured in this blockhouse. By this magnificent act of courage he undoubtedly saved what might have been a serious check to the whole advance, at the same time saving a great number of lives.'

Cooper knew nothing of his VC recommendation until he arrived at King's Cross station on his way home on leave: 'I accidentally knocked a newspaper on to the floor … It opened out and there was an account about nine new VCs and I was surprised to see my name among them.'[7] Press reporting seems also to have been helped at about this time since Sergeant Cooper's citation is the first Green Jacket citation to be published in *The London Gazette* naming the recipient's home-town, information which is included with all subsequent citations.

Meanwhile, on the announcement of her son's award, Sergeant Cooper's mother was asked if he had told her anything about his doings. 'Oh, no,' she said, 'he would never do that. He is not that kind of boy; he would be too much afraid that anyone would make a fuss about it. He writes regularly, but all we get to know from him is that he has been very busy.'[8]

After receiving his VC from King George V at Buckingham Palace on 26 September 1917, Cooper returned to France and took part in the Battle of Cambrai in November. He then returned to England to undergo officer training before being commissioned on 25 June 1918, rejoining 12 KRRC on 4 September and serving with the Battalion until the end of the War.

In 1918 Cooper received the French Médaille Militaire for rescuing wounded men under shellfire on the Menin Road, near Ypres, an action almost certainly relating to his bravery during the Third Battle of Ypres in 1917 (*London Gazette*, 10 September 1918). Cooper, however, was less certain about the reason, stating: 'Everyone makes a song and dance about the French decoration. I have no idea why it was awarded to me. Perhaps it was for the same [VC] action, but I honestly do not know.'[9]

Lieutenant Cooper was demobilised on 27 January 1919 and on return to civilian life went back to work for the Co-operative Society. In 1926 he moved to Sunderland as a warehouse manager, returning to Stockton-on-Tees in 1938 as manager of the fruit department, a position he held until his retirement, aged 65, in 1961. During the Second World War he served in the Home Guard and was promoted to Major in command of G (Thornaby) Company of the 9th (North Riding) Battalion. He also assumed many civic responsibilities and was a Justice of the Peace for 20 years from 1949–68, but his chief interests were helping church, youth and ex-Service organisations. He never missed a reunion of VC holders and took great pride in his honour despite his embarrassment at all the adulation. On 24 July 1985 he was made a Freeman of the Borough of Stockton-on-Tees, as proud of Stockton as the citizens of Stockton were proud of him. Within a matter of weeks he suffered a heart attack and died in North Tees General Hospital on 19 August 1985, aged 89.

Prior to his death Cooper was the last survivor among the 61 men to receive VCs for their acts of gallantry during the Third Battle of Ypres and the last living Green Jacket to have been awarded a VC.

Photograph courtesy of Imperial War Museum, London

Arras, 9 April 1917

Photograph courtesy of Imperial War Museum, London

Messines Ridge, near Ypres, 12 June 1917

Menin Road, 20–25 September 1917

The third act in eight parts at Passchendaele was an attack on an eight-mile frontage by the British to seize the high ground known as the Menin Road ridge near Ypres. 16 RB, a part of 39 Division, was close to the extreme right of the assaulting force, south-east of Ypres. The 2nd/8th (City of London) Battalion, The London Regiment (Post Office Rifles), a part of 58 Division, was near the centre, just to the north-east of Ypres. On the opening day of the attack, a member of each battalion performed acts of bravery that resulted in the award of VCs.

Sergeant W.F. Burman VC

Sergeant William Burman was born on 30 August 1897 at Stepney in the East End of London. While at school he became a cadet in what is now the City of London and North East Sector Army Cadet Force affiliated to The Royal Green Jackets. In 1911 he left school, aged 14. He subsequently enlisted in The Rifle Brigade on 23 March 1915, aged 17, and was posted to 16 RB, accompanying the Battalion to France on 8 March 1916. A month later, on 20 April 1916, he was promoted to Sergeant at the young age of 18, most probably because of his previous experience of the Army as a cadet.

On 14 September 1917 a five-day artillery barrage was directed at the German positions on the Menin Road ridge. At 5.40 a.m. on 20 September the British assault began. 16 RB's objectives lay near Bulgar Wood, south-east of Ypres. The Battalion attacked with two companies in the first wave and two companies immediately behind. Sergeant Burman was a member of C Company, the right-hand company in the second wave.

The assault started punctually in thick fog, which necessitated the use of the compass to maintain direction. The Germans, alerted by the artillery barrage, were expecting an attack. Within minutes of leaving the start line the assaulting troops were under heavy fire. Despite mounting casualties, the leading companies managed to achieve their initial objectives and the second wave passed through to attack the final objectives. It was during this second phase that Sergeant Burman determined the outcome. His VC citation describes the crucial part he played:

For most conspicuous bravery when the advance of his Company was held up by an enemy machine gun firing at point blank range. He shouted to the man next to him to wait a few minutes, and going forward to what seemed certain death, killed the enemy gunner and carried the gun to the Company's objective, where he subsequently used it with great effect. By this exceptionally gallant deed the progress of the attack was assured. About 15 minutes later it was observed that the battalion on the right was being impeded by a party of about 40 of the enemy, who were enfilading them. Sjt. Burman with two others ran forward and got behind the enemy, killing 6 and capturing 2 officers and 29 other ranks.

By 7 a.m., due largely to the cool courage and initiative of Sergeant Burman, 16 RB achieved its objectives for the loss of 29 men killed and 179 wounded – all in the space of 90 minutes. Burman's Company Commander later wrote home:'Sergeant Burman is the finest fellow that ever lived, standing only 5 ft 4 in, but with the heart of a lion, knowing no fear. When we had gone half-way to our objective a machine-gun opened fire at us from 30 yd range in a shell-hole position, and my poor fellows were falling down everywhere. Sgt Burman went on all alone in face of what appeared to be certain death, killed the three gunners and captured the gun, saving, by his gallant deed, the lives of his chums behind and allowing the company to continue to advance. He carried the gun all the way to the final objective, and turned it on the retiring enemy, and his courage and fortitude throughout were amazing to see. He is the hero of the battalion today, and he is my company, hence my pride, and I do sincerely he hope he gets his VC. He thoroughly deserves it ten times over.'[10]

When *The London Gazette* announced Burman's VC award, the Mayor of Stepney opened a public fund which raised £220. He was also given a hero's reception at his old school and while he '"was too modest to speak of his exploits", the local newspaper recorded:"The cheering of the boys was terrific, and … might have been heard in the trenches".'[11]

Sergeant Burman was demobilised on 7 March 1919 and for the next 30 years was a chauffeur for the managing director of the *Daily Mirror*. He then started his own car hire business before retiring in 1964. Seven years later, in 1971, he moved into a Royal British Legion Home at Cromer in Norfolk, where he died on 23 October 1974, aged 77.

Throughout his later life 'Burman remained unaffected by his signal honour and was not much given to discussing his exploits. Once when he did, he was almost apologetic as he confided:"I couldn't help it. It was a case of going on or going back. I couldn't go back."'[12]

Sergeant A.J. Knight VC
(Later Second Lieutenant A.J. Knight VC MBE)

Sergeant Knight was born at Ladywood, Birmingham, on 24 August 1888. On leaving school he joined the Post Office and was employed as a clerical assistant in Birmingham before transferring to Nottingham in 1912. On 26 October 1914 he enlisted in the 2nd/8th (City of London) Battalion, The London Regiment, known as the 2nd Post Office Rifles, a Territorial battalion of The Rifle Brigade. After a lengthy period in England, he accompanied the Battalion to France in February 1917. On 14 May 1917 he distinguished himself as a Lance-Sergeant at Bullecourt during the final stages of the Battle of Arras, receiving a special certificate from his Divisional Commander for bringing in wounded men under heavy fire. He was also promoted to Sergeant.

On 20 September 1917 the 2nd Post Office Rifles had the unenviable task of attacking the German positions on a spur of the main Ypres ridge, which bristled with strong points, machine-gun posts and barbed wire. Because the positions were known to be so strong, the plan was to conduct a feint frontal assault, while the main attack was mounted on a flank with the intention of establishing a breakthrough and assaulting the German positions on the spur from the rear. Even so, a number of German strong points had still to be overcome on the flank, with each company of the 2nd Post Office Rifles assigned to specific objectives. B Company, with Sergeant Knight in command of 6 Platoon, was responsible for clearing Hubner Trench and then two clusters of pillboxes around Hubner Farm.

The attack was launched at 5.40 a.m. at the same moment as Sergeant Burman and 16 RB were assaulting Bulgar Wood some five miles to the south. Progress was initially slow due to the nature of the ground, with handfuls of Germans offering stubborn resistance from Hubner Trench. Maintaining the momentum of the attack was crucial. Knight's VC citation provides a full description of his actions:

For most conspicuous bravery and devotion to duty during the operations against the enemy positions. Sjt. Knight did extraordinary good work, and showed exceptional bravery and initiative when his platoon was attacking an enemy strong point, and came under very heavy fire from an enemy machine gun. He rushed through our own barrage, bayoneted the enemy gunner, and captured the position single-handed. Later, twelve of the enemy with a machine gun, were encountered in a shell-hole. He again rushed forward by himself, bayoneted two and shot a third and caused the remainder to scatter. Subsequently, during the attack on a fortified farm, when entangled up to his waist in mud, and seeing a number of the enemy firing on our troops, he immediately opened fire on them without waiting to extricate himself from the mud, killing six of the enemy. Again, noticing the company on his right flank being held up in their attack on another farm, Sjt. Knight collected some men and took up a position on the flank of this farm, from where he brought a heavy fire to bear on the farm as a result of which the farm was captured. All the platoon officers of the company had become casualties before the first objective was reached, and this gallant N.C.O. took command of all the men of his own platoon and of the platoons without officers. His energy in consolidating and reorganising was untiring. His several single-handed actions showed exceptional bravery, and saved a great number of casualties in the company. They were performed under heavy machine gun and rifle fire, and without regard to personal risk, and were the direct cause of the objectives being captured.

The similarity between Sergeant Knight and Sergeant Burman's VC actions carried out five miles apart at exactly the same time is uncanny, although not wholly unexpected, since success in operations of the sort in which they were engaged is so often dependent upon the courage, initiative and leadership of junior officers and NCOs. Fortune also sometimes favours the brave, since Knight survived the assault completely unharmed. 'There had, however, been many near misses. Years later, he [Knight] recalled being fascinated "by the pattern made all the way round me in the mud by the German bullets". He referred to his survival as a "miracle", and added: "All my kit was shot away almost as soon as we were in it. Everything went, in fact. Bullets rattled on my steel helmet – there were several significant dents and one hole in it I found later – and part of a book was shot away in my pocket. A photograph-case and a cigarette-case probably saved my life from one bullet, which must have passed just under my arm-pit – quite close enough to be comfortable!"'[13]

By 6.30 a.m. the 2nd Post Office Rifles had achieved all their objectives in less than an hour at a cost of 65 killed and 182 wounded or missing. In addition to Knight's VC, a DSO, eight MCs, two DCMs and 28 MMs were awarded for individual acts of bravery by the members of this most distinguished Territorial Battalion.[14]

Soon after the fighting at Hubner Farm, Knight became a training instructor. In December 1917 he returned to England on leave and was honoured with civic receptions in Nottingham and Birmingham. In Nottingham he received a silver tea service and a £100 War Bond. He also received an inscribed marble clock from the postal workers and another clock from the citizens of Birmingham. He became a magnet for journalists, although he always insisted of his VC action that: 'I hardly know myself how it all happened.'[15]

On 17 March 1919 Knight was commissioned as a Second Lieutenant in The Sherwood Foresters but was demobilised soon afterwards, resuming his career in the Post Office. In 1920 he transferred to the Ministry of Labour, becoming a senior manager and remaining an employee until his retirement in 1951, being awarded an MBE (Civil) for his services. He died suddenly at his home at Edgbaston, Birmingham, on 4 December 1960, aged 72.

Battle of Cambrai, 20 November to 6 December 1917

The final five acts in the eight-act tragedy at Passchendaele were played out in a sea of mud between 26 September and 10 November 1917. As the battle ground to a halt, the British decided to switch their main effort and mount a major attack on the German positions south-west of Cambrai, where the ground was considered suitable for armour, even in wet weather. 378 battle tanks, plus a further 90 support tanks and six infantry divisions, took part in the opening attack launched on a six-mile frontage at 6.20 a.m. on 20 November. 12 KRRC, a part of the 20th (Light) Division, was one of the battalions in the six assaulting divisions.

Rifleman A.E. Shepherd VC

(Later Corporal A.E. Shepherd VC)

Rifleman Albert Shepherd was born at Royston, near Barnsley, Yorkshire, on 11 January 1897, and was a pony driver at New Monckton Colliery before enlisting in The King's Royal Rifle Corps on 4 August 1915. He was posted to 12 KRRC in France and served with the Battalion during the Battle of the Somme and the Third Battle of Ypres.

On 20 November 1917, 12 KRRC's objective at Cambrai was a series of German trenches on the strongly fortified Hindenburg Line. Two companies provided intimate support to the tanks, one company was in close support, and B Company was in Battalion Reserve. Rifleman Shepherd was B Company Commander, Captain A. Hoare's orderly. After early success in achieving the Battalion's intermediary objectives, B Company was ordered to push on at once and capture the final objective. What happened next is described in detail in the Regimental Annals:

Captain Hoare led his company forward. The first enemy trench was crossed without opposition, but in the support line the platoon, under command of 2nd Lieutenant H.T. Paul, met with a party of the enemy. A hand-to-hand fight ensued, in which 2nd Lieutenant Paul was, unfortunately, killed, together with 3 of his men. Five Germans lay dead in front of him. The remainder of the enemy fled. Captain Hoare left the rest of this platoon to hold that part of the support line, and himself advanced with his other two platoons. Between the support line and the third line was a little mound, which, as appeared afterwards, contained a dug-out. On reaching this our men came under very severe fire from snipers and machine guns ...

Round and upon the mound Captain Hoare and 14 other riflemen were killed, and many others wounded. The last remaining N.C.O., Sergeant Rowland, at once took command of the Company, and endeavoured to advance, when he, too, was wounded.

Rifleman Shepherd, who was Captain Hoare's orderly, then took command. He ordered the others to keep up a steady fire, and by his gallant example encouraged them and inspired them with confidence. In spite of the severe and accurate fire, he then got up and walked back over some 70 yards of open ground to get assistance from a tank which he had noticed approaching. He succeeded in attracting the attention of the crew, and the tank moved forward to deal with the enemy. Rifleman Shepherd then returned, still under heavy fire, to the Company. Already that day he had rushed a machine gun single-handed, and taken it after killing the gun team. Not many actions have been more gallant than those of this rifleman. ... On calling the roll after the fight it was found that only 34 survived out of 3 officers and 94 N.C.O.s and riflemen of B Company who had gone into action. But the Company took its objective.[16]

135

Shepherd's VC citation provides more detail about his first action as well as confirming the second. It reads: 'For most conspicuous bravery as a company runner. When his company was held up by a machine gun at point blank range he volunteered to rush the gun, and, though ordered not to, rushed forward and threw a Mills bomb, killing two gunners and capturing the gun. The company, on continuing its advance, came under heavy enfilade machine-gun fire. When the last officer and the last non-commissioned officer had become casualties, he took command of the company, ordered the men to lie down, and himself went back some seventy yards under severe fire to obtain the help of a tank. He then returned to his company, and finally led them to their last objective. He showed throughout conspicuous determination and resource.'

On receipt of his VC, Shepherd returned to Royston on leave to be met at the station by thousands of people. The Patriotic Fund presented him with a gold watch and chain at the Royston Palace. He also received a Bible from the scholars of the Primitive Methodist Chapel, with which he was formerly connected.

Back in France Shepherd was promoted to Lance-Corporal on 28 August 1918 and to Corporal a month later. He was wounded three times during the War and, in addition to the VC, was awarded the French Croix de Guerre and Médaille Militaire. He was demobilised in January 1919 and returned to Yorkshire where he died on 24 October 1966, aged 69.

In an obituary notice Major (formerly Sergeant) E. Cooper VC, who served with Shepherd in 12 KRRC and also came from Yorkshire, wrote: 'Whilst not an original 12th Battalion man, he came to us in a replacement draft, and quickly endeared himself to his platoon comrades. His small stature, boyish appearance, cheerful disposition, and ready Yorkshire humour made him a general favourite with both officers and men. … In his native town of Royston, near Barnsley, where he returned after his discharge from the forces, he was equally respected and loved, for his sincerity, unassuming modesty, his willingness to serve in the British Legion, and on any committee which had for its purpose the welfare of the ex-service man. … Though handicapped for the last $3\frac{1}{2}$ years of his life by ill health, and for the last 18 months confined to a wheel chair, he still continued to the end of his days to display those qualities of fortitude and courage friends had learned to expect from him.'[17]

Palestine, 1917

In August 1914 the British closed the Suez Canal for passage by ships from hostile nations. In February 1915 the Turks and Germans advanced from Palestine across the Sinai in an unsuccessful attempt to seize the Canal. Throughout 1915 the British defended the Egyptian side and the

Turks and the Germans remained on the other. In early 1916 Lieutenant-General Sir Archibald Murray assumed command of all troops in the Eastern Mediterranean theatre and was ordered to advance up the coast towards Palestine. Some progress was made but operations were not well conducted and in April 1917 a failed attempt to capture Gaza resulted in Murray being replaced by Lieutenant-General Sir Edmund Allenby. After receiving substantial reinforcements, Allenby mounted an offensive against the Turks and Germans. On 31 October Beersheba fell to the British and Gaza soon thereafter. On 11 December 1917 Allenby made a triumphal entry into Jerusalem. But there was much bitter fighting along the way and in the immediate aftermath as the Turks and Germans fought fiercely to counter the British offensive. Between 27 October and the end of December eight members of Allenby's Egyptian Expeditionary Force performed acts of gallantry that were to result in the award of VCs.

Lieutenant-Colonel A.D. Borton VC DSO, 2nd/22nd (County of London) Battalion, The London Regiment (The Queen's)

Lieutenant-Colonel Arthur ('Boskey') Borton was awarded a VC for his bravery and leadership in command of the 2nd/22nd (County of London) Battalion, The London Regiment, during a dawn attack on 7 November 1917 at Tel-el-Sheria between Beersheba and Jerusalem. Quoting from his VC citation: 'Under most difficult circumstances in darkness and in unknown country, he deployed his battalion for attack, and at dawn led his attacking companies against the strongly-held position. When the leading waves were checked by a withering machine-gun fire, Lt.-Col. Borton showed an utter contempt for danger, and moved freely up and down his lines under heavy fire. Reorganising his command, he led his men forward, and captured the position. At a later stage of the fight, he led a party of volunteers against a battery of field guns in action at point-blank range, capturing the guns and the detachments.'

Borton was a former Regular officer in The King's Royal Rifle Corps, who joined the Regiment in South Africa in 1902, later serving with 2 KRRC in India before being obliged to retire from the Army on medical grounds in 1910. He then moved to the west coast of America and became a fruit farmer, supplying ice to the Transcontinental Railway during the hard winter months from a lake on his property. His business did not prosper and at the start of the First World War he managed to make his way back to England, joining the Royal Flying Corps as an observer. In January 1915 he accompanied No. 8 Squadron to France. On 5 March 1915 his machine crashed during a reconnaissance flight and his neck was broken in two places. He was declared unfit and invalided out of the Army for a second time. Three months later he talked his way into the Royal Naval Volunteer Reserve, becoming a Lieutenant-Commander in command of two squadrons of motor machine guns. He was present at the landings at Suvla Bay in August 1915 and was later awarded a DSO for his services at Gallipoli. In June 1916 he joined the 2nd/22nd (County of London) Battalion, a regiment unconnected to either The King's Royal Rifle Corps or The Rifle Brigade. Initially he served with the 2nd/22nd in France, then in Salonika before it moved to Palestine. He was appointed commanding officer of the 2nd/22nd in May 1917, later receiving a CMG to add to his VC and DSO.

For many years it was erroneously thought within the Green Jackets that Borton was a 60th officer attached to the 2nd/22nd at the time of his VC action, and hence his name used to appear on the list of VC recipients. He ceased, however, to have a direct service link with The King's Royal Rifle Corps in 1910, although he retained many friends within the Regiment. He died prematurely at Southwold in Suffolk on 5 January 1933, aged 49. Quoting from his obituary, 'Boskey, to those who knew him intimately, was a splendid and very gallant character. … No one ever heard him say an unkind thing about anyone.'[18]

Lance-Corporal J.A. Christie VC

Lance-Corporal John (Jock) Christie was born to Scottish parents in Edmonton, London, on 14 May 1895. After leaving school he joined the London and North Western Railway Company (L&NWR) and was a parcels clerk at Euston Station. In September 1914 he joined the 1st/11th (County of London) Battalion, The London Regiment (Finsbury Rifles), a Territorial battalion of The King's Royal Rifle Corps. In August 1915 he landed with the Battalion at Suvla Bay during the Gallipoli campaign, and was wounded in the head by shrapnel at Chocolate Hill. He was evacuated to Egypt and then England, rejoining the Battalion in November 1915, just prior to the withdrawal of the Allies from the Dardanelles. The 1st Finsbury Rifles then became a part of General Murray's Egyptian Expeditionary Force advancing up the Mediterranean coastline towards Gaza, during which Christie suffered severe sunstroke during a 100-mile march across the Sinai desert before taking part in the unsuccessful battles at Gaza in March/April 1917.

In the autumn of 1917 the 1st Finsbury Rifles joined the renewed offensive in Palestine, where during the night of 21/22 December 1917 at Fejja, near Jerusalem, 10 days after Allenby's triumphal entry into the city, Lance-Corporal Christie performed the act of gallantry recorded in his VC citation: 'For most conspicuous bravery when after a position had been captured, the enemy immediately made counter and bombing attacks up communication trenches. L./Cpl. Christie, realising the position, took a supply of bombs over the top, proceeding alone about fifty yards in the open along the communication trench and bombed the enemy. He continued to do this alone in spite of very heavy opposition until a block had been established. Returning towards our lines he heard voices behind him; he at once turned back and bombed another party moving up the trench, entirely breaking up a further bombing attack. By his prompt and effective action he undoubtedly cleared a difficult position at a most critical time and saved many lives. Throughout he was subjected to heavy machine-gun fire and shell fire. He showed the greatest coolness and a total disregard for his own safety.'

Further information about Christie's action, which took place as Allenby's forces sought to exploit north and east of Jerusalem, is lacking. Torrential rain also intervened to bring the campaign to a halt until March 1918, when, in a further action at Medjelyaba, Christie was again wounded, this time in the knee and wrist. He received some recompense, however, when HRH The Duke of Connaught visited him in hospital near Jaffa and presented him with his VC medal ribbon. However, he had to wait until 18 November 1918 to receive the medal from King George V at Buckingham Palace.

In January 1919 Christie was presented with a mahogany bureau and cheque by the L&NWR station staff at Euston and had a locomotive named after him. He also received a silver salver from the citizens of Islington, where he had moved before the War. However, he did not rejoin the L&NWR, becoming a commercial traveller. He then entered the catering and wine business. During the 1926 General Strike he drove a food wagon on the streets of London and during the Second World War was a driver in the Auxiliary Fire Service and a Sergeant in the Special Constabulary. He was a founder member of the VC Association and at the time of his death at Bramhall, Cheshire, on 10 September 1967, aged 72, he was Honorary Treasurer.

1918

For the Germans the situation at the beginning of 1918 was obvious; after signing an armistice with Russia on 17 December 1917, the Allies had to be defeated on the Western Front before the Americans arrived in France in sufficient strength to ensure an Allied victory. The Allies, on the other hand, had every reason to favour defence while the Americans assembled their forces. The outcome was predictable and anticipated – a German offensive.

First German Offensive, 21 March to 5 April 1918

The Germans chose to mount their offensive against the BEF between Arras and La Fère, with the main effort on a 20-mile front west of St Quentin. They did so with a numerical superiority of three to one, having redeployed 30 divisions from the Eastern Front. Early on 21 March a huge bombardment began, after which wave after wave of German storm troopers overwhelmed the British front line. Many small parties fought gallantly to a finish, while those who were able conducted a fighting withdrawal. On 4/5 April the German advance, which had penetrated 40 miles, was eventually halted 10 miles east of Amiens.

Captain A.M. Toye VC MC, The Middlesex Regiment

On 25 March 1918 Acting Captain Maurice Toye was commanding C Company, 2nd Battalion, The Middlesex Regiment, as the Battalion tried desperately to stem the German advance across the River Somme near Péronne. During the fighting Toye displayed conspicuous bravery, three times recapturing a trench occupied by the enemy. In all he was wounded twice in 10 days as he repeatedly rallied his men in opposing the German advance. He was later awarded a VC for his fine leadership in critical circumstances. He also received a MC for his actions during the Third Battle of Ypres and was mentioned in despatches three times during the War.

On 26 April 1924 Captain Toye, who rose through the ranks of the Royal Engineers before being commissioned into The Middlesex Regiment in 1917, transferred to The Oxfordshire and Buckinghamshire Light Infantry. From 1925–35 he was Chief Instructor at the Royal Egyptian Military College, Cairo. He was promoted to Major in March 1938 serving briefly as a company commander in the 1st Battalion (43rd) before being promoted to Brevet Lieutenant-Colonel on 1 July 1939 and Acting Colonel in August 1940. In 1943 he became an instructor at the Staff College, Camberley, and later a Brigadier on the staff at GHQ Middle East Command. He retired from the Army on 19 January 1949 and was Commandant of the Civil Defence College at Bristol. He died of cancer on 6 September 1955, aged 58.

While there are four known instances of officers who have served in the antecedent regiments of The Royal Green Jackets being awarded VCs after transferring to other regiments,[19] Toye is the only person known to have done the opposite and transferred into the Regiment having already received a VC.

Second German Offensive, 9 to 29 April 1918

On 5 April 1918 the Germans ceased their offensive in Picardy and turned their attention to Flanders. On 9 April they attacked between Ypres and Neuve Chapelle on a smaller scale than on 21 March but with a numerical superiority that was just as great. By 12 April the situation was so desperate that Field Marshal Haig issued an order to his forces that: 'Every position must be held to the last man: there must be no retirement. With our backs to the wall and believing in the justice of our cause, each one of us must fight on to the end.'[20]

Photograph courtesy of Imperial War Museum, London

A village on the Somme, March 1918

Photograph courtesy of Imperial War Museum, London

German prisoners-of-war, March 1918

Chapter 8

Lance-Sergeant J.E. Woodall VC

(Later Captain J.E. Woodall VC)

Lance-Sergeant Joseph Woodall was born at Salford, Manchester, on 1 June 1896. He was the eldest of 10 children. His father was a L&NWR train driver. After leaving school he had a number of jobs before enlisting in The Rifle Brigade on 2 September 1914 and being posted to the 1st Battalion.

When the Second German Offensive began on 9 April 1918, 1 RB was in reserve recovering from its part in halting the First German Offensive near Arras. Over the next few days the Battalion moved up to the front line, occupying defensive positions along the La Bassée Canal, at the southern extreme of the German line of attack. During the night of 21/22 April 1 RB crossed the canal and early on 22 April attacked the German positions on the far bank, during which Lance-Sergeant Woodall especially distinguished himself.

Woodall's VC citation reads: 'For most conspicuous bravery and fine leadership during an attack. Sjt. Woodall was in command of a platoon, which, during the advance, was held up by a machine gun. On his own initiative he rushed forward and, single-handed, captured the gun and eight men. After the objective had been gained, heavy fire was encountered from a farmhouse some 200 yards in front. Sjt. Woodall collected ten men and, with great dash and gallantry, rushed the farm and took thirty prisoners. Shortly afterwards, when the officer in charge was killed, he took entire command, reorganised the two platoons, and disposed of them skilfully. Throughout the day, in spite of intense shelling and machine-gun fire, this gallant N.C.O. was constantly on the move, encouraging the men and finding out and sending back invaluable information. The example set by Sjt. Woodall was simply magnificent, and had a marked effect on the troops. The success of the operation on this portion of the front is attributed almost entirely to his coolness, courage, and utter disregard for his own personal safety.'

The fighting over this period was severe. 1 RB lost 43 men killed and 112 wounded or missing. Across the front the German advance was first slowed and then held. On 29 April, after a final attempt to breakthrough the British lines had failed, Ludendorff, the German Commander-in-Chief, called off the offensive with both sides exhausted.

Lance-Sergeant Woodall was at home on leave when the award of his VC was announced. He immediately responded by disappearing to a friend's home to avoid all the enthusiasm and fuss it created. He was eventually tracked down and presented with the proceeds of a public fund initiated in his honour. He did not, however, receive his VC from the hands of the King until 23 November 1918, after the War had ended. He then stayed in the Army for a while and was commissioned on 7 March 1919. He retired as an Honorary Captain on 1 September 1921. Thereafter he went to work in a mill at Oldham but lost part of his arm while operating some unfenced machinery. He was retrained and found alternative employment, eventually moving to Dun Laoghaire in Eire in 1955. He died in a Dublin hospital on 2 January 1962, aged 65.

Bucquoy, 8 May 1918

The end of the German Second Offensive on 29 April 1918 was followed by an operational pause before Ludendorff, on 27 May, launched a Third Offensive, this time against the French on the Aisne, near Soissons.

Meanwhile, 13 RB was doing its turn in the newly-established front line at the village of Bucquoy, north of Albert, where observation of the German lines to the east of the village was poor. It was therefore decided to mount a 'minor operation' without artillery support to eject the Germans from their positions on the eastern outskirts of the village and bring the German positions in the valley beyond under better view. 13 RB was selected for the task which was timed to begin at 2 p.m. on 8 May 1918, with two companies leading the assault and two in direct support. A Company, to which Sergeant Gregg and Rifleman Beesley belonged, was the right assault company. What happened next is described in the Regimental History:

The attack started punctually and it was soon found that the right company [A Company] *would have trouble from the Cemetery and Crucifix* [on the eastern edge of the village]. *The parties of this company got on with varying success, but machine-gun fire from these two places caused many casualties. Two parties detailed for the attack on the Cemetery rushed a machine-gun and killed the team. There were at least thirty Germans in the Cemetery, of whom eleven were sent back as prisoners and the remainder killed. 2nd-Lieutenant G. D. Fraser having been* [mortally] *wounded in the Cemetery, Serjeant Gregg took command and the parties pushed on to the Crucifix, which they occupied, as well as posts to the north. The enemy counter-attacked from a support trench and got round the right flank, whereupon the parties fell back to the edge of the Cemetery; here they were reinforced by a section of the support company and, returning to the charge, bombed the enemy back. They remained there until, under orders, they withdrew at 5.40 p.m., having lost half their strength.*

The next party on the left, a platoon, came under enfilade machine-gun fire and lost the platoon serjeant and three section commanders killed, or wounded. Rifleman Beesley took command and continued to advance.

First, with a Lewis-gun, he engaged an enemy machine-gun and knocked it out; continuing, he encountered four enemy posts, one of which he rushed single-handed; from this he extracted five German officers, of whom he killed one, wounded one, and disarmed three, sending them back as prisoners.

Next Rifleman Beesley single-handed rushed a post on the left, the machine-gun post referred to above, and found one dead and two live Germans; the latter he disarmed and sent back. Having obtained touch with the section on the left, he returned to the captured machine-gun position and mounted his Lewis-gun there, the No. 2 (the only other survivor of the section) having arrived with the gun. There he remained with the No. 2 (whose name, unhappily, is not recorded), who, although wounded about 7.0 p.m., remained until the pair brought their gun back into the line at 10.0 p.m. During these activities Rifleman Beesley did considerable execution with the 600–800 rounds he fired, whilst he also rescued a valuable disposition map which a German officer was about to destroy.[21]

The opposition experienced by 13 RB during the attack, plus the fact that the positions occupied did not offer any better observation than before, resulted in the Battalion being ordered to withdraw to its original start-point, having lost around 100 men killed, wounded or missing.

Sergeant W. Gregg VC DCM MM

Sergeant William (Bill) Gregg was born at Heanor, Derbyshire, on 27 January 1890. After leaving school he worked as a miner at Shipley Colliery and was married on 25 June 1910. Responding to Kitchener's call for volunteers, he enlisted in The Rifle Brigade on 24 November 1914 and was posted to 2 RB in France. When 13 RB arrived in 1915 he was transferred to it, rising to the rank of Sergeant by the end of 1917 and remaining with 13 RB until the end of the War.

In 1916 Gregg was wounded on the Somme. On 26 March 1917 *The London Gazette* announced the award to him of a MM for his role in a daylight reconnaissance patrol in February 1917, during which he secured important information from a dead German whose body was lying in a crater. On 6 February 1918 *The London Gazette* announced the further award to him of a DCM for his role in November 1917 in carrying messages across a road swept by machine-gun fire and for leading a counter-attack that drove off the enemy.

Gregg's VC citation resulting from the action at Bucquoy on 8 May 1918 reads: 'For most conspicuous bravery and brilliant leadership in action. Two companies of his unit attacked the enemy's outpost position without artillery preparation. Sergeant Gregg was with the right company, which came under heavy fire from the right flank as it advanced. All the officers of the company were hit. He at once took command of the attack. He rushed an enemy post and personally killed an entire machine-gun team and captured the gun and four men in a dug-out near by. He then rushed another post, killed two men and captured another. In spite of heavy casualties he reached his objective, and started consolidating the position. By this prompt and effective action this gallant N.C.O. saved the situation at a critical time and

The medals of Sergeant W. Gregg VC DCM MM (RGJ Museum)

ensured the success of the attack. Later, Sjt. Gregg's party were driven back by an enemy counter-attack, but, reinforcements coming up, he led a charge, personally bombed a hostile machine gun, killed the crew, and captured the gun. Once again he was driven back. He led another successful attack, and hung on to the position until ordered by his company commander to withdraw. Although under very heavy rifle and machine-gun fire for several hours, Sjt. Gregg displayed throughout the greatest coolness and contempt of danger, walking about encouraging his men and setting a magnificent example.'

Within 13 RB Sergeant Gregg established a great reputation as a fighting soldier. One of his platoon corporals said of him: 'He was

completely fearless. He came through action after action unscathed. In
fact, he went looking for trouble, particularly at night in No-Mans-Land,
observing and searching for information of value. Indeed a fine fighting
man and one we would follow anywhere.'[22]

In 1919 Gregg was demobilised and returned to work in the mines.
When War was declared in 1939, he joined the National Defence
Company of The Sherwood Foresters, 'saying that if the Country was
worth living in, it was worth defending',[23] but left in 1941 when he
reached the upper age limit. He later served on one of the ferries
evacuating survivors from the Dieppe Raid in August 1942. After the
War he again returned to the mines before retiring in the 1950s due to
ill health.

Gregg was a founder member of the Heanor Branch of the Royal
British Legion 'of whom we were all very proud, but he was just as much
admired as a quite [quiet] unassuming, hard working family man who
shunned the limelight'.[24] He died at Heanor on 9 August 1969, aged 79.
His widow, who was married to him for 59 years, died in 1993, aged 101.

Sergeant Gregg was the first soldier in the First World War to be
awarded a VC, DCM and MM.[25]

Rifleman W. Beesley VC

(Later Corporal W. Beesley VC)

Rifleman William Beesley was born on 5 October 1895 at Burton-on-
Trent, Staffordshire, later moving to Nuneaton. After leaving school he
worked as a miner at Haunchwood and Tunnel Collieries. Towards the
end of 1914 he enlisted in The King's Royal Rifle Corps, accompanying
9 KRRC to France in May 1915. He was soon in action near Ypres and
was wounded twice during the year. On recovering he was posted to a
machine-gun section in 13 RB and took part in the Battle of the Somme.

Beesley's VC citation resulting from the action at Bucquoy on 8 May
1918 reads:'For most conspicuous bravery. The enemy's outpost position
was attacked by two companies of his unit without artillery preparation.
Pte. Beesley was in the leading wave of the left company, which came
under heavy fire as it approached the enemy's front line. His platoon
serjeant and all the section commanders were killed. This young soldier,
realising the situation at once, took command and led the assault. Single-
handed he rushed a post, and with his revolver killed two of the enemy
at a machine gun. He then shot dead an officer who ran across from a
dug-out to take their place at the machine gun. Three more officers
appeared from the dug-out. These he called on to surrender; seeing one
of them trying to get rid of a map he shot him and obtained the map. He
took four more prisoners from a dug-out and two others from a shelter
close by, disarmed them and sent them back to our lines. At this moment
his Lewis gun was brought up by a comrade, who was acting as a carrier.
Pte. Beesley at once brought it into action, and used it with great effect

against the enemy as they bolted towards their support line, inflicting many casualties. For four hours Private Beesley and his comrade held on to the position under very heavy machine-gun and rifle fire. The enemy then advanced to counter-attack, and the other soldier was wounded. Pte. Beesley carried on by himself, and actually maintained his position until 10 p.m., long after the posts on his right and left had been practically wiped out and the survivors had fallen back. It was mainly due to his action that the enemy were prevented from rushing the position, and that the remnants of his company, when compelled to withdraw, were able to do so without further loss. When darkness set in Pte. Beesley made his way back to the original line from which the attack had started, bringing with him the wounded carrier and the Lewis gun. He at once mounted the Lewis gun in the trench and remained in action until things had quietened down. The indomitable pluck, skilful shooting and good judgement in economising ammunition displayed by Pte. Beesley stamp the incident as one of the most brilliant actions in recent operations.'

Nearly 40 years later Beesley described the action: 'It was half-past two in the afternoon, I remember. A boiling hot day. Three trench mortars were the signal to go over and it was every man for himself. We had no artillery barrage; the Germans loosed every thing they had got.' Recalling the No. 2 on the Lewis gun who acted as a carrier: 'He was a lad called Douglas, and he had dropped his shovel in the support trenches when he saw the way things were going and dashed up the ridge [to join me]. We stuck it out, me and this kid. I don't know whether we were scared or not.'[26]

Beesley was promoted to Corporal on 28 June 1918, the day that the award of his VC was announced in *The London Gazette*. He was subsequently invited to tea in the trenches with his Commanding Officer and to lunch with his Divisional Commander who also gave him a box of chocolates. On 9 August 1918 he and Sergeant Gregg received their VCs together from King George V at a field investiture at HQ Third Army at Frohen-le-Grand.

On 14 July 1919 Beesley was awarded the French Médaille Militaire for an earlier undocumented action during the War. He was demobilised in the same year and returned to work in the mines. During the Second World War he joined the Royal Artillery but was discharged in 1941 due to his age. After the War he worked for a manufacturing company at Coventry before retiring in 1960. He died on holiday at Abergavenny in South Wales on 23 September 1966, aged 70.

Allied Offensive, 18 July to 11 November 1918

By the end of May 1918 the Americans had 650,000 men in France, with the first troops deployed in the line to halt the Third German Offensive. The Fourth and Fifth German Offensives followed and were similarly halted. The strategic initiative now passed to the Allies who, on 18 July, launched a major counter-offensive between the Aisne and the Marne and, on 8 August, at Amiens, which soon developed into an advance along the whole Allied line against a German army that was becoming increasingly dispirited. In September the Germans withdrew to the Hindenburg Line, whence they had mounted their offensive in March. By October they were forced to abandon the Hindenburg Line with their withdrawal fast becoming a rout. The Germans, bereft of reserves, sued for peace. On 6 November the last act of gallantry on the Western Front resulting in the award of a VC took place.[27] On 11 November the Armistice was signed.

Meanwhile, losses during the First German Offensive earlier in the year had resulted in a reorganisation of the BEF and the amalgamation of many under-strength battalions, including the absorption of the 2nd/1st Buckinghamshire Battalion into the 2nd/4th Battalion, The Oxfordshire and Buckinghamshire Light Infantry.

On 11 September 1918 the 2nd/4th moved forward to the front line as a preliminary to mounting an attack to capture a German position, known as Junction Post, near the town of Laventie, north of Neuve Chapelle. This post was a grass-bound breastwork, where the enemy offered strong resistance. On 12 September the attack was launched.

Lance-Corporal A. Wilcox VC

Lance-Corporal Alfred Wilcox was born at Aston, Birmingham, on 16 December 1884. In 1902 he enlisted in the 1st Royal Warwickshire Volunteer Battalion, before moving to Liverpool and becoming a member of the Territorial Force, reaching the rank of Corporal before leaving in 1909. On 25 March 1915 he joined The Royal Buckinghamshire Hussars as a Trooper, later transferring to the 2nd/4th Battalion, The Oxfordshire and Buckinghamshire Light Infantry, as a Private, when dismounted soldiers were in greater demand than cavalry. During the First German Offensive in March 1918 he was extremely fortunate to escape when the 2nd/4th was surrounded by overwhelming numbers of Germans close to St Quentin. In the following month he was promoted to Lance-Corporal.

The 1918 Regimental Chronicle has the following report on the action at Laventie on 12 September:

During a local operation on the morning of 12th September, 1918, in front of Laventie, the flank platoon of A Company, 2/4th Battalion Oxford and Bucks Light Infantry, was held up by heavy and persistent machine-gun fire from a trench about 70 yards distant. Finding it impossible to advance, Lance-Corporal Wilcox crawled towards the trench with 4 men, bombed it, and finally rushed the gun nearest to him, disposed of the gunner, and, being unable to take the gun along with him, put it out of action.[28]

Recording his own version of events, Wilcox later wrote:

My battalion was ordered to take what was known as Junction Point – believed to be strongly held by machine-guns. I was in charge of the leading section; my duty was to cut through the wire and locate the posts. Having got to the wire and successfully cut it, I went back for my section, which I had left in a shell hole a hundred yards to the rear, only to find all but one wounded. That one I told to follow me. Getting through the gap I had already cut, and making my way in the trench the enemy was holding, I got into it, and, bombing my way, captured my first gun. Being quite safe from enemy fire, I still proceeded up the trench, capturing a second gun after a hand-to-hand struggle, in which I bayoneted my man; then bombing a third post, killing five. My own rifle by this time being clogged with mud, I had to resort to German stick bombs, which accounted for a fourth post with its gun. I carried on, driving the remainder of the post right away, leaving behind them about twelve dead in all and four guns (one light, three heavy). I then returned to the guns. Finding I could not remove the three latter, I put them out of action, and had to withdraw owing to lack of support and no fire-arms, my own gun having been dumped for the free use of German stick bombs.[29]

Wilcox's VC citation is similar to his own account in some but not all respects: 'For most conspicuous bravery and initiative in attack when his company was held up by heavy and persistent machine-gun fire at close range. On his own initiative, with four men he rushed forward to the nearest enemy gun, bombed it, killed the gunner and put the gun out of action. Being then attacked by an enemy bombing party, Cpl. Wilcox picked up enemy bombs and led his company against the next gun, finally capturing and destroying it. Although left with only one man, he continued bombing and captured a third gun. He again bombed up the trench, captured a fourth gun, and then rejoined his platoon. Cpl. Wilcox displayed in this series of successful individual enterprises exceptional valour, judgement and initiative.'

Lance-Corporal Wilcox's action was unarguably an 'individual enterprise of exceptional valour, judgement, and initiative' for which he was decorated with the VC by King George V on 26 November 1918. He was subsequently discharged on 2 May 1919, maintaining his links thereafter with the regiments with which he had served and veterans' organisations. He died at his home at Small Heath, Birmingham, on 30 March 1951, aged 69.

In 1949 Wilcox's nephew, Charles Wilcox, was awarded the Edward Medal, which he exchanged for a GC in 1971 (see page 12), for rescuing a man trapped on the ledge of a building in Birmingham.

Summary of First World War VC Awards

Lance-Corporal Wilcox was the last member of the antecedent regiments of The Royal Green Jackets to be awarded a VC during the First World War. It was fitting, too, that he should have been a Territorial, since those serving in the 48 front-line Service and Territorial battalions had distinguished themselves with valour in every respect equal to those serving in the 10 Regular battalions.

VCs Awarded

Regiment	Regular	Service	Territorial	Total
Oxf & Bucks LI	–	–	2	2
KRRC	5	2	2	9
RB	5	5	2	12
Total	10	7	6	23

In addition to the 23 VCs recorded above, two were awarded to Regimental Medical Officers serving with Green Jacket battalions and two to officers who had previously served in The King's Royal Rifle Corps.

Most memorable of all, however, The Rifle Brigade achieved a remarkable double, with Major Billy Congreve the first officer ever to be awarded a VC, DSO and MC, and Sergeant Gregg the first non-commissioned rank ever to be awarded a VC, DCM and MM. The Territorial battalions, too, led the way, with Second Lieutenant Woolley of Queen Victoria's Rifles the first Territorial, and Lance-Sergeant Belcher of the London Rifle Brigade the first Territorial non-commissioned rank, ever to be awarded VCs. It is a unique record of which every Rifleman today may and should be extremely and justifiably proud.

Chapter 9

The Second World War: 1939–45

During the Second World War the antecedent regiments of The Royal Green Jackets contributed 19 Regular and Territorial battalions to front-line service overseas, compared to 58 Regular, Service and Territorial battalions during the First World War.

During the First World War, 628 VCs were awarded, including to 23 members of the antecedent regiments. During the Second World War 182 VCs were awarded, with two to Green Jackets.

This chapter concentrates on the two Green Jacket awards, each of which resulted from acts of gallantry in North Africa. It also focuses on an award to a former officer in The Oxfordshire and Buckinghamshire Light Infantry resulting from his extraordinary acts of bravery at Arnhem.

North Africa, 1940–1

In June 1940 Italy declared war on Britain, threatening British domination of the Mediterranean, its important bases in Egypt, and its lines of communication to India and the Persian Gulf.

Libya was an Italian colony with 250,000 troops based there, greatly outnumbering the 36,000 British and Dominion soldiers in Egypt. An extensive barbed-wire fence marked the frontier between the two countries. As soon as war was declared, the Allies took the offensive, patrolling aggressively across the border, establishing moral ascendancy over the Italians. In September 1940 the Italians responded by invading Egypt, advancing 60 miles to Sidi Barrani. In December General Wavell, Commander-in-Chief, Middle East Command, launched an Allied counter-offensive, which, in the space of 10 weeks, forced the Italians out of Egypt and Cyrenaica to El Agheila, over 700 miles by road and track to the west.

On 5 February 1941, Hitler, fearing an Italian collapse, decided to send General Rommel and two German divisions to Libya to oppose the Allies. Arriving in some secrecy and quicker than expected, the Germans wrong-footed Wavell, who had reduced the strength of his forces in Cyrenaica. On 31 March Rommel initiated an offensive which, within a few weeks, drove the Allies all the way back to Egypt, whence they had started in December, with only the garrison at Tobruk holding firm. In May and June attempts to force the Germans to withdraw failed. During the next four

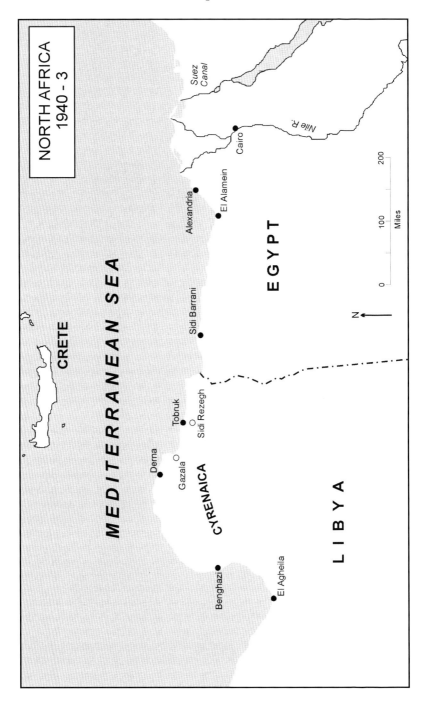

months between July and October 1941 a relative lull occurred as each side sought to build up its strength for future operations.

By November 1941 the newly created Eighth Army, consisting of two army corps, was sufficiently strong for General Auchinleck, who had replaced Wavell, to accede to Churchill's pressure to move on to the offensive. Meanwhile, Rommel was planning the capture of Tobruk. On 18 November Auchinleck pre-empted Rommel by launching Operation Crusader, with 13 Corps tying down the Axis forces on the Egyptian frontier, while 30 Corps outflanked the German positions to the south with the aim of defeating Rommel's armour and relieving Tobruk.

Sidi Rezegh, 21/22 November 1941

1 KRRC and 2 RB were both motor battalions forming a part of 7th Armoured Division's Support Group in 30 Corps. At 5.50 a.m. on 18 November the advance began.

> *By the evening of 20 November* [1 KRRC] *had reached the south side of Sidi Rezegh airfield, which was situated on flat ground above an escarpment overlooking the main road bypassing Tobruk. German and some Italian troops occupied the area north of the airfield where the escarpment lay. In the early hours of 21 November Lieutenant-Colonel De Salis* [Commanding Officer] *issued orders to the Battalion to seize the ground occupied by the enemy so that gunner observation posts might be positioned to enable shelling of the bypass road. Despite conducting reconnaissance patrols during the night, the extent of the enemy position was not fully realised. There was no alternative to a frontal assault over 2,000 yards of flat, open ground, with three scout platoons in Bren carriers leading, and the motor platoons following dismounted. The Battalion was less one of its motor companies and had two* [artillery] *batteries of 25 pounders under command, but no tanks in support.*
>
> *The attack, which was mounted at 8.30 a.m. with around 300 officers and Riflemen in the assaulting force, achieved remarkable success, over-running an enemy that was later assessed to have been 1,000 strong, including a German machine-gun company. 700 prisoners were taken. For much of the three hours that it took to capture the escarpment, it was a platoon and section commander's battle, with Riflemen skirmishing forward in pairs in the manner of their forebears in the Peninsula. Many acts of great gallantry were performed including an action for which Rifleman Beeley was subsequently awarded a posthumous Victoria Cross, the only Victoria Cross awarded to a member of the Regiment* [KRRC] *during the Second World War. The Battalion lost three officers and twenty-six other ranks killed and fifty wounded.*[1]

*Rifleman John Beeley VC killed in action at Sidi Rezegh,
21 November 1941*

*HRH The Duke of Gloucester and Lieutenant-General Willoughby Norrie
at the grave of Rifleman Beeley VC, May 1942*

Rifleman J. Beeley VC†

Rifleman John Beeley was one of twin boys born in Manchester on 8 February 1918. After leaving school he became a stonemason before enlisting in The King's Royal Rifle Corps on 4 August 1938, later being posted to 1 KRRC in the Western Desert.

On 21 November 1941 Rifleman Beeley was a member of a motor platoon in A Company, which was the centre company of the three 1 KRRC companies assaulting dismounted across the airfield at Sidi Rezegh. Quoting from the Regimental Annals: 'Practically no fire was encountered crossing the landing ground itself ... The Companies, which moved in perfect extended order, were therefore able to cross at normal walking speed without getting down at all, and no casualties were suffered during this stage of the advance. As soon as the far side of the landing-ground was reached, however, all companies came under very severe fire from all arms and were forced to get down. From then on progress was only possible by fire and movement.'[2]

A Company was opposite the most strongly held enemy positions and 'were [sic] eventually pinned down and unable to proceed any farther, though they were within one hundred yards of their objective and could clearly hear German and Italian voices giving orders in the enemy posts'.[3] It was at this point that Rifleman Beeley acted in the manner described in his VC citation:

On the 21st November, 1941, during the attack by a Battalion of The King's Royal Rifle Corps at Sidi Rezegh against a strong enemy position, the Company to which Rifleman Beeley belonged was pinned down by heavy fire at point-blank range from the front and flank on the flat open ground of the aerodrome. All the officers but one of the Company and many of the other ranks had been either killed or wounded. On his own initiative, and when there was no sort of cover, Rifleman Beeley got to his feet carrying a Bren gun and ran towards a strong enemy post containing an anti-tank gun, a heavy machine gun and a light machine gun. He ran thirty yards and discharged a complete magazine at the post from a range of twenty yards, killing or wounding the entire crew of the anti-tank gun. The post was silenced and Rifleman Beeley's platoon was enabled to advance, but Rifleman Beeley fell dead across his gun, hit in at least four places. Rifleman Beeley went to certain death in a gallant and successful attempt to carry the day. His courage and self-sacrifice was [sic] a glorious example to his comrades and inspired them to further efforts to reach their objective, which was eventually captured by them, together with 700 prisoners.

It is open to speculation why Beeley should have acted in the way described in his citation without any apparent prompting. Maybe he was frustrated by the actions of the enemy or those around him to the point of feeling obliged to act. That he did so without regard for his own safety, and in a manner which some would term foolhardy, is self-evident since he paid the ultimate price of losing his life at the age of 23. It was, however, a truly brave act, bearing many similarities to that of Lieutenant-Colonel 'H' Jones's well-publicised VC action in the Falkland Islands on 28 May 1982.

Soon after Beeley's act of great courage and self-sacrifice, an artillery bombardment of the enemy's positions led to their surrender. However, without armoured support the Battalion 'was extremely vulnerable against a German tank attack. Hence there was little it could do when, at 1.30 p.m. on 22 November, a huge force of about eighty tanks with supporting infantry and artillery assaulted the rear of the position and overwhelmed the companies and the commanding officer's tactical headquarters. Five officers and fifty other ranks escaped, but the majority were captured, including Lieutenant-Colonel De Salis. It was an unfortunate sequel to one of the finest actions fought by the Regiment during the War. Fortunately, one of the motor companies had survived, which, together with those who escaped, provided the nucleus around which the Battalion was quickly re-formed.'[4]

Rifleman Beeley was married in 1940 to Elizabeth Davy, serving in the Auxiliary Territorial Service, Royal Artillery. On 20 October 1942 she received her late husband's VC from King George VI during an investiture at Buckingham Palace. There were no children from the marriage.

North Africa, 1942–3

Although tactically the Germans often had the edge over the Allies during the confused tank battles south of Tobruk in November 1941, operationally Rommel's losses mattered more as his lines of communication were extended and he lacked immediate replacements. He therefore abandoned his plan to capture Tobruk and withdrew his forces back to El Agheila, whence he had come eight months previously. After a short pause to reconstitute, he reverted to the offensive on 21 January 1942, precipitating an abrupt Allied withdrawal to Gazala and the re-capture of the port of Benghazi through which Rommel was able to reinforce and re-supply his army.

On 26 May 1942 Rommel resumed the offensive, attacking the British positions south of Gazala and eventually forcing the Allies to withdraw a further 350 miles to El Alamein, 60 miles west of Alexandria. On 20/21 June the Germans captured Tobruk.

The El Alamein line stretched 38 miles south from the Mediterranean coast to the Qattara Depression. Although the German High Command originally wanted Rommel to pause at this point, the prize of achieving a rapid breakthrough to the Nile Delta was too tempting. Between July and September 1942 Rommel's forces tried time and again to breach the

Eighth Army's positions, and time and again they were repulsed; and as the Germans dissipated their strength in attack, the Eighth Army under General Montgomery, who assumed command in August, built up theirs in defence.[5]

Battle of El Alamein, 23 October to 3 November 1942

By October Montgomery was sufficiently confident that the Germans were close to their limit to order the Allies on to the offensive. His intention was to breach the extensive minefields forward of the Allied positions at El Alamein and defeat Rommel's army in place.

The Battle of El Alamein began during the evening of 23 October 1942. Four days of heavy fighting followed as the Eighth Army sought to clear a way through the minefields. It was during this period that 2 KRRC and 2 RB, motor battalions in the 7th Motor Brigade, were ordered to seize a feature known as Kidney Ridge as a pivot around which British armoured forces could subsequently manoeuvre. 2 KRRC was directed to the north part of the feature known as 'Woodcock' and 2 RB to the south part known as 'Snipe'. It was here that 2 RB carried out one of the most heroic actions in the Regiment's history resulting in the award of a VC to the Battalion's Commanding Officer, Lieutenant-Colonel V.B. Turner.

Lieutenant-Colonel V.B. Turner VC
(Later Lieutenant-Colonel V.B. Turner VC CVO)

Lieutenant-Colonel Victor (Vic) Turner was born at Thatcham in Berkshire on 17 January 1900, into a family of which the father and all four sons (there was also a daughter) were, or came to be, distinguished soldiers and sailors. They were also renowned for their bravery, Vic Turner's eldest brother, Alexander, being awarded a posthumous VC for his gallantry while serving as a Second Lieutenant with The Royal Berkshire Regiment at Loos on 28 September 1915.

After being educated at Wellington College and RMC Sandhurst, Vic Turner was commissioned into The Rifle Brigade on 20 December 1918. He subsequently served in Iraq in 1919–20 and with 1 RB in India. He was Adjutant of the 1st Battalion from 1931–4 and of the London Rifle Brigade from 1934–8. At the outbreak of the Second World War he was Second-in-Command of The Rifle Depot at Winchester, rejoining 1 RB when the Battalion was re-formed after the majority of its members were captured following their vain but heroic defence of Calais in May 1940. Arriving with 1 RB in North Africa in November 1941, he became a victim in January 1942 of Rommel's rapid advance from El Agheila to Gazala. Quoting from the Regimental History:

No one had a more exciting experience than Vic Turner, whose vehicle had been knocked out in the early stages of operations. He, together with Geoffrey Fletcher[6] and several riflemen, set out to walk back across that endless desert [to Gazala]. To anyone who knows the desert the idea of walking across it is quite fantastic. But they set out, lying up by day and walking at night. After six nights, during each of which they walked for ten hours, torrential rain added to their discomfort and they decided they must somehow secure a vehicle. They laid an ambush, featuring the apparently bloodstained body of a rifleman, and waited. For two days nothing came. On the third day a German staff car appeared and stopped to investigate. They set on the crew, seized the car and drove off across the desert, leaving the astonished Germans still standing with their hands above their head. Their troubles were not over, although the car was full of petrol and carried a reserve. When they were almost within our lines, the car broke down and the little party had to start off again on foot. They rejoined the Battalion after a memorable trek, avoiding capture by refusing to accept the apparently inevitable. They must have covered a hundred sandy miles on foot![7]

In May 1942 Vic Turner had another close shave when an armour-piercing shell penetrated the command vehicle in which he was travelling, killing one occupant and seriously wounding the driver. Turner was unhurt. In July 1942 he assumed command of 2 RB, just over three months before 'Snipe'.

There are many accounts of the action at 'Snipe', of which the most full and best is by C.E. Lucas Phillips in his book, *Alamein*.[8] Quoting from the book: 'In short terms, what Turner was called upon to do … was to make a night dash [26/27 October] through enemy-held country, to establish an island of resistance until the arrival of 24th Armoured Brigade next morning and to continue holding it while the tanks operated forward.'[9] Lucas Phillips also wrote that 'it ['Snipe'] was to illustrate in the most vivid fashion how the mischances, misunderstandings and dark uncertainties that beset the soldier in a vague and confused situation can be overcome by his own self-reliance and battle discipline'.[10]

This is not the place to describe what happened in detail. Suffice it to state that all did not go well in the lead up to occupation of the position at 'Snipe'. The difficulties of navigation at night and uncertainty about the exact position to be occupied resulted in 2 RB finishing up 900 yards SSE of where the Battalion was supposed to be, in a scrubby depression previously occupied by a German engineer-stores depot and close to the night leaguers of two German battle groups. There were problems, too, moving forward the anti-tank guns, ammunition and Regimental Aid Post, while, most seriously of all, the Gunner forward observation officer lost his way and the Battalion was without artillery support. In the end Turner's force at 'Snipe' comprised some 300 men, including 16 Sappers from 7 Field Squadron, Royal Engineers, and

Lieutenant-Colonel Vic Turner VC

'Snipe' action, 27 October 1942. Painting by Terence Cuneo.

159

19 six-pounder anti-tank guns, of which six belonged to 239 Anti-Tank Battery, Royal Artillery.

The action began before dawn as the Germans became aware of the British presence in their midst. 'Full daylight [also] revealed to Turner only too clearly the nakedness of his position. ... To north, west and south enemy movement and activity of all sorts was to be seen.'[11] At 8 a.m. 24th Armoured Brigade arrived on the scene, but was soon obliged to withdraw. From 9 a.m. onwards and throughout the rest of the day, Turner's force was on its own, fighting for survival but extracting huge toll on the enemy's armour.

Turner's VC citation describes his part: 'For most conspicuous gallantry and devotion to duty on the 27th October, 1942, in the Western Desert. Lieutenant-Colonel Turner led a Battalion of the Rifle Brigade at night for 4,000 yards through difficult country to their objective, where 40 German prisoners were captured. He then organised the captured position for all-round defence; in this position he and his Battalion were continuously attacked from 5.30 a.m. to 7 p.m., unsupported and so isolated that replenishment of ammunition was impossible owing to the concentration and accuracy of the enemy fire. During this time the Battalion was attacked by not less than 90 German tanks which advanced in successive waves. All of these were repulsed with a loss to the enemy of 35 tanks which were in flames, and not less than 20 more which had been immobilised. Throughout the action Lieutenant-Colonel Turner never ceased to go to each part of the front as it was threatened. Wherever the fire was heaviest, there he was to be found. In one case, finding a solitary six-pounder gun in action (the others being casualties) and manned only by another officer and a Sergeant, he acted as loader and with these two destroyed 5 enemy tanks. While doing this he was wounded in the head, but he refused all aid until the last tank was destroyed. His personal gallantry and complete disregard of danger as he moved about encouraging his Battalion to resist to the last, resulted in the infliction of a severe defeat on the enemy tanks. He set an example of leadership and bravery which inspired his whole Battalion and which will remain an inspiration to the Brigade.'

Lieutenant-Colonel Turner's action as a loader took place shortly after 1 p.m. when eight Italian tanks and a 105-mm Semovente self-propelled field gun approached 2 RB's position from the south-west. C.E. Lucas Phillips describes the action, which later became the subject of Terence Cuneo's famous painting of 'Snipe':

Here [in the south west] *there was now only one gun in action that could bear. It was that commanded by Sergeant Charles Calistan. ... He was alone, one of his detachment lying wounded and the others having, on his orders, crawled away to fetch more ammunition. Seeing his predicament, Turner himself and Jack Toms* [anti-tank platoon commander] *ran to join him. Calistan took post on the left of the gun as a layer, Turner on the right as loader, and Toms behind as No. 1.*

Turner ordered fire to be held until the enemy tanks were within 600 yards. The sergeant and the two officers then opened a devastating fire. Five of the eight tanks and the Semovente were hit very quickly one after the other and burst into flames. The three remaining tanks still came on, ... machine-gunning hard, and there were only two rounds of ammunition left. Toms ran to his jeep, which was a hundred yards away, and quickly loaded several boxes of ammunition from a gun out of action. He drove back with the machine-gun bullets from the three tanks streaming down on him. It was an almost suicidal act. The jeep was riddled and burst into flames ten yards short of Calistan's gun. Turner ran to the jeep. So also did Corporal Francis, who had doubled over from Hine's gun [nearby] to give a hand. Turner, Toms and Francis lugged the ammunition from the burning vehicle and dragged it to the gun. At this point a shell splinter penetrated Turner's steel helmet and wounded him severely in the skull. He keeled over sideways beside the gun, the blood streaming down over his eyes.

Toms and Calistan carried on, joined now by Corporal Barnett as loading number. The three remaining Italian tanks, their machine guns blazing, were now within 200 yards. ... Calistan, who all this time had been keeping them in his sight with the utmost unconcern, while he waited for the ammunition, laid with coolness and deliberation. With three shots he killed all three tanks, which added their conflagrations to those of the other six.

... Turner, having lain down for a while under a camel's thorn bush near Calistan's gun, insisted, against all persuasion, on visiting his guns once more, but the effort was too severe and he had to be taken down into the small headquarters dug-out where Marten [the Adjutant] and the wireless were. Even from here he occasionally sallied out to give encouragement and example, but later in the day he began to suffer from the hallucination that he was defending a harbour against hostile warships. On seeing a tank, he would exclaim 'Open fire on that destroyer'. It was, indeed, a very good simile and an hallucination of the sort that showed the spirit in the man. At length his officers had to restrain him physically.[12]

At last light, after a number of further unsuccessful attacks on 2 RB's position, the Germans and Italians had had enough and departed to the west to leaguer for the night. With no prospect of relief, 2 RB was later ordered to withdraw under cover of darkness to the comparative safety of the British lines. During the course of the battle out of the original 300 men at 'Snipe', 72 Gunners, Sappers and Riflemen were killed or wounded, and out of the 19 anti-tank guns on the position, only six remained in action and only one was recovered.

Less than four weeks afterwards, *The London Gazette* announced the award of a VC for Lieutenant-Colonel Turner. Field Marshal Lord Alexander later described Turner's award as 'one of the finest VCs of the War'.

Meanwhile the Battle of El Alamein was won and Rommel forced to begin a retreat, which, by May 1943, was to end in the destruction of his army in Tunisia and the eviction or surrender of all Axis forces in North Africa.

As to Vic Turner, after he had recovered from his wound, he spent some months in training appointments in Egypt before returning to England in mid-1943 and assuming command of 9 RB (2 Motor Training Battalion) at Ranby Camp, Retford, in Nottinghamshire from 1943–5. He then commanded 2 RB again from 1946–8 before retiring from the Army on 9 March 1949.

Lieutenant-Colonel Turner never married, nor did his two surviving brothers[13] or his sister, Jane. After his retirement they all lived together in a cottage at Ditchingham in Suffolk. He was a member of The King's/Queen's Bodyguard of the Yeoman of the Guard from 1950–67 and was awarded a CVO in 1966. He was Lieutenant of the Body Guard from 1967–70. He was also a staunch supporter of the Regiment and every year would visit Sandhurst to cast an eye over those aspiring to be Green Jacket officers. He died at Ditchingham on 7 August 1972, aged 72. His sister died in 1996, aged 101. Quoting from his obituary in the Regimental Chronicle:

> *For a whole generation of Riflemen, officers and men, he* [Turner] *more than any other single person embodied the virtues and character of the Regiment.... It may be that in our Regiment's star-studded history some, but not many, have reached a wider fame and others have attained higher rank, but surely none has loved the Regiment more devotedly or served it more single-heartedly. It is certain that none has done it more honour.*[14]

Sergeant (later Lieutenant) C. Calistan DCM MM

Sergeant Charles Calistan, whose actions were in part described above, was typical of the many quick-witted Cockneys who joined the Green Jackets and whose upbringing in the East End of London ensured they knew how to look after themselves in a tight corner. After his Commanding Officer had served as his loader at 'Snipe', he continued to operate his anti-tank gun for the rest of the day, receiving orders after dark to withdraw with the rest of his company. Quoting from a part of the citation recommending him for a VC: 'He set off to walk the quarter of a mile back under heavy machine-gun fire from three German tanks, carrying one of the wounded members of his crew; the wounded man was hit and killed in his arms. He immediately returned to his troop position to fetch the last remaining wounded men, whom he brought back safely, still under intense and accurate fire. Throughout the ['Snipe'] action the quality of his determination was such that when the last point of endurance and ability to continue to fight had been reached Sergeant Calistan took a new lease of courage. This he communicated to all around him and with their help he saved the day ... During this action his superb gallantry was outstanding among many courageous acts performed.'

Disappointingly, as he assuredly deserved it, Sergeant Calistan did not receive a VC, but was awarded a DCM to add to the MM he had already received for his conduct during the Allied withdrawal to El Alamein in June 1942. He was later commissioned and was killed on 30 July 1944 while serving with 7 RB in Italy.

In total, one VC, two DSOs, five MCs, three DCMs and 11 MMs were awarded for the action at 'Snipe', including a bar to his MC for Lieutenant Toms and a MM for Corporal Francis and Corporal Barnet.

Arnhem, 1944

On 6 June 1944 the Allies landed in Normandy. After weeks of fierce fighting they eventually overcame strong German resistance and, between 17 and 21 August, annihilated the German Seventh Army at Falaise. They then swept through northern France and into Belgium, reaching Brussels on 3 September. However, the lines of communication reaching back to Normandy were overstretched. The advance slowed. Clearing the Germans from the Scheldt estuary and gaining ship access to the port of Antwerp became a strategic priority. Meanwhile the Germans regrouped and prepared defensive positions forward of the River Rhine.

Montgomery, commanding 21st Army Group, was anxious to maintain the momentum of the Allied advance and to seize an intact bridge over the Rhine as a preliminary to launching a narrow British-led thrust into the German industrial heartland of the Ruhr. On 17 September 1944 he initiated Operation Market Garden, a combined airborne and ground offensive to capture, inter alia, the bridge at Arnhem, an objective indelibly associated in the public mind with *A Bridge Too Far*, the title of Cornelius Ryan's 1974 book on the subject.

What happened at Arnhem is generally well known, with the heroic attempts of the 2nd Battalion, The Parachute Regiment, under Lieutenant-Colonel John Frost, to capture the bridge being especially well remembered. The operation, however, failed and on 21 September, with their supply of food and ammunition exhausted, the 2nd Battalion surrendered. Of the 10,600 men of 1st Airborne Division who fought at Arnhem, only 2,400 escaped.

Lieutenant John Grayburn, formerly of the 1st Battalion, The Oxfordshire and Buckinghamshire Light Infantry (43rd), was one of five individuals – four in the Army and one in the RAF – to be awarded VCs for their exceptional bravery at Arnhem. Grayburn's was posthumous.

Chapter 9

Lieutenant J.H. Grayburn VC†

Lieutenant John Grayburn was born at Karachi on 30 January 1918 and was educated at Sherborne School before working for the Hong Kong and Shanghai Bank. On 14 September 1940 he was granted a Regular Army Emergency Commission in the 1st Battalion, The Oxfordshire and Buckinghamshire Light Infantry (43rd), which after recovering from the evacuation of the BEF from Dunkirk was stationed in England. In March 1942 he was promoted to Lieutenant and on 21 May 1942 to Temporary Captain. On 27 June 1943 'Captain Grayburn, tired of inactivity, left to become a parachutist',[15] reverting to the rank of Lieutenant, first on secondment and later on transfer to the 2nd Battalion, The Parachute Regiment. Quoting from the 43rd's 1939/45 Roll of Honour: 'Among his own men in the Carrier Platoon, he [Grayburn] was affectionately known as "Mad Jack", forever endeavouring to keep them on their toes with his infectious enthusiasm. He combined a thorough and detailed care of his men with reckless dash in all training exercises. … His departure for the paratroopers came as a disappointment to many but at least they knew he would uphold the name of the 43rd wherever he went.'

Lieutenant Grayburn was one of Lieutenant-Colonel Frost's men at the bridge at Arnhem. His VC citation provides a detailed description of his actions over the period 17–20 September 1944:

For supreme courage, leadership and devotion to duty.

Lieutenant Grayburn was a platoon commander of the [2nd] *Parachute Battalion which was dropped on 17th September, 1944, with the task of seizing and holding the bridge over the Rhine at Arnhem. The North end of the bridge was captured and, early in the night, Lieutenant Grayburn was ordered to assault and capture the Southern end with his platoon. He led his platoon on to the bridge and began the attack with the utmost determination, but the platoon was met by a hail of fire from two 20 mm. quick firing guns, and from the machine guns of an armoured car. Almost at once, Lieutenant Grayburn was shot through the shoulder. Although there was no cover on the bridge, and in spite of his wound, Lieutenant Grayburn continued to press forward with the greatest dash and bravery until casualties became so heavy that he was ordered to withdraw. He directed the withdrawal from the bridge personally and was himself the last man to come off the embankment into comparative cover. Later, his platoon was ordered to occupy a house which was vital to the defence of the bridge and he personally organised the occupation of the house.*

Throughout the next day and night [18 September] *the enemy made ceaseless attacks on the house, using not only infantry with mortars and machine guns but also tanks and self-propelled guns. The house was very exposed and difficult to defend and the fact that it did not fall to the enemy must be attributed to Lieutenant*

164

Grayburn's great courage and inspiring leadership. He constantly exposed himself to the enemy's fire while moving among, and encouraging, his platoon, and seemed completely oblivious to danger.

On 19th September, 1944, the enemy renewed his attacks, which increased in intensity, as the house was vital to the defence of the bridge. All attacks were repulsed, due to Lieutenant Grayburn's valour and skill in organising and encouraging his men, until eventually the house was set on fire and had to be evacuated. Lieutenant Grayburn then took command of elements of all arms, including the remainder of his own company, and reformed them into a fighting force. He spent the night organising a defensive position to cover the approach to the bridge.

On 20th September, 1944, he extended his defence by a series of fighting patrols which prevented the enemy gaining access to the houses in the vicinity, the occupation of which would have prejudiced the defence of the bridge. This forced the enemy to bring up tanks which brought Lieutenant Grayburn's positions under such heavy fire that he was forced to withdraw to an area farther North. The enemy now attempted to lay demolition charges under the bridge and the situation was critical. Realising this, Lieutenant Grayburn organised and led a fighting patrol which drove the enemy off temporarily, and gave time for the fuzes to be removed. He was again wounded, this time in the back, but refused to be evacuated. Finally, an enemy tank, against which Lieutenant Grayburn had no defence, approached so close to his position that it became untenable. He then stood up in full view of the tank and personally directed the withdrawal of his men to the main defensive perimeter to which he had been ordered. He was killed that night.

From the evening of September 17th until the night of September 20th, 1944, a period of over three days, Lieutenant Grayburn led his men with supreme gallantry and determination. Although in pain and weakened by his wounds, short of food and without sleep, his courage never flagged. There is no doubt that, had it not been for this officer's inspiring leadership and personal bravery, the Arnhem bridge could never have been held for this time.

Although lengthy, Grayburn's VC citation is reproduced in full because it records such a remarkable story of supreme courage and bravery in adversity, with which not only The Parachute Regiment but also Green Jackets should be extremely proud to be associated.

Grayburn's body now lies buried in the Oosterbeek War Cemetery at Arnhem. He died aged 26. His VC is held by the Airborne Forces Museum, but he will long be remembered for upholding the name of the 43rd.

Reflections

Bravery in battle is a quality that most, if not all of us, admire in others. We are filled with admiration especially because in the dark recesses of our mind, however brave in battle we think we may be, doubts linger. Reading about the bravery of others sets us wondering and maybe even fearing how we would behave in similar circumstances.

The previous chapters provide plenty of examples to stimulate such thought and from which to draw our own conclusions. Whatever those conclusions may be, it would be difficult, however, as we have found in writing this book, not to be moved, humbled and inspired by the courage, selflessness and modesty of the individuals whose extraordinary acts of valour we have recorded. We have also often been struck by their youth, with ten out of the 59 VC recipients upon whom this book focuses aged 21 or under at the time of their bravery. In an era when it is fashionable to seek role models for the young, one need look no further than Rifleman Peachment, aged 18, Second Lieutenant Woodroffe, aged 19, or Rifleman Shepherd, aged 20, all awarded VCs during the First World War.

Even so, and as the table below shows, twenty-four of the Regiment's VC recipients, just over 40%, were aged 30 and over, with the oldest, Lieutenant-Colonel Vic Turner, aged 42. This belies any thought that acts of gallantry are the preserve of the young or that older, more mature men are inherently more cautious about placing their lives at risk. Nevertheless, it is a sad fact that seven out of the ten who received posthumous awards were aged 25 or under, including Peachment and Woodroffe.

Ages of Regimental VC Recipients

	21 and under	22–25	26–29	30 and over	Total
Before 1914	3	8	6	16	33
1914 onwards	7	7	3	8	25
Total	10	15	9	24	58[a]

[a] Rifleman Shaw's age is not known, hence the total is 58 not 59.

While the thought of young men sacrificing their lives for others is arresting enough, it is evident that some of those awarded VCs were simply born to lead and that courage and fearlessness were in their genes. Lieutenant Clifford in the Crimea, Ensigns Heathcote and Lisle Phillipps at Delhi, Redvers Buller at Hlobane, Billy Congreve and Sergeant Gregg during the First World War, and Vic Turner during the Second World War, were all imbued with a fighting spirit that naturally resulted in them being in the forefront of battle, inspiring others to follow them. These men seemed to thrive on a diet of danger, repeatedly risking their lives in their determination to succeed in battle; witness the remarkable circumstances of Billy Congreve being awarded a VC, DSO and MC while a staff officer, and Sergeant Gregg receiving a VC, DCM and MM all in the space of 15 months.

Success, however, is not a pre-condition for the award of a VC; indeed, some of the best remembered and most heroic acts relate to disasters, for example, Captain Walter Congreve and Lieutenant Roberts at Colenso in 1899. The acts, though, that have mattered the most and merit the greatest praise are often the least remembered, in particular those involving little-known junior officers and non-commissioned ranks whose enterprise at critical moments averted failure – to name but a few, Second Lieutenant Woolley, CSM Brooks, Sergeants Burman, Cooper and Knight, and Lance-Sergeants Belcher and Woodall. Their leadership and courage during the First World War were, and remain today, a shining example to all.

Interestingly, while the majority of the Regiment's 59 VCs arose from acts involving direct engagement with the enemy, usually at close quarters, a significant number, one-third, involved rescuing colleagues under fire and/or tending the wounded. Two of these acts were particularly poignant with Rifleman Peachment, aged 18, and Corporal Drake, aged 21, both dying by the side of the officers for whom they were caring, each of whom survived. To repeat the passage from St John: 'Greater love hath no man than this, that a man lay down his life for his friends.' Similarly, there is no sadder or more moving entry in this book than the letter written by General Sir Walter Congreve VC after being present at the burial of his son, Billy, on the Somme in July 1916.

It is, though, a truism that not all those who deserve VCs receive them. This book has highlighted several instances, including Lieutenant Tryon at Sebastopol in 1854 and Sergeant Calistan at 'Snipe' in 1942. Almost certainly, too, there are some who received awards who were less deserving than those who did not. There can be little doubt, however, that the five members of the 1st/60th at Delhi who were chosen to receive a VC by ballot were, in the eyes of their peers, which really counts, the most deserving.

Most VC actions recorded in this book resulted from individuals responding to circumstance by instinct, which is almost certainly why so many VC recipients are unable to explain with clarity why they did what they did when they did. There are very few examples of pre-meditated acts of bravery. An interesting exception concerns Rifleman Mariner whose readiness as a very junior rank to leave the safety of his trench in May 1915 in order single-handedly to silence a German machine gun was an extraordinary act of courage markedly different in context to those conducted in the heat of battle. Furthermore, at the age of 32, he might reasonably have had a keen predisposition for self-preservation.

While luck and opportunity all play a part in determining the award of VCs, high morale is a key ingredient. Units with low morale, lacking regimental pride and without concern for their reputation or performance in battle are unlikely to generate many VCs. It is no surprise, therefore, that the antecedent regiments of The Royal Green Jackets have received so many awards. High morale, resulting from good, caring leadership at every rank level, underpinned by the emphasis placed upon Riflemen thinking and acting imaginatively and sensibly on their own initiative, has seen to it. It was high morale, too, that resulted in 2 RB's extraordinary success against the odds at 'Snipe' and in the award of a VC to the Commanding Officer, Vic Turner, in recognition not just of his own performance but that of the Battalion as a whole.

Vic Turner's VC is one of 30 VCs held in trust on behalf of the Regiment at The Royal Green Jackets Museum in Winchester. A further four are presently held on loan. Each is treasured, not for its monetary value (a VC is worth over £150,000), but because of what it symbolises and the nature of the act that led to its award.

The changing face of battle means that VCs are now less easy to come by than they used to be. They are, however, just as 'highly prized and eagerly sought after' as Queen Victoria intended when she signed the Royal Warrant instituting the Victoria Cross on 29 January 1856. Paradoxically, though, it is a characteristic of VC recipients that so many seek thereafter to shun the limelight; indeed, it is the usual comment of the majority that they were only ordinary men doing their duty. Maybe – but in the eyes of the rest of us they were *remarkable* men, doing their duty but doing it in a manner and to a degree that has inspired, and will no doubt continue to inspire, all who admire bravery in others and who would want to be as brave themselves.

Appendix A

Citations of Regimental Recipients of the VC

^c = elected by ballot   [†] = posthumous award

Notes:

1. Ranks, decorations and ages were those held at the time of the act of gallantry for which the VC was awarded.
2. Privates were known as Riflemen, although the rank was not formally approved until 1923.

CRIMEAN WAR, 1854–6

RIFLEMAN F. WHEATLEY VC

(Later Rifleman F. Wheatley VC DCM) (1821–65)

1st Battalion, The Rifle Brigade

Date of Act: 12 October 1854
Place: Sebastopol, Crimea
Age: 33
Citation: 'For throwing a live shell over the parapet of the trenches.' (*London Gazette*, 24 February 1857)
Investiture: Queen Victoria, Hyde Park, 26 June 1857
VC: RGJ Museum

LIEUTENANT THE HON. H.H. CLIFFORD VC

(Later Major-General Sir Henry Clifford VC KCMG CB) (1826–83)

The Rifle Brigade (Staff)

Date of Act: 5 November 1854
Place: Inkerman, Crimea
Age: 28
Citation: 'For conspicuous courage at the Battle of Inkerman, in leading a charge and killing one of the enemy with his sword, disabling another, and saving the life of a soldier.' (*London Gazette*, 24 February 1857)
Investiture: Queen Victoria, Hyde Park, 26 June 1857
VC: Not publicly held

Lieutenant Clifford's cousin, Ensign E.A. Lisle Phillipps of the 1st/60th, KRRC, received a VC for gallantry during the Indian Mutiny.

LIEUTENANT C.T. BOURCHIER VC

(Later Colonel C.T. Bourchier VC) (1831-77)

1st Battalion, The Rifle Brigade

Date of Act: 20 November 1854
Place: Sebastopol, Crimea
Age: 23
Citation: 'Highly distinguished at the capture of the Rifle Pits, 20th November, 1854. His gallant conduct was recorded in the French General Orders.' (*London Gazette*, 24 February 1857)
Investiture: Queen Victoria, Hyde Park, 26 June 1857
VC: RGJ Museum

Lieutenant Bourchier's act of gallantry was performed jointly with Lieutenant Cuninghame VC.

LIEUTENANT W.J.M. CUNINGHAME VC

(Later Colonel Sir William Cuninghame, Bt., VC) (1834-97)

1st Battalion, The Rifle Brigade

Date of Act: 20 November 1854
Place: Sebastopol, Crimea
Age: 20
Citation: 'Highly distinguished at the capture of the Rifle Pits, 20th November, 1854. His gallant conduct was recorded in the French General Orders.' (*London Gazette*, 24 February 1857)
Investiture: Queen Victoria, Hyde Park, 26 June 1857
VC: RGJ Museum

Lieutenant Cuninghame's act of gallantry was performed jointly with Lieutenant Bourchier VC.

RIFLEMAN J. BRADSHAW VC

(Later Corporal J. Bradshaw VC) (1835–75)

2nd Battalion, The Rifle Brigade

Date of Act: 22 April 1855
Place: Sebastopol, Crimea
Age: 19
Citation: 'A Russian Rifle Pit, situated among the rocks overhanging the Woronzoff Road, between the 3rd parallel, Right Attack, and the Quarries (at that period in possession of the enemy), was occupied every night by the Russians, and their Riflemen commanded a portion of the Left Attack, and impeded the work in a new battery then being erected on the extreme right front of the 2nd parallel, Left Attack. It was carried in daylight on the 22nd of April, 1855, by two Riflemen, one of whom was Private Bradshaw; he has since received the French War Medal. The Rifle Pit was subsequently destroyed on further support being obtained.' (*London Gazette*, 24 February 1857)
Investiture: Queen Victoria, Hyde Park, 26 June 1857
VC: RGJ Museum

Rifleman Bradshaw's act of gallantry was performed jointly with Rifleman Humpston VC and Rifleman McGregor VC.

RIFLEMAN R. HUMPSTON VC

(1832–84)

2nd Battalion, The Rifle Brigade

Date of Act: 22 April 1855
Place: Sebastopol, Crimea
Age: 22/23
Citation: 'A Russian Rifle Pit, situated among the rocks overhanging the Woronzoff Road, between the 3rd parallel, Right Attack, and the Quarries (at that period in possession of the enemy), was occupied every night by the Russians, and their Riflemen commanded a portion of the Left Attack, and impeded the work in a new battery then being erected on the extreme right front of the 2nd parallel, Left Attack. It was carried in daylight on the 22nd of April, 1855, by two Riflemen, one of whom was Private Humpston. The Rifle Pit was subsequently destroyed on further support being obtained. He received a gratuity of 5*l*., and was promoted.' (*London Gazette*, 24 February 1857)
Investiture: Queen Victoria, Hyde Park, 26 June 1857
VC: RGJ Museum (on loan)

Rifleman Humpston's act of gallantry was performed jointly with Rifleman Bradshaw VC and Rifleman McGregor VC.

RIFLEMAN R. McGREGOR VC

(1824-88)

2nd Battalion, The Rifle Brigade

Date of Act: 22 April 1855 (see below)
Place: Sebastopol, Crimea
Age: 32/33
Citation: 'For courageous conduct when employed as a sharpshooter in the advanced trenches in the month of July, 1855; a Rifle Pit was occupied by two Russians, who annoyed our troops by their fire. Private McGregor crossed the open space under fire, and taking cover under a rock, dislodged them, and occupied the pit.' (*London Gazette*, 24 February 1857)
Investiture: Queen Victoria, Hyde Park, 26 June 1857
VC: RGJ Museum

Although Rifleman McGregor's citation refers to July 1855, it is widely believed, and recorded in the Regimental History, that his VC action took place on 22 April 1855, at the same time as, and in conjunction with, the acts of gallantry of Rifleman Bradshaw VC and Rifleman Humpston VC (see pages 26-7)).

LIEUTENANT J.S. KNOX VC

(Later Brevet Major J.S. Knox VC) (1828-97)

2nd Battalion, The Rifle Brigade

Date of Acts: 5 November 1854 and 18 June 1855
Places: Alma and Sebastopol, Crimea
Age: 25/26
Citation: 'When serving as a Serjeant in the Scots Fusilier Guards, Lieutenant Knox was conspicuous for his exertions in reforming the ranks of the Guards at the Battle of the Alma. Subsequently, when in the Rifle Brigade, he volunteered for the ladder-party in the attack on the Redan, on the 18th of June, and (in the words of Captain Blackett, under whose command he was,) behaved admirably, remaining on the field until twice wounded.' (*London Gazette*, 24 February 1857)
Investiture: Queen Victoria, Hyde Park, 26 June 1857
VC: Not publicly held

INDIAN MUTINY, 1857–9

RIFLEMAN S. TURNER VC

(1826–68)

1st/60th, The King's Royal Rifle Corps

Date of Act: 19 June 1857
Place: Delhi, India
Age: 31
Citation: 'For having, at Delhi, on the night of the 19th of June, 1857, during a severe conflict with the Enemy, who attacked the rear of the Camp, carried off on his shoulders, under a heavy fire, a mortally wounded Officer, Lieutenant Humphreys, of the Indian Service. During this service, Private Turner was wounded by a sabre cut in the right arm. His gallant conduct saved the above-named Officer from the fate of others, whose mangled remains were not recovered until the following day.' (*London Gazette*, 20 January 1860)
Investiture: Umballa, India, December 1860
VC: Not publicly held

COLOUR-SERGEANT S. GARVIN VC

(Later Colour-Sergeant S. Garvin VC DCM) (1826–74)

1st/60th, The King's Royal Rifle Corps

Date of Act: 23 June 1857
Place: Delhi, India
Age: 30/31
Citation: 'For daring and gallant conduct before Delhi on the 23rd June, 1857, in volunteering to lead a small party of men, under a heavy fire, to the "Sammy House" for the purpose of dislodging a number of the enemy in position there, who kept up a destructive fire on the advanced battery of heavy guns, in which, after a sharp contest, he succeeded. Also recommended for gallant conduct throughout the operations before Delhi.' (*London Gazette*, 20 January 1860)
Investiture: Queen Victoria, Windsor Home Park, 9 November 1860
VC: Not publicly held

ENSIGN A.S. HEATHCOTE VC^e

(Later Captain A.S. Heathcote VC) (1832–1912)

1st/60th, The King's Royal Rifle Corps

Date of Acts: June to September 1857
Place: Delhi, India
Age: 25
Citation: 'For highly gallant and daring conduct at Delhi throughout the Siege, from June to September, 1857, during which he was wounded. He volunteered for services of extreme danger, especially during the six days of severe fighting in the streets after the assault. Elected by the Officers of his Regiment.' (*London Gazette*, 20 January 1860)
Investiture: Lieutenant-General Sir James Hope-Grant, China, 11 January 1861.
VC: Victoria Barracks, Sydney, Australia

COLOUR-SERGEANT G. WALLER VC^e

(1827–77)

1st/60th, The King's Royal Rifle Corps

Date of Acts: 14 and 18 September 1857
Delhi: Delhi, India
Age: 30
Citation: 'For conspicuous bravery at Delhi, on 14th September, 1857, in charging and capturing the Enemy's guns near the Cabul Gate; and again, on the 18th of September, 1857, in the repulse of a sudden attack made by the enemy on a gun near the Chandney Chouk. Elected by the Non-Commissioned Officers of the Regiment.' (*London Gazette*, 20 January 1860)
Investiture: Queen Victoria, Windsor Home Park, 9 November 1860
VC: RGJ Museum

RIFLEMAN W.J. THOMPSON VC^e

(1829–91)

1st/60th, The King's Royal Rifle Corps

Date of Act: 9 July 1857
Place: Delhi, India
Age: 27/28
Citation: 'For gallant conduct in saving the life of his Captain (Captain Wilton), on the 9th of July, 1857, by dashing forward to his relief, when that Officer was surrounded by a party of Ghazees, who made a sudden rush on him from a Serai, – and killing two of them before further assistance could reach. Also recommended for conspicuous conduct throughout the Siege. Wounded. Elected by the Privates of the Regiment.' (*London Gazette*, 20 January 1860)
Investiture: Queen Victoria, Windsor Home Park, 9 November 1860
VC: RGJ Museum

RIFLEMAN J. DIVANE VC[e]

(John Duane) (1822–88)

1st/60th, The King's Royal Rifle Corps

Date of Act: 10 September 1857
Place: Delhi, India
Age: 34/35
Citation: 'For distinguished gallantry in heading a successful charge made by the Beeloochee and Sikh troops on one of the Enemy's trenches before Delhi, on the 10th of September, 1857. He leaped out of our trenches, closely followed by the Native Troops, and was shot down from the top of the Enemy's breastworks. Elected by the Privates of the Regiment.' (*London Gazette*, 20 January 1860)
Investiture: Queen Victoria, Windsor Home Park, 9 November 1860
VC: Not publicly held

BUGLER W. SUTTON VC[e]

(1830–88)

1st/60th, The King's Royal Rifle Corps

Date of Acts: 2 August and 13 September 1857
Place: Delhi, India
Age: 26/27
Citation: 'For gallant conduct at Delhi on the 13th of September, 1857, the night previous to the Assault, in volunteering to reconnoitre the breach. This Soldier's conduct was conspicuous throughout the operations, especially on the 2nd of August, 1857, on which occasion during an attack by the Enemy in force, he rushed forward over the trenches, and killed one of the Enemy's Buglers, who was in the act of sounding. Elected by the Privates of the Regiment.' (*London Gazette*, 20 January 1860)
Investiture: Queen Victoria, Windsor Home Park, 9 November 1860
VC: RGJ Museum (replaced in 1872 – original lost)

BUGLER R. HAWTHORNE VC

(1822-79)

52nd (Oxfordshire) Light Infantry

Date of Act: 14 September 1857
Place: Delhi, India
Age: 34/35
Citation: 'Bugler Hawthorne, who accompanied the explosion party, not only performed the dangerous duty on which he was employed, but previously attached himself to Lieutenant Salkeld, of the Engineers, when dangerously wounded, bound up his wounds under a heavy musketry fire, and had him removed without further injury. (General Order of Major-General Sir Archdale Wilson, Bart., K.C.B., dated Head Quarters, Delhi City, September 21, 1857.)' (*London Gazette*, 27 April 1858)
Investiture: Not known
VC: RGJ Museum

LANCE-CORPORAL H. SMITH VC

(Later Sergeant H. Smith VC) (1825-62)

52nd (Oxfordshire) Light Infantry

Date of Act: 14 September 1857
Place: Delhi, India
Age: 31/32
Citation: 'Lance Corporal Smith most gallantly carried away a wounded comrade under a heavy fire of grape and musketry on the Chaundee Chouck, in the city of Delhi, on the morning of the assault on the 14th September 1857. (General Order of Major-General Sir Archdale Wilson, Bart., K.C.B., dated Head Quarters, Delhi City, September 21, 1857.)' (*London Gazette*, 27 April 1858)
Investiture: India, 1858
VC: RGJ Museum

ENSIGN E.A. LISLE PHILLIPPS VC[†]

(1835-57)

1st/60th, The King's Royal Rifle Corps

Date of Acts: 30 May to 18 September 1857
Place: Delhi, India
Age: 22
Citation: 'Ensign Everard Aloysius Lisle Phillipps, of the 11th Regiment of Bengal Native Infantry, would have been recommended to Her Majesty for the decoration of the Victoria Cross, had he survived, for many gallant deeds which he performed during the siege of Delhi, during which he was wounded three times. At the assault of that city he captured the Water Bastion with a small party of men and was finally killed in the streets of Delhi on the 18th of September.' (Memorandum to *London Gazette*, 21 October 1859, confirmed as a posthumous award, *London Gazette*, 15 January 1907)
Investiture: None (deceased) - posted to his brother, 6 February 1907
VC: Not publicly held

Ensign Lisle Phillipps was erroneously listed in *The London Gazette* as an officer in the 11th Regiment of Bengal Native Infantry. His date of death was 17 and not 18 September 1857. His cousin, Lieutenant the Hon. H.H. Clifford of The Rifle Brigade, received a VC for gallantry during the Crimean War.

CAPTAIN H. WILMOT VC

(Later Colonel Sir Henry Wilmot, Bt., VC KCB) (1831-1901)

2nd Battalion, The Rifle Brigade

Date of Act: 11 March 1858
Place: Lucknow, India
Age: 27
Citation: 'For conspicuous gallantry at Lucknow on the 11th March, 1858. Captain Wilmot's Company was engaged with a large body of the enemy, near the Iron Bridge. That officer found himself at the end of a street with only four of his men, opposed to a considerable body. One of the four was shot through both legs and became utterly helpless: the two men lifted him up, and although Private Hawkes was severely wounded, he carried him for a considerable distance, exposed to the fire of the enemy, Captain Wilmot firing with the men's rifles, and covering the retreat of the party. Despatch of Brigadier-General Walpole, C.B., dated 20th of March, 1858.' (*London Gazette*, 24 December 1858)
Investiture: GOC India, 1859
VC: RGJ Museum (on loan)

Captain Wilmot's act of gallantry was performed at the same time/place as Corporal Nash VC and Rifleman Hawkes VC.

CORPORAL W. NASH VC

(Later Sergeant W. Nash VC) (1824–75)

2nd Battalion, The Rifle Brigade

Date of Act: 11 March 1858
Place: Lucknow, India
Age: 27
Citation: 'For conspicuous gallantry at Lucknow on the 11th March, 1858. Captain Wilmot's Company was engaged with a large body of the enemy, near the Iron Bridge. That officer found himself at the end of a street with only four of his men, opposed to a considerable body. One of the four was shot through both legs and became utterly helpless: the two men lifted him up, and although Private Hawkes was severely wounded, he carried him for a considerable distance, exposed to the fire of the enemy, Captain Wilmot firing with the men's rifles, and covering the retreat of the party. Despatch of Brigadier-General Walpole, C.B., dated 20th of March, 1858.' (*London Gazette*, 24 December 1858)
Investiture: GOC India, 1859
VC: Not publicly held

Corporal Nash's act of gallantry was performed at the same time/place as Captain Wilmot VC and Rifleman Hawkes VC.

RIFLEMAN D. HAWKES VC

(1822–58)

2nd Battalion, The Rifle Brigade

Date of Act: 11 March 1858
Place: Lucknow, India
Age: 27
Citation: 'For conspicuous gallantry at Lucknow on the 11th March, 1858. Captain Wilmot's Company was engaged with a large body of the enemy, near the Iron Bridge. That officer found himself at the end of a street with only four of his men, opposed to a considerable body. One of the four was shot through both legs and became utterly helpless: the two men lifted him up, and although Private Hawkes was severely wounded, he carried him for a considerable distance, exposed to the fire of the enemy, Captain Wilmot firing with the men's rifles, and covering the retreat of the party. Despatch of Brigadier-General Walpole, C.B., dated 20th of March, 1858.' (*London Gazette*, 24 December 1858)
Investiture: None (deceased) – posted to his father, 10 February 1859
VC: Not publicly held

Rifleman Hawkes's act of gallantry was performed at the same time/place as Captain Wilmot VC and Corporal Nash VC.

RIFLEMAN V. BAMBRICK VC

(1837–64)

1st/60th, The King's Royal Rifle Corps

Date of Act: 6 May 1858
Place: Bareilly, India
Age: 21
Citation: 'For conspicuous bravery at Bareilly, on the 6th of May, 1858, when in a Serai, he was attacked by three Ghazees, one of whom he cut down. He was wounded twice on this occasion.' (*London Gazette*, 24 December 1858)
Investiture: GOC India, 1859
VC: Not publicly held – thought to have been returned to the War Office on forfeiture

Rifleman Bambrick later served in the 87th (Royal Irish Fusiliers) and is one of eight VC recipients to have had his name erased from the VC Register and to forfeit his medal. Although his name has never been formally reinstated, King George V's opposition to forfeiture effectively annulled the entry.

RIFLEMAN S. SHAW VC

(d. 1859)

3rd Battalion, The Rifle Brigade

Date of Act: 13 June 1858
Place: Nawabgunge, India
Age: Not known
Citation: 'For the Act of Bravery recorded in a despatch from Major-General James Hope-Grant, K.C.B., Commanding the Lucknow Field Force, to the Deputy Adjutant-General of the army, of which the following is an extract: Nowabgunge [sic], 17th June, 1858. "I have to bring to notice the conduct of Private Same Shaw, of the 3rd Battalion, Rifle Brigade, who is recommended by his Commanding Officer for the Victoria Cross. An armed rebel had been sent to enter a tope of trees. Some officers and men ran into the tope in pursuit. This man was a Ghazee. Private Shaw drew his short sword, and with that weapon rushed single-handed on the Ghazee. Shaw received a severe tulwar wound, but after a desperate struggle, he killed the man. I trust his Excellency will allow me to recommend this man for the Victoria Cross, and that he will approve of my having issued a Division Order, stating that I have done so.' (*London Gazette*, 26 October 1858)
Investiture: India, February 1859
VC: RGJ Museum

PRIVATE H. ADDISON VC

(1821–87)

43rd (Monmouthshire) Light Infantry

Date of Act: 2 January 1859
Place: Near Kurrereah, India
Age: 37
Citation: 'For gallant conduct on the 2nd of January, 1859, near Kurrereah, in defending, against a large force, and saving the life of Lieutenant Osborn, Political Agent, who had fallen on the ground wounded. Private Addison received two dangerous wounds, and lost a leg, in this gallant service.' (*London Gazette*, 2 September 1859)
Investiture: Queen Victoria, Windsor Home Park, 9 November 1860
VC: RGJ Museum

NEW ZEALAND, 1864

CAPTAIN F.A. SMITH VC

(Later Lieutenant-Colonel F.A. Smith VC) (1826–87)

43rd (Monmouthshire) Light Infantry

Date of Act: 21 June 1864
Place: Tauranga, New Zealand
Age: 38
Citation: 'For his distinguished conduct during the engagement at Tauranga, on the 21st of June. He is stated to have led on his Company in the most gallant manner at the attack on the Maories' position, and, although wounded previously to reaching the Rifle Pits, to have jumped down into them, where he commenced a hand to hand encounter with the Enemy, thereby giving his men great encouragement, and setting them a fine example.' (*London Gazette*, 4 November 1864)
Investiture: None – posted to him, 31 January 1865
VC: Not publicly held

CANADA, 1866

RIFLEMAN T. O'HEA VC

(1843-74)

1st Battalion, The Prince Consort's Own Rifle Brigade

Date of Act: 9 June 1866
Place: Danville, Canada
Age: 22
Citation: 'For his courageous conduct on the occasion of a Fire which occurred in a Railway Car containing ammunition, between Quebec and Montreal, on the 9th of June last. The Serjeant in charge of the Escort states that, when at Danville Station, on the Grand Trunk Railway, the alarm was given that the Car was on fire; it was immediately disconnected, and, whilst considering what was best to be done, Private O'Hea took the keys from his hand, rushed to the Car, opened it, and called out for water and a ladder. It is stated that it was due to his example that the fire was suppressed.' (*London Gazette*, 1 January 1867)
Investiture: Colonel T.H. Pakenham, Quebec, 26 April 1867
VC: RGJ Museum

Rifleman O'Hea is one of only six men to have been awarded a VC for an act of gallantry not performed 'in the presence of the enemy', and the only man to have been awarded a VC for valour in Canada.

ZULU WAR, 1879

BREVET LIEUTENANT-COLONEL R.H. BULLER VC CB

(Later General Sir Redvers Buller VC GCB GCMG) (1839-1908)

The 60th, The King's Royal Rifle Corps (Frontier Light Horse)

Date of Act: 28 March 1879
Place: Inhlobana (Hlobane), Zululand
Age: 39
Citation: 'For his gallant conduct at the retreat at Inhlobana, on the 28th March, 1879, in having assisted, whilst hotly pursued by Zulus, in rescuing Captain C. D'Arcy, of the Frontier Light Horse, who was retiring on foot, and carrying him on his horse until he overtook the rearguard. Also for having on the same date and under the same circumstances, conveyed Lieutenant C. Everitt, of the Frontier Light Horse, whose horse had been killed under him, to a place of safety. Later on, Colonel Buller, in the same manner, saved a trooper of the Frontier Light Horse, whose horse was completely exhausted, and who otherwise would have been killed by the Zulus, who were within 80 yards of him.' (*London Gazette*, 17 June 1879)
Investiture: Queen Victoria, Balmoral, 9 September 1879
VC: RGJ Museum (on loan)

EGYPT, 1882

RIFLEMAN F. CORBETT VC

(David Embleton) (1853-1912)

3rd Battalion, The King's Royal Rifle Corps (Mounted Infantry)

Date of Act: 5 August 1882
Place: Kafr Dowar, Egypt
Age: 30
Citation: 'During the reconnaissance upon Kafr Dowar, on 5th August, 1882, the Mounted Infantry, with which Private Corbett was serving, came under a hot fire from the enemy and suffered some loss, including Lieutenant Howard-Vyse, mortally wounded. This officer fell in the open, and there being then no time to move him, Private Corbett asked and obtained permission to remain by him, and though under a constant fire, he sat down and endeavoured to stop the bleeding of this officer's wounds, until the Mounted Infantry received orders to retire, when he rendered valuable assistance in carrying him off the field.' (*London Gazette*, 16 February 1883)
Investiture: Field Marshal Lord Napier of Magdala, Cairo, 2 March 1883
VC: RGJ Museum

Rifleman Corbett later served in the Royal Horse Artillery and is one of eight VC recipients to have had his name erased from the VC Register and to forfeit his medal. Although his name has never been formally reinstated, King George V's opposition to forfeiture effectively annulled the entry.

SUDAN, 1884

LIEUTENANT P.S. MARLING VC

(Later Colonel Sir Percival Marling, Bt., VC CB) (1861-1936)

3rd Battalion, The King's Royal Rifle Corps (Mounted Infantry)

Date of Act: 13 March 1884
Place: Tamaai, Sudan
Age: 23
Citation: 'For his conspicuous bravery at the battle of Tamai [sic], on the 13th March last, in risking his life to save that of Private Morley, Royal Sussex Regiment, who, having been shot, was lifted and placed in front of Lieutenant Marling on his horse. He fell off almost immediately, when Lieutenant Marling dismounted, and gave up his horse for the purpose of carrying off Private Morley, the enemy pressing close on to them until they succeeded in carrying him about 80 yards to a place of comparative safety.' (*London Gazette*, 21 May 1884)
Investiture: General Sir Frederick Stephens, Cairo, July 1884
VC: Not publicly held

SOUTH AFRICAN WAR, 1899–1902

CAPTAIN W.N. CONGREVE VC

(Later General Sir Walter Congreve VC KCB MVO)
(1862-1927)

The Rifle Brigade (The Prince Consort's Own) (Staff)

Date of Act: 15 December 1899
Place: Colenso, South Africa
Age: 37
Citation: 'At Colenso on the 15th December, 1899, the detachments serving the guns of the 14th and 66th Batteries, Royal Field Artillery, had all been either killed, wounded, or driven from their guns by Infantry fire at close range, and the guns were deserted. About 500 yards behind the guns was a donga in which some of the few horses and drivers left alive were sheltered. The intervening space was swept with shell and rifle fire. Captain Congreve, Rifle Brigade, who was in the donga, assisted to hook a team into a limber, went out, and assisted to limber up a gun. Being wounded, he took shelter; but, seeing Lieutenant Roberts fall, badly wounded, he went out again and brought him in. Captain Congreve was shot through the leg, through the toe of his boot, grazed on the elbow and the shoulder, and his horse shot in three places.' (*London Gazette*, 2 February 1900)
Investiture: Field Marshal Lord Roberts, Pretoria, 25 October 1900
VC: RGJ Museum

Captain Congreve's act of gallantry was performed at the same time/place as Lieutenant Roberts VC. His son was awarded a VC in 1917. They are one of three pairs of fathers and sons to be awarded VCs and the only pair to have served in the same regiment.

LIEUTENANT THE HON. F.H.S. ROBERTS VC†
(1872-1899)

The King's Royal Rifle Corps (Staff)

Date of Act: 15 December 1899
Place: Colenso, South Africa
Age: 27
Citation: 'At Colenso on the 15th December, 1899, the detachments serving the guns of the 14th and 66th Batteries, Royal Field Artillery, had all been either killed, wounded, or driven from their guns by Infantry fire at close range, and the guns were deserted. About 500 yards behind the guns was a donga in which some of the few horses and drivers left alive were sheltered. The intervening space was swept with shell and rifle fire. Captain Congreve, Rifle Brigade, who was in the donga, assisted to hook a team into a limber, went out, and assisted to limber up a gun. Being wounded, he took shelter; but, seeing Lieutenant Roberts fall, badly wounded, he went out again and brought him in. Captain Congreve was shot through the leg, through the toe of his boot, grazed on the elbow and the shoulder, and his horse shot in three places. Lieutenant Roberts assisted Captain Congreve. He was wounded in three places.' (*London Gazette*, 2 February 1900)
Investiture: None (deceased) – despatched to his mother by Queen Victoria
VC: National Army Museum

Lieutenant Roberts's act of gallantry was performed at the same time/place as Captain Congreve VC. His father, Field Marshal Lord Roberts, was awarded a VC during the Indian Mutiny. They are one of three pairs of fathers and sons to be awarded VCs.

RIFLEMAN A.E. DURRANT VC
(Later Acting Corporal A.E. Durrant VC) (1864-1933)

2nd Battalion, The Rifle Brigade (The Prince Consort's Own)

Date of Act: 27 August 1900
Place: Bergendal, South Africa
Age: 35
Citation: 'At Bergendal, on the 27th August, 1900, Acting-Corporal Weller having been wounded, and being somewhat dazed, got up from his prone position in the firing line, exposing himself still more to the enemy's fire, and commenced to run towards them. Private Durrant rose, and, pulling him down endeavoured to keep him quiet, but finding this impossible he took him up and carried him back for 200 yards under heavy fire to shelter, returning immediately to his place in the firing line.' (*London Gazette*, 18 October 1901)
Investiture: Lieutenant-General Lord Kitchener, Pretoria, 6 June 1902
VC: RGJ Museum

LIEUTENANT L.A.E. PRICE-DAVIES VC DSO

(Later Major-General L.A.E. Price-Davies VC CB CMG DSO)
(1878–1965)

The King's Royal Rifle Corps (24th Mounted Infantry)

Date of Act: 17 September 1901
Place: Blood River Poort
Age: 23
Citation: 'At Blood River Poort, on the 17th September, 1901, when the Boers had overwhelmed the right of the British column, and some 400 of them were galloping round the flank and rear of the guns, riding up to the drivers (who were trying to get the guns away) and calling upon them to surrender, Lieutenant Price-Davies, hearing an order to fire upon the charging Boers, at once drew his revolver and dashed in among them, firing at them in a most gallant and desperate attempt to rescue the guns. He was immediately shot and knocked off his horse, but was not mortally wounded, although he had ridden to what seemed to be almost certain death without a moment's hesitation.' (*London Gazette*, 29 November 1901)
Investiture: Lieutenant-General Lord Kitchener, Pretoria, 8 June 1902
VC: RGJ Museum

SOMALILAND, 1903

BREVET MAJOR J.E. GOUGH VC

(Later Brigadier-General Sir John Gough VC KCB CMG)
(1871–1915)

The Prince Consort's Own Rifle Brigade (Staff)

Date of Act: 22 April 1903
Place: Daratoleh, Somaliland
Age: 31
Citation: 'During the action of Daratoleh, on 22nd April last, Major Gough assisted Captains Walker and Rolland in carrying back the late Captain Bruce (who had been mortally wounded) and preventing that Officer from falling into the hands of the enemy. Captains Walker and Rolland have already been awarded the Victoria Cross for their gallantry on this occasion, but Major Gough (who was in command of the column) made no mention of his own conduct, which has only recently been brought to notice.' (*London Gazette*, 15 January 1904)
Investiture: King Edward VII, St James's Palace, 29 February 1904
VC: RGJ Museum

Major Gough's father, General Sir Charles Gough, and his uncle, General Sir Hugh Gough, were both awarded VCs during the Indian Mutiny. Major Gough and his father are one of three pairs of fathers and sons to be awarded VCs.

FIRST WORLD WAR, 1914–18

LIEUTENANT J.H.S. DIMMER VC

(Later Lieutenant-Colonel J.H.S. Dimmer VC MC) (1883–1918)

2nd Battalion, The King's Royal Rifle Corps

Date of Act: 12 November 1914
Place: Klein Zillebeke, Belgium
Age: 31
Citation: 'This officer served his Machine Gun during the attack on the 12th November at Klein Zillebeke until he had been shot five times – three times by shrapnel and twice by bullets, and continued at his post until his gun was destroyed.' (*London Gazette*, 19 November 1914)
Investiture: King George V, Buckingham Palace, 13 January 1915
VC: RGJ Museum

LIEUTENANT J.F.P. BUTLER VC

(Later Captain J.F.P. Butler VC DSO) (1888–1916)

The King's Royal Rifle Corps (Gold Coast Regiment)

Date of Acts: 17 November and 27 December 1914
Place: Cameroons, West Africa
Age: 26
Citation: 'For most conspicuous bravery in the Cameroons, West Africa. On 17th November, 1914, with a party of 13 men, he went into the thick bush and at once attacked the enemy, in strength about 100, including several Europeans, defeated them, and captured their machine-gun and many loads of ammunition. On 27th December, 1914, when on patrol duty, with a few men, he swam the Ekam River, which was held by the enemy, alone and in the face of brisk fire, completed his reconnaissance on the further bank, and returned in safety. Two of his men were wounded while he was actually in the water.' (*London Gazette*, 23 August 1915)
Investiture: King George V, Buckingham Palace, 24 August 1915
VC: RGJ Museum

COMPANY SERGEANT-MAJOR H. DANIELS VC

(Later Lieutenant-Colonel H. Daniels VC MC) (1884–1953)

2nd Battalion, The Rifle Brigade (The Prince Consort's Own)

Date of Act: 12 March 1915
Place: Neuve Chapelle, France
Age: 30
Citation: 'For most conspicuous bravery on the 12th March, 1915, at Neuve Chapelle. When their Battalion was impeded in the advance to the attack by wire entanglements, and subjected to a very severe machine-gun fire, CSM Daniels and Corporal Noble voluntarily rushed in front and succeeded in cutting the wires. They were both wounded at once, and Corporal Noble has since died of his wounds.' (*London Gazette*, 27 April 1915)
Investiture: King George V, Buckingham Palace, 15 May 1915
VC: RGJ Museum

Company Sergeant-Major Daniels's act of gallantry was performed at the same time/place as Corporal Noble VC.

ACTING CORPORAL C.R. NOBLE VC†

(1891–1915)

2nd Battalion, The Rifle Brigade (The Prince Consort's Own)

Date of Act: 12 March 1915
Place: Neuve Chapelle, France
Age: 30
Citation: 'For most conspicuous bravery on the 12th March, 1915, at Neuve Chapelle. When their Battalion was impeded in the advance to the attack by wire entanglements, and subjected to a very severe machine-gun fire, CSM Daniels and Corporal Noble voluntarily rushed in front and succeeded in cutting the wires. They were both wounded at once, and Corporal Noble has since died of his wounds.' (*London Gazette*, 27 April 1915)
Investiture: King George V to his mother, Buckingham Palace, 29 November 1916
VC: Not publicly held

Corporal Noble's act of gallantry was performed at the same time/place as CSM Daniels VC.

SECOND LIEUTENANT G.H. WOOLLEY VC

(Later The Revd. G.H. Woolley VC OBE MC) (1892–1968)

1st/9th (County of London) Battalion, The London Regiment (Queen Victoria's Rifles)

Date of Act: 20/21 April 1915
Place: Hill 60, near Ypres, Belgium
Age: 22
Citation: 'For most conspicuous bravery on "Hill 60" during the night of 20th-21st April, 1915. Although the only Officer on the hill at the time, and with very few men, he successfully resisted all attacks on his trench, and continued throwing bombs and encouraging his men until relieved. His trench during all this time was being heavily shelled and bombed and was subjected to heavy machine gun fire by the enemy.' (*London Gazette*, 22 May 1915)
Investiture: King George V, Buckingham Palace, July 1915
VC: Not publicly held

Second Lieutenant Woolley was the first Territorial to be awarded a VC during the First World War.

LANCE-SERGEANT D.W. BELCHER VC

(Later Captain D.W. Belcher VC) (1889–1953)

1st/5th (City of London) Battalion, The London Regiment (London Rifle Brigade)

Date of Act: 13 May 1915
Place: Ypres, Belgium
Age: 25
Citation: 'On the early morning of 13th May, 1915, when in charge of a portion of an advanced breastwork south of the Wieltje–St. Julien Road during a very fierce and continuous bombardment by the enemy, which frequently blew in the breastwork, Lance-Serjeant Belcher, with a mere handful of men elected to remain and endeavour to hold his position after the troops near him had been withdrawn. By his skill and great gallantry he maintained his position during the day, opening rapid fire on the enemy, who were only 150 to 200 yards distant, whenever he saw them collecting for an attack. There is little doubt that the bold front shown by Lance-Serjeant Belcher prevented the enemy breaking through on the Wieltje road, and averted an attack on the flank of one of our Divisions.' (*London Gazette*, 23 June 1915)
Investiture: King George V, Buckingham Palace, 12 July 1915
VC: RGJ Museum

Lance-Sergeant Belcher was the first Territorial soldier holding non-commissioned rank to be awarded a VC during the First World War.

RIFLEMAN W. MARINER VC

(William Wignall) (1882–1916)

2nd Battalion, The King's Royal Rifle Corps

Date of Act: 22 May 1915
Place: Festubert, France
Age: 32
Citation: 'During a violent thunderstorm on the night of the 22nd May, 1915, he left his trench near Cambrin, France, and crept out through the German wire entanglements till he reached the emplacement of a German machine gun which had been damaging our parapets and hindering our working parties. After climbing on the top of the German parapet he threw a bomb in under the roof of the gun emplacement and heard some groaning and the enemy running away. After about a quarter of an hour he heard some of them coming back again and climbed up on the other side of the emplacement and threw another bomb among them left-handed. He then lay still while the Germans opened a heavy fire on the wire entanglements behind him, and it was only after about an hour that he was able to crawl back to his own trench. Before starting out he had requested a sergeant to open fire on the enemy's trenches as soon as he had thrown his bombs. Rifleman Mariner was out alone for one and a half hours carrying out this gallant work. (*London Gazette*, 23 June 1915)
Investiture: King George V, Buckingham Palace, 12 July 1915
VC: Not publicly held

SECOND LIEUTENANT S.C. WOODROFFE VC†

(1895–1915)

8th (Service) Battalion, The Rifle Brigade
(The Prince Consort's Own)

Date of Act: 30 July 1915
Place: Hooge, Belgium
Age: 19
Citation: 'For most conspicuous bravery on the 30th July, 1915, at Hooge. The enemy having broken through the centre of our front trenches, consequent on the use of burning liquids, this Officer's position was heavily attacked with bombs from the flank and subsequently from the rear, but he managed to defend his post until all his bombs were exhausted, and then skilfully withdrew his remaining men. This very gallant Officer immediately led his party forward in a counter-attack under an intense rifle and machine-gun fire, and was killed while in the act of cutting the wire obstacles in the open.' (*London Gazette*, 6 September 1915)
Investiture: King George V to his parents, Buckingham Palace, 29 November 1916
VC: Not publicly held

189

RIFLEMAN G.S. PEACHMENT VC†

(1897-1915)

2nd Battalion, The King's Royal Rifle Corps

Date of Act: 25 September 1915
Place: Loos, France
Age: 18
Citation: 'For most conspicuous bravery near Hulluch on the 25th September, 1915. During very heavy fighting, when our front line was compelled to retire in order to reorganize, Private Peachment, seeing his Company Commander, Captain Dubs, lying wounded, crawled to assist him. The enemy's fire was intense, but, though there was a shell hole quite close, in which a few men had taken cover, Private Peachment never thought of saving himself. He knelt in the open by his Officer and tried to help him, but while doing this he was first wounded by a bomb and a minute later mortally wounded by a rifle bullet. He was one of the youngest men in his battalion, and gave this splendid example of courage and self-sacrifice.' (*London Gazette*, 18 November 1915)
Investiture: King George V to his mother, Buckingham Palace, 29 November 1916
VC: Not publicly held

CORPORAL A.G. DRAKE VC†

(1893-1915)

8th (Service) Battalion, The Rifle Brigade
(The Prince Consort's Own)

Date of Act: 23 November 1915
Place: La Brique, Belgium
Age: 21
Citation: 'For conspicuous bravery on the night of 23rd November, 1915, near La Brique, France. He was one of a patrol of four which was reconnoitring towards the German lines. The patrol was discovered when close to the enemy, who opened heavy fire with rifles and a machine gun, wounding the Officer and one man. The latter was carried back by the last remaining man. Corporal Drake remained with his Officer and was last seen kneeling beside him and bandaging his wounds regardless of the enemy's fire. Later, a rescue party crawling near the German lines found the Officer and Corporal, the former unconscious but alive and bandaged, Corporal Drake beside him dead and riddled with bullets. He had given his own life and saved his Officer.' (*London Gazette*, 22 January 1916)
Investiture: King George V to his father, Buckingham Palace, 16 November 1916
VC: Not publicly held

BREVET MAJOR W. La T. CONGREVE VC DSO MC†

(1891–1916)

The Rifle Brigade (The Prince Consort's Own) (Staff)

Date of Acts: 6 to 20 July 1916
Place: Somme, France
Age: 25
Citation: 'For most conspicuous bravery during a period of fourteen days preceding his death in action. This officer constantly performed acts of gallantry and showed the greatest devotion to duty; and by his personal example inspired all those around him with confidence at critical periods of the operations. During preliminary preparations for the attack he carried out personal reconnaissances of the enemy lines, taking out parties of officers and non-commissioned officers for over 1,000 yards in front of our line, in order to acquaint them with the ground. All these preparations were made under fire. Later, by night, Major Congreve conducted a battalion to its position of employment, afterwards returning to it to ascertain the situation after assault. He established himself in an exposed forward position from whence he successfully observed the enemy, and gave orders necessary to drive them from their position. Two days later, when Brigade Headquarters was heavily shelled and many casualties resulted, he went out and assisted the medical officer to remove the wounded to places of safety, although he was himself suffering severely from gas and other shell effects. He again on a subsequent occasion showed supreme courage in tending wounded under heavy shell fire. He finally returned to the front line to ascertain the situation after an unsuccessful attack, and whilst in the act of writing his report, was shot and killed instantly.'
(*London Gazette*, 26 October 1916)
Investiture: King George V to his widow, Buckingham Palace, 1 November 1916
VC: RGJ Museum

Major Congreve was the first of 23 officers in the First World War to be awarded a VC, DSO and MC. His father was awarded a VC in 1899. They are one of three pairs of fathers and sons to be awarded VCs and the only pair to have served in the same regiment.

SERGEANT A. GILL VC[†]

(1879-1916)

1st Battalion, The King's Royal Rifle Corps

Date of Act: 27 July 1916
Place: Somme, France
Age: 36
Citation: 'For most conspicuous bravery. The enemy made a very strong counter-attack on the right flank of the battalion, and rushed the bombing post after killing all the company bombers. Sergeant Gill at once rallied the remnants of his platoon, none of whom were skilled bombers, and reorganized his defences, a most difficult and dangerous task, the trench being very shallow and much damaged. Soon afterwards the enemy nearly surrounded his men by creeping up through the thick undergrowth, and commenced sniping at about twenty yards range. Although it was almost certain death, Sergeant Gill stood boldly up in order to direct the fire of his men. He was killed almost at once, but not before he had shown his men where the enemy were, and thus enabled them to hold up their advance. By his supreme devotion to duty and self-sacrifice he saved a very dangerous situation.' (*London Gazette*, 26 October 1916)
Investiture: King George V to his widow, Buckingham Palace, 29 November 1916
VC: Not publicly held

SECOND LIEUTENANT G.E. CATES VC[†]

(1892-1917)

2nd Battalion, The Rifle Brigade (The Prince Consort's Own)

Date of Act: 8 March 1917
Place: Bouchavesnes, near Péronne, France
Age: 24
Citation: 'For most conspicuous gallantry and self-sacrifice. When engaged with some other men in deepening a captured trench this officer struck with his spade a buried bomb, which immediately started to burn. 2nd Lt. Cates, in order to save the lives of his comrades, placed his foot on the bomb, which immediately exploded. He showed the most conspicuous gallantry and devotion to duty in performing the act which cost his life, but saved the lives of others.' (*London Gazette*, 11 May 1917)
Investiture: King George V to his father, Hyde Park, 2 June 1917
VC: RGJ Museum (replaced in 1951 – original destroyed in a fire)

COMPANY SERGEANT-MAJOR E. BROOKS VC

(1883–1944)

2nd/4th Battalion, The Oxfordshire and Buckinghamshire Light Infantry

Date of Act: 28 April 1917
Place: Fayet, near St Quentin, France
Age: 34
Citation: 'For most conspicuous bravery. This Warrant Officer, while taking part in a raid on the enemy's trenches, saw that the front wave was checked by an enemy machine gun at close quarters. On his own initiative, and regardless of personal danger, he rushed forward from the second wave with the object of capturing the gun, killing one of the gunners with his revolver and bayoneting another. The remainder of the gun's crew then made off, leaving the gun in his possession. C. S./M. Brooks then turned the machine gun on to the retreating enemy, after which he carried it back into our lines. By his courage and initiative he undoubtedly prevented many casualties, and greatly added to the success of the operations.' (*London Gazette*, 27 June 1917)
Investiture: King George V, Buckingham Palace, 21 July 1917
VC: RGJ Museum

SERGEANT E. COOPER VC

(Later Major E. Cooper VC) (1896–1985)

12th (Service) Battalion, The King's Royal Rifle Corps

Date of Act: 18 August 1917
Place: Langemarck, Belgium
Age: 21
Citation: 'For most conspicuous bravery and initiative in attack. Enemy machine guns from a concrete blockhouse, 250 yards away, were holding up the advance of the battalion on his left, and were also causing heavy casualties to his own battalion. Sjt. Cooper, with four men, immediately rushed towards the blockhouse, though heavily fired on. About 100 yards distant he ordered his men to lie down and fire at the blockhouse. Finding this did not silence the machine guns, he immediately rushed forward straight at them and fired his revolver into an opening in the blockhouse. The machine guns ceased firing and the garrison surrendered. Seven machine guns and forty-five prisoners were captured in this blockhouse. By this magnificent act of courage he undoubtedly saved what might have been a serious check to the whole advance, at the same time saving a great number of lives.' (*London Gazette*, 14 September 1917)
Investiture: King George V, Buckingham Palace, 26 September 1917
VC: Preston Hall Museum, Stockton-on-Tees

SERGEANT W.F. BURMAN VC

(1897–1974)

*16th (Service) Battalion, The Rifle Brigade
(The Prince Consort's Own)*

Date of Act: 20 September 1917
Place: Bulgar Wood, near Ypres, Belgium
Age: 20
Citation: 'For most conspicuous bravery when the advance
                 of his Company was held up by an enemy
                 machine gun firing at point blank range. He
                 shouted to the man next to him to wait a few
                 minutes, and going forward to what seemed
                 certain death, killed the enemy gunner and
                 carried the gun to the Company's objective,
                 where he subsequently used it with great effect.
                 By this exceptionally gallant deed the progress of
                 the attack was assured. About 15 minutes later it
                 was observed that the battalion on the right was
                 being impeded by a party of about 40 of the
                 enemy, who were enfilading them. Sjt. Burman
                 with two others ran forward and got behind the
                 enemy, killing 6 and capturing 2 officers and 29
                 other ranks.' (*London Gazette*, 26 November
                 1917)
Investiture: King George V, Buckingham Palace, 19 December
                 1917
VC: Imperial War Museum

SERGEANT A.J. KNIGHT VC

(Later Second Lieutenant A.J. Knight VC MBE) (1888–1960)

*2nd/8th (City of London) Battalion, The London Regiment
(Post Office Rifles)*

Date of Act: 20 September 1917
Place: Hubner Farm, near Ypres, Belgium
Age: 29
Citation: 'For most conspicuous bravery and devotion to
                 duty during the operations against the enemy
                 positions. Sjt. Knight did extraordinary good work,
                 and showed exceptional bravery and initiative
                 when his platoon was attacking an enemy strong
                 point, and came under very heavy fire from an
                 enemy machine gun. He rushed through our own
                 barrage, bayoneted the enemy gunner, and
                 captured the position single-handed. Later, twelve
                 of the enemy with a machine gun, were
                 encountered in a shell-hole. He again rushed
                 forward by himself, bayoneted two and shot a
                 third and caused the remainder to scatter.
                 Subsequently, during the attack on a fortified farm,
                 when entangled up to his waist in mud, and
                 seeing a number of the enemy firing on our

194

troops, he immediately opened fire on them without waiting to extricate himself from the mud, killing six of the enemy. Again, noticing the company on his right flank being held up in their attack on another farm, Sjt. Knight collected some men and took up a position on the flank of this farm, from where he brought a heavy fire to bear on the farm as a result of which the farm was captured. All the platoon officers of the company had become casualties before the first objective was reached, and this gallant N.C.O. took command of all the men of his own platoon and of the platoons without officers. His energy in consolidating and reorganising was untiring. His several single-handed actions showed exceptional bravery, and saved a great number of casualties in the company. They were performed under heavy machine gun and rifle fire, and without regard to personal risk, and were the direct cause of the objectives being captured.' (*London Gazette*, 8 November 1917)

Investiture: King George V, Buckingham Palace, 19 December 1917

VC: National Postal Museum, London

RIFLEMAN A.E. SHEPHERD VC

(Later Corporal A.E. Shepherd VC) (1897–1966)

12th (Service) Battalion, The King's Royal Rifle Corps

Date of Act: 20 November 1917
Place: Cambrai, France
Age: 20
Citation: 'For most conspicuous bravery as a company runner. When his company was held up by a machine gun at point blank range he volunteered to rush the gun, and, though ordered not to, rushed forward and threw a Mills bomb, killing two gunners and capturing the gun. The company, on continuing its advance, came under heavy enfilade machine-gun fire. When the last officer and the last non-commissioned officer had become casualties, he took command of the company, ordered the men to lie down, and himself went back some seventy yards under severe fire to obtain the help of a tank. He then returned to his company, and finally led them to their last objective. He showed throughout conspicuous determination and resource.' (*London Gazette*, 13 February 1918)

Investiture: King George V, Buckingham Palace, 9 March 1918
VC: RGJ Museum

LANCE-CORPORAL J.A. CHRISTIE VC

(1895–1967)

*1st/11th (County of London) Battalion,
The London Regiment (Finsbury Rifles)*

Date of Act: 21/22 December 1917
Place: Fejja, near Jerusalem, Palestine
Age: 22
Citation: 'For most conspicuous bravery when after a position had been captured, the enemy immediately made counter and bombing attacks up communication trenches. L./Cpl. Christie, realising the position, took a supply of bombs over the top, proceeding alone about fifty yards in the open along the communication trench and bombed the enemy. He continued to do this alone in spite of very heavy opposition until a block had been established. Returning towards our lines he heard voices behind him; he at once turned back and bombed another party moving up the trench, entirely breaking up a further bombing attack. By his prompt and effective action he undoubtedly cleared a difficult position at a most critical time and saved many lives. Throughout he was subjected to heavy machine-gun fire and shell fire. He showed the greatest coolness and a total disregard for his own safety.' (*London Gazette*, 27 February 1918)
Investiture: King George V, Buckingham Palace, 18 November 1918
VC: Not publicly held

LANCE-SERGEANT J.E. WOODALL VC

(Later Captain J.E. Woodall VC) (1896–1962)

1st Battalion, The Rifle Brigade (The Prince Consort's Own)

Date of Act: 22 April 1918
Place: La Bassée Canal, near Neuve Chapelle, France
Age: 21
Citation: 'For most conspicuous bravery and fine leadership during an attack. Sjt. Woodall was in command of a platoon which, during the advance, was held up by a machine gun. On his own initiative he rushed forward and, single-handed, captured the gun and eight men. After the objective had been gained, heavy fire was encountered from a farmhouse some 200 yards in front. Sjt. Woodall collected ten men and, with great dash and gallantry, rushed the farm and took thirty prisoners. Shortly afterwards, when the officer in charge was killed, he took entire command, reorganised the two platoons, and disposed of them skilfully. Throughout the day, in spite of intense shelling and machine-gun fire, this gallant N.C.O. was constantly on the move, encouraging the men and finding out and sending back invaluable information. The example set by

Sjt. Woodall was simply magnificent, and had a marked effect on the troops. The success of the operation on this portion of the front is attributed almost entirely to his coolness, courage, and utter disregard for his own personal safety.' (*London Gazette*, 28 June 1918)

Investiture: King George V, Buckingham Palace, 23 November 1918
VC: RGJ Museum (on loan)

SERGEANT W. GREGG VC DCM MM

(1890–1969)

13th (Service) Battalion, The Rifle Brigade
(The Prince Consort's Own)

Date of Act: 8 May 1918
Place: Bucquoy, France
Age: 28
Citation: 'For most conspicuous bravery and brilliant leadership in action. Two companies of his unit attacked the enemy's outpost position without artillery preparation. Sergeant Gregg was with the right company, which came under heavy fire from the right flank as it advanced. All the officers of the company were hit. He at once took command of the attack. He rushed an enemy post and personally killed an entire machine-gun team and captured the gun and four men in a dug-out near by. He then rushed another post, killed two men and captured another. In spite of heavy casualties he reached his objective, and started consolidating the position. By this prompt and effective action this gallant N.C.O. saved the situation at a critical time and ensured the success of the attack. Later, Sjt. Gregg's party were driven back by an enemy counter-attack, but, reinforcements coming up, he led a charge, personally bombed a hostile machine gun, killed the crew, and captured the gun. Once again he was driven back. He led another successful attack, and hung on to the position until ordered by his company commander to withdraw. Although under very heavy rifle and machine-gun fire for several hours, Sjt. Gregg displayed throughout the greatest coolness and contempt of danger, walking about encouraging his men and setting a magnificent example.' (*London Gazette*, 28 June 1918)

Investiture: King George V, Frohen-le-Grand, 9 August 1918
VC: RGJ Museum

Sergeant Gregg was the first of eight soldiers in the First World War to be awarded a VC, DCM and MM. His act of gallantry was performed at the same time/place as Rifleman Beesley VC.

RIFLEMAN W. BEESLEY VC

(Later Corporal W. Beesley VC) (1895-1966)

13th (Service) Battalion, The Prince Consort's Own Rifle Brigade

Date of Act: 8 May 1918
Place: Bucquoy, France
Age: 22
Citation: 'For most conspicuous bravery. The enemy's outpost position was attacked by two companies of his unit without artillery preparation. Pte. Beesley was in the leading wave of the left company, which came under heavy fire as it approached the enemy's front line. His platoon serjeant and all the section commanders were killed. This young soldier, realising the situation at once, took command and led the assault. Single-handed he rushed a post, and with his revolver killed two of the enemy at a machine gun. He then shot dead an officer who ran across from a dug-out to take their place at the machine gun. Three more officers appeared from the dug-out. These he called on to surrender; seeing one of them trying to get rid of a map he shot him and obtained the map. He took four more prisoners from a dug-out and two others from a shelter close by, disarmed them and sent them back to our lines. At this moment his Lewis gun was brought up by a comrade, who was acting as a carrier. Pte. Beesley at once brought it into action, and used it with great effect against the enemy as they bolted towards their support line, inflicting many casualties. For four hours Private Beesley and his comrade held on to the position under very heavy machine-gun and rifle fire. The enemy then advanced to counter-attack, and the other soldier was wounded. Pte. Beesley carried on by himself, and actually maintained his position until 10 p.m., long after the posts on his right and left had been practically wiped out and the survivors had fallen back. It was mainly due to his action that the enemy were prevented from rushing the position, and that the remnants of his company, when compelled to withdraw, were able to do so without further loss. When darkness set in Pte. Beesley made his way back to the original line from which the attack had started, bringing with him the wounded carrier and the Lewis gun. He at once mounted the Lewis gun in the trench and remained in action until things had quietened down. The indomitable pluck, skilful shooting and good judgement in economising ammunition displayed by Pte. Beesley stamp the incident as one of the most brilliant actions in recent operations.' (*London Gazette*, 28 June 1918)

Investiture: King George V, Frohen-le-Grand, 9 August 1918
VC: RGJ Museum

Rifleman Beesley's act of gallantry was performed at the same time/place as Sergeant Gregg VC DCM MM.

LANCE-CORPORAL A. WILCOX VC

(1884–1954)

2nd/4th Battalion, The Oxfordshire and Buckinghamshire Light Infantry

Date of Act: 12 September 1918
Place: Laventie, France
Age: 33
Citation: 'For most conspicuous bravery and initiative in attack when his company was held up by heavy and persistent machine-gun fire at close range. On his own initiative, with four men he rushed forward to the nearest enemy gun, bombed it, killed the gunner and put the gun out of action. Being then attacked by an enemy bombing party, Cpl. Wilcox picked up enemy bombs and led his company against the next gun, finally capturing and destroying it. Although left with only one man, he continued bombing and captured a third gun. He again bombed up the trench, captured a fourth gun, and then rejoined his platoon. Cpl. Wilcox displayed in this series of successful individual enterprises exceptional valour, judgement and initiative.' (*London Gazette*, 15 November 1918)
Investiture: King George V, Buckingham Palace, 26 November 1918
VC: Not publicly held

SECOND WORLD WAR, 1939–45

RIFLEMAN J. BEELEY VC†
(1918-41)

1st Battalion, The King's Royal Rifle Corps

Date of Act: 21 November 1941
Place: Sidi Rezegh, North Africa
Age: 23
Citation: 'On the 21st November, 1941, during the attack by a Battalion of The King's Royal Rifle Corps at Sidi Rezegh against a strong enemy position, the Company to which Rifleman Beeley belonged was pinned down by heavy fire at point-blank range from the front and flank on the flat open ground of the aerodrome. All the officers but one of the Company and many of the other ranks had been either killed or wounded. On his own initiative, and when there was no sort of cover, Rifleman Beeley got to his feet carrying a Bren gun and ran towards a strong enemy post containing an anti-tank gun, a heavy machine gun and a light machine gun. He ran thirty yards and discharged a complete magazine at the post from a range of twenty yards, killing or wounding the entire crew of the anti-tank gun. The post was silenced and Rifleman Beeley's platoon was enabled to advance, but Rifleman Beeley fell dead across his gun, hit in at least four places. Rifleman Beeley went to certain death in a gallant and successful attempt to carry the day. His courage and self-sacrifice was a glorious example to his comrades and inspired them to further efforts to reach their objective, which was eventually captured by them, together with 700 prisoners.' (*London Gazette*, 21 April 1942)

Investiture: King George VI to his widow, Buckingham Palace, 20 October 1942
VC: RGJ Museum

Appendix A

LIEUTENANT-COLONEL V.B. TURNER VC

(Later Lieutenant-Colonel V.B. Turner VC CVO) (1900–72)

2nd Battalion, The Rifle Brigade

Date of Act: 27 October 1942
Place: El Alamein, North Africa
Age: 42
Citation: 'For most conspicuous gallantry and devotion to duty on the 27th October, 1942, in the Western Desert. Lieutenant-Colonel Turner led a Battalion of the Rifle Brigade at night for 4,000 yards through difficult country to their objective, where 40 German prisoners were captured. He then organised the captured position for all-round defence; in this position he and his Battalion were continuously attacked from 5.30 a.m. to 7 p.m., unsupported and so isolated that replenishment of ammunition was impossible owing to the concentration and accuracy of the enemy fire. During this time the Battalion was attacked by not less than 90 German tanks which advanced in successive waves. All of these were repulsed with a loss to the enemy of 35 tanks which were in flames, and not less than 20 more which had been immobilised. Throughout the action Lieutenant-Colonel Turner never ceased to go to each part of the front as it was threatened. Wherever the fire was heaviest, there he was to be found. In one case, finding a solitary six-pounder gun in action (the others being casualties) and manned only by another officer and a Sergeant, he acted as loader and with these two destroyed 5 enemy tanks. While doing this he was wounded in the head, but he refused all aid until the last tank was destroyed. His personal gallantry and complete disregard of danger as he moved about encouraging his Battalion to resist to the last, resulted in the infliction of a severe defeat on the enemy tanks. He set an example of leadership and bravery which inspired his whole Battalion and which will remain an inspiration to the Brigade.'
(*London Gazette*, 20 November 1942)

Investiture: King George VI, Buckingham Palace, 27 July 1943
VC: RGJ Museum

Lieutenant-Colonel Turner's eldest brother, Second Lieutenant A.B. Turner of The Royal Berkshire Regiment, was awarded a posthumous VC in 1915. They are one of four pairs of brothers to be awarded VCs.

Appendix B
Royal Warrant of 29 January 1856 Instituting the VC[1]

Appd. Victoria R

Victoria by the Grace of God of the United Kingdom of Great Britain and Ireland Queen Defender of the Faith &c. To all to whom these Presents shall come Greeting! Whereas We taking into Our Royal consideration that there exists no means of adequately rewarding the individual gallant services either of Officers of the lower grades in Our Naval and Military Service or of Warrant and Petty Officers Seamen and Marines in Our Navy and Non-commissioned Officers and Soldiers in Our Army. And Whereas the third Class of Our Most Honorable Order of the Bath is limited except in very rare cases to the higher ranks of both Services and the granting of Medals both in Our Navy and Army is only awarded for long service or meritorious conduct, rather than for bravery in Action or distinction before an enemy, such cases alone excepted while [sic] a general Medal is granted for a particular Action or Campaign or a Clasp added to the Medal for some special engagement, in both of which cases all share equally in the boon and those who by their valour have particularly signalized themselves remain undistinguished from their comrades. Now for the purpose of attaining an end so desirable as that of rewarding individual instances of merit and valour We have instituted and created and by these Presents for Us Our Heirs and Successors institute and create a new Naval and Military Decoration, which We are desirous should be highly prized and eagerly sought after by the Officers and Men of Our Naval and Military Services and are graciously pleased to make ordain and establish the following rules and ordinances for the government of the same which shall from henceforth be inviolably observed and kept.

Firstly It is ordained that the distinction shall be styled and designated the 'Victoria Cross' and shall consist of a Maltese Cross of Bronze with Our Royal Crest in the centre and underneath which an Escroll bearing this inscription 'For Valour'.

Secondly It is ordained that the Cross shall be suspended from the left breast by a Blue Riband for the Navy and by a Red Riband for the Army.

Thirdly It is ordained that the names of those upon whom We may be pleased to confer the decoration shall be published in the *London*

---

[1] Public Record Office WO 98/1.

Gazette and a registry thereof kept in the office of Our Secretary of State for War.

Fourthly It is ordained that anyone who, after having received the Cross, shall again perform an Act of bravery which, if he had not received such Cross would have entitled him to it, such further act shall be recorded by a Bar attached to the riband by which the Cross is suspended and for every additional act of bravery an additional Bar may be added.

Fifthly It is ordained that the Cross shall only be awarded to those Officers or Men who have served Us in the presence of the Enemy and shall then have performed some signal act of valour or devotion to their Country.

Sixthly It is ordained with a view to place all persons on a perfectly equal footing in relation to eligibility for the Decoration that neither rank nor long service nor wounds nor any other circumstance or condition whatsoever save the merit of conspicuous bravery shall be held to establish a sufficient claim to the honour.

Seventhly It is ordained that the Decoration may be conferred on the spot where the act to be rewarded by the grant of such Decoration has been performed under the following circumstances:

I. When the Fleet or Army in which such Act has been performed is under the eye and command of an Admiral or General Officer commanding the Forces.

II. Where the Naval or Military Force is under the eye and command of an Admiral or Commodore Commanding a Squadron or detached Naval Force or of a General Commanding a Corps or Division or Brigade on a distinct and detached Service when such Admiral Commodore or General Officer shall have the power of conferring the Decoration on the spot subject to confirmation by Us.

Eighthly It is ordained where such act shall not have been performed in sight of a Commanding Officer as aforesaid then the claimant for the honour shall prove the act to the satisfaction of the Captain or Officer Commanding his Ship or to the Officer Commanding the Regiment to which the Claimant belongs and such Captain or such Commanding Officer shall report the same through the usual channel to the Admiral or Commodore Commanding the Force employed on the Service or to the Officer Commanding the Forces in the Field who shall call for such description and attestation of the act as he may think requisite and on approval shall recommend the grant of the Decoration.

Ninthly It is ordained that every person selected for the Cross under rule seven shall be publicly decorated before the Naval or Military Force or body to which he belongs and with which the act of bravery for which he is to be rewarded shall have been performed and his name shall be recorded in a General Order together with the cause of his especial distinction.

Tenthly It is ordained that every person selected under rule eight shall receive his Decoration as soon as possible and his name shall likewise appear in a General Order as above required, such General Order to be issued by the Naval or Military Commander of the Forces employed on the Service.

Eleventhly It is ordained that the General Orders above referred to shall from time to time be transmitted to our Secretary of State for War to be laid before Us and shall be by him registered.

Twelfthly It is ordained that as cases may arise not falling within the rules above specified or in which a claim though well founded may not have been established on the spot We will on the joint submission of Our Secretary of State for War and of Our Commander-in-Chief of Our army or on that of Our Lord High Admiral or Lords Commissioners of the Admiralty in the case of the Navy confer the Decoration but never without conclusive proof of the performance of the act of bravery for which the claim is made.

Thirteenthly It is ordained that in the event of a gallant and daring act having been performed by a Squadron Ship's Company a detached body of Seamen and Marines not under fifty in number or by a Brigade Regiment Troop or Company in which the Admiral General or other Officer Commanding such Forces may deem that all are equally brave and distinguished and that no special selection can be made by them, Then in such case the Admiral General or other Officer Commanding may direct that for any such body of Seamen and Marines or for every Troop or Company of Soldiers one Officer shall be selected by the officers engaged for the Decoration; and in like manner one Petty Officer or Non-commissioned Officer shall be selected by the Petty Officers and Non-commissioned Officers engaged; and two Seamen or Private Soldiers or Marines shall be selected by the Seamen or Private Soldiers or Marines engaged respectively for the Decoration; and the names of those selected shall be transmitted by the Senior Officer in Command of the Naval Force Brigade Regiment Troop or Company to the Admiral or General Officer Commanding who shall in due manner confer the Decoration as if the acts were done under his own eye.

Fourteenthly It is ordained that every Warrant Officer Petty Officer Seaman or Marine or Non-Commissioned Officer or Soldier who shall have received the Cross shall from the date of the act by which the Decoration has been gained be entitled to a Special Pension of Ten pounds a year; and each additional bar conferred under rule four on such Warrant or Petty Officers or Non-Commissioned Officers or Men, shall carry with it an additional pension of Five Pounds per annum.

Fifteenthly In order to make such additional provision as shall effectually preserve pure this Most Honorable distinction it is ordained that if any person on whom such distinction shall be conferred be convicted of Treason, Cowardice, Felony or of any infamous Crime, or if he be accused of any such offence and doth not after a reasonable time surrender himself to be tried for the same his name shall forthwith be erased from the Registry of Individuals upon whom the said Decoration shall have been conferred by an especial Warrant under Our Royal Sign Manual, and the pension conferred under rule fourteen shall cease and determine from the date of such Warrant. It is hereby further declared that We Our Heirs and Successors shall be the sole judge of the circumstances demanding such expulsion; moreover We shall at all times have power to restore such persons as may at any time have been expelled, both to the enjoyment of the Decoration and Pension.

Given at Our Court at Buckingham Palace this twenty-ninth day of January in the Nineteenth Year of Our Reign and in the Year of Our Lord One Thousand Eight Hundred and Fifty Six.

By Her Majesty's Command
Panmure
To Our Principal Secretary of State for War.

Appendix C

Design and Manufacture of the VC

Technical Information[1]

Description:	A bronze cross pattée rather than a Maltese cross as described in the original Warrant.
Obverse:	A lion passant gardant standing on the Royal Crown; and below, on a scroll, the words FOR VALOUR. The cross has a raised edge, 3/16 inch wide, with a beading of the same width and at that distance running round inside.
Reverse:	A raised circle in the centre and the same beaded edges and lining as the obverse.
Naming:	The recipient's name, rank, and unit are hand-engraved at the back of the suspender; the date of the act(s), which gained the award, is engraved in the circle at the centre of the reverse. In the event of a Bar being awarded, the date of the act is engraved on the reverse of the Bar.
Size/Weight:	1.375 inches wide, weighing, including the suspender bar and link, 0.87 ounces.
Ribbon:	1.5 inches wide. The colour was originally dark blue for the Navy and red (crimson) for the Army. In 1918, following the creation of the Royal Air Force, a red ribbon was adopted and applied retrospectively for all awards regardless of the Service of the recipient. In 1916 a bronze miniature cross was added to the medal ribbon when worn 'in khaki' without a medal, with, from 1917, a second miniature cross indicating receipt of a Bar.
Suspension:	A loop at the top of the cross is joined by a ring to a Roman 'V' which is part of a straight flat suspender ornamented with laurel leaves. The ribbon is threaded through a slot at the top of the suspender.

General Information

VCs are presently cast from the gunmetal (bronze) from the cascabels[2] of two Chinese cannon allegedly captured from the Russians at Sebastopol during the Crimean War and now on display (without their cascabels) at Woolwich. However, in his recent book, *Bravest of the Brave*,[3] John Glanfield states that, contrary to popular belief, close examination of the historical record and scientific analysis show that not all VCs were cast from the Sebastopol cannon and that prior to 1914 bronze from another cannon was used. He also states that five VCs awarded between 1942 and 1945 were made from a different source at a time when, apparently, the remaining Sebastopol gunmetal had temporarily disappeared. Sufficient metal remains, closely guarded at an Army depot at Donnington, for approximately a further 84 Crosses (1 May 2006).

The manufacturing process, which has been carried out exclusively by Messrs Hancock since the first VCs were cast in 1856, is basic. The hot metal is poured into a sand-filled mould, with 12 Crosses normally produced at any one time in batches of four. When the metal has cooled the rough Crosses are cut from the metal 'casting tree' before each is hand chased and then treated chemically to produce the familiar fine dark-brown finish.

Replacement of VCs is permitted in instances of proven loss or theft. In some instances also, duplicates were prepared. Thus, occasionally, and usually prior to sale, more than one VC awarded to an individual is found to be in existence. There have also been a number of attempts at forgery. Since 1906 identification of the original has been aided by the imprint of a secret mark of authenticity known only to Messrs Hancock.

Since 1916 a miniature VC has been worn with evening or mess dress instead of the full-sized medal.

---

[1] Information sourced primarily from *British Orders and Awards* (London: Kaye & Ward, Revised 1968), 23–7.
[2] A cascabel is the large knob behind the base-ring at the rear of a cannon for affixing a rope when moving it.
[3] John Glanfield, *Bravest of the Brave: The Story of the VC* (Stroud: Sutton, 2005).

Appendix D

Some Facts and Frequently Asked Questions about VCs

As at 1 May 2006

The Victoria Cross is Britain's highest award for gallantry and first in the Order of Precedence of Orders, Decorations and Medals conferred by the Crown. It may be awarded to a Serviceman or woman of any rank. It was instituted by Royal Warrant of 29 January 1856 (see Appendix B) and made retrospective to the outbreak of the Crimean War in March 1854. Prior to this conflict the Sovereign had no means of rewarding junior officers and non-commissioned ranks in the Army and Royal Navy for 'signal acts of valour or devotion to their Country in the presence of the enemy'.

There have been various changes to the eligibility rules for award of the VC since its inception. For example, in October 1857 members of the Honourable East India Company became eligible, but not native Indians, who had to wait until 1911 to qualify. Members of the Colonial Forces in New Zealand and other parts of the Empire were included in 1867.

The present Warrant states that the VC 'shall only be awarded for conspicuous bravery or some daring or pre-eminent act of valour or self-sacrifice or extreme devotion to duty in the presence of the enemy'.

Awards do not have to relate to a single incident but may relate to several.

Frequently Asked Questions
How are VCs awarded?

VCs are awarded on the recommendation of a superior officer 'who shall call for such description, conclusive proof as far as the circumstances will allow, and attestation of the act as he may think requisite'. Recommendations need to be supported at each higher level of command and subsequently be approved by the Sovereign. Once approved, notification of the award, usually including the citation, is published in *The London Gazette* ('gazetted') and the recipient invited to attend an Investiture, usually at Buckingham Palace.

How many VCs have been awarded?

1,355 – 1,351 to individuals, plus three Bars. A further VC was awarded to the American Unknown Warrior of the First World War. See also the table on page xi.

The VC awarded to the American Unknown Warrior was presented by Admiral of the Fleet Lord Beatty on behalf of King George V at Arlington National Cemetery on 11 November 1921. This followed receipt of the US Congressional Medal of Honor awarded to the British Unknown Warrior in Westminster Abbey on 17 October 1921.

What is the breakdown of awards by Service and to Commonwealth countries?

See the table at the end of this Appendix (page 214).

Who are the three individuals who received a Bar to their VC?

- Lieutenant A. Martin-Leake, Royal Army Medical Corps (1902 and 1914)
- Captain N.G. Chavasse, Royal Army Medical Corps (1916 and 1917)
- Captain C.H. Upham, New Zealand Military Forces (1941 and 1942)

How many officers have been awarded a VC, DSO and MC?

Twenty-four: twenty-three during the First World War and one during the Second World War. Brevet Major W. La T. Congreve of The Rifle Brigade was the first officer to be awarded a VC, DSO and MC.

How many soldiers have been awarded a VC, DCM and MM?

Eight, all during the First World War. Sergeant W. Gregg of The Rifle Brigade was the first soldier to be awarded a VC, DCM and MM.

Have any VCs been awarded to civilians?

Yes, to five civilians under military command. The last was the Reverend J.W. Adams of the Bengal Ecclesiastical Department in 1879.

Have any VCs been awarded to nationalities other than British or Commonwealth citizens?

Yes – five Americans, one Belgian, three Danes, two Germans, one Swede, a Swiss and a Ukrainian, all while serving with British or Commonwealth forces.

Appendix D

Who was the first person to be awarded a VC?

Mate C.D. Lucas, Royal Navy, in the Baltic during the Crimean War, 21 June 1854.

Who was the last person to be awarded a VC?

Private J.G. Beharry, The Princess of Wales's Royal Regiment, for two individual acts of gallantry on 1 May and 11 June 2004 in Iraq.

Who are the youngest persons to be awarded a VC?

Drummer Thomas Flinn, 64th (2nd Staffordshire) Regiment, in 1857, and Andrew Fitzgibbon, a hospital apprentice attached to the 67th (South Hampshire) Regiment, in 1860. Both were aged 15 years and 3 months.

Who is the oldest person to be awarded a VC?

Lieutenant W. Raynor, Bengal Veterans Establishment, in 1857, aged 61 years.

Who was the first black man to be awarded a VC?

Able Seaman W.N. Hall of the Royal Navy (Naval Brigade) on 16 November 1857 at Lucknow during the Indian Mutiny. Hall was a freed black slave who settled in Canada before joining, first, the US Navy and, then, the Royal Navy. He was also the first Canadian sailor to be awarded a VC.

Can VCs be awarded as a result of ballot?

Yes. Recommendations for awards to individuals may be submitted as a result of election by ballot among their comrades when units perform collective acts of gallantry where all are deemed to be equally brave, the number of awards being dictated by the size of the unit involved.

How often have VCs been awarded by ballot?

Forty-six VCs have been awarded by ballot, 29 during the Indian Mutiny. Among the first to benefit were five members of 1st/60th, KRRC, who received VCs for their part during the relief and recapture of Delhi during the Indian Mutiny in 1857. On the last occasion four awards were made following the Zeebrugge Raid on 23 April 1918.

Can VCs be awarded posthumously?

Yes, but not initially. Although the Royal Warrant of 29 January 1856 did not expressly exclude such awards, it was decided against awarding VCs posthumously. Instead, in circumstances in which a potential recipient was killed, a Memorandum was inserted in *The London Gazette* announcing that had the individual survived he would have been recommended for the VC. Six such entries were made between 1859 and 1897, including for Ensign E.A. Lisle Phillipps (KRRC). However, in 1902, King Edward VII assented to six posthumous awards arising from acts of gallantry during the South African War. On 15 January 1907 he assented to six further posthumous awards to the persons named in Memoranda between 1859 and 1897. Thereafter, recommendations for posthumous awards were accepted.

How many VCs have been awarded posthumously?

There have been 293 posthumous awards (22% of the total number of VCs awarded), including 10 awards to members of the antecedent regiments of The Royal Green Jackets. However, the count of posthumous awards often varies dependent upon the definition and application of the word 'posthumous'.

When was the earliest act of gallantry resulting in a posthumous VC?

On 17 September 1857 Ensign E.A. Lisle Phillipps was killed on the streets of Delhi while serving with the 1st/60th, KRRC. On 21 October 1859 a Memorandum appeared in *The London Gazette* announcing that, had he survived, he would have been recommended for the VC for his many gallant deeds during the relief and recapture of Delhi. On 15 January 1907 his acts of gallantry resulted in Royal assent to the award of a posthumous VC.

What is the largest number of VCs awarded on the same day?

Twenty-four, on 16 November 1857 at the second relief of Lucknow.

What is the largest number of VCs awarded for a single action?

Eleven, on 22/23 January 1879 at Rorke's Drift during the Anglo-Zulu War.

Have VCs ever been awarded for acts of gallantry 'not in the presence of the enemy'?

Yes, six. A Royal Warrant was signed on 10 August 1858 permitting awards 'under circumstances of extreme danger' not in the presence of the enemy. As a consequence Rifleman T. O'Hea (RB) was awarded a VC for his gallantry in extinguishing a fire on an ammunition train in Canada on 9 June 1866. A further five VCs were awarded following a ship-to-shore rescue in the Andaman Islands in 1867. The introduction of the Royal Warrant was not popular, little publicised and ceased to have effect after 1881.

Has a woman ever been awarded a VC?

Women are eligible but no award has yet been made.

Have members of the same family ever been awarded VCs?

Yes, on three occasions to a father and son, and on four occasions to brothers. Those relating to the antecedent regiments of The Royal Green Jackets are:

- Captain W.N. Congreve (RB) received a VC for his gallantry at Colenso (1899). His son, Brevet Major W. La T. Congreve (RB), received a posthumous VC for his gallantry on the Somme (1916). This is the only instance of a father and son in the same regiment being awarded VCs.
- Lieutenant the Hon F.H.S. Roberts (KRRC) received a VC for his gallantry at Colenso (1899). His father, Lieutenant F.S. (later Field Marshal Lord) Roberts, was awarded a VC while serving with the Bengal Artillery during the Indian Mutiny (1858).
- Brevet Major J.E. Gough (RB) received a VC for his gallantry in Somaliland (1903). His father, Major C.J.S. (later General Sir Charles) Gough, was awarded a VC for saving the life of his brother while serving with the 5th Bengal Cavalry during the Indian Mutiny (1857). Charles's brother, Lieutenant H.H. (later General Sir Hugh) Gough, was also awarded a VC for gallantry during the Indian Mutiny (1857).
- Lieutenant-Colonel V.B. Turner (RB) received a VC for gallantry during the 'Snipe' action at El Alamein (1942). His eldest brother, Second Lieutenant A.B. Turner serving with The Royal Berkshire Regiment, was awarded a posthumous VC during the First World War (1915).

Does the award of a VC result in any financial benefit?

Yes. Initially all VC recipients, except officers, were entitled to an annual pension (annuity) of £10, with a further £5 for a Bar. In 1890 this was changed to allow officers who were awarded a VC prior to commissioning to retain their annuity. On 1 August 1959 all officers became eligible for an annuity. The annuity, which is subject to regular review, presently amounts to £1,495 (tax free).

Can a recipient be required to forfeit his VC?

Yes. Originally erasure of the recipient's name from the Register and forfeiture of his VC and pension were required as a consequence of relatively minor cases of misconduct. However, King George V felt very strongly that the medal should never be forfeited – 'even were a VC to be sentenced to be hanged for murder, he should be allowed to wear his VC on the scaffold'. While the Royal Warrant continues to provide for annulment of an award, there has been no case of forfeiture since 1908, with the names of those who were earlier struck off the Register subsequently restored to the roll.

How many persons have been required to forfeit their VC?

Eight, including Rifleman Bambrick (KRRC) in 1863, after transfer to the 87th (Royal Irish Fusiliers), for assault and theft of a comrade's medals, and Rifleman Corbett (KRRC) in 1884, after transfer to the Royal Artillery, for embezzlement and theft from an officer.

VC Awards by Service and Country: 1854–2005

	1856-1913	1914-18	1919-38	1939-45	1946 onwards	Total
Royal Navy & R Marines	45	48	3	2	–	**119**
Army	357	409 incl 2 Bars	3	61	8	**838**
Royal Flying Corps & RAF	–	10	–	22	–	**32**
East India Company & Indian Army	83	19	4	30	–	**136**
Australian Forces	5	63	–	19	4	**91**
Canadian Forces	4	63	–	13	–	**80**
South African Forces	21	4	–	3	–	**28**
New Zealand Forces	2	11	–	9 incl 1 Bar	–	**22**
Newfoundland	–	1	–	–	–	**1**
Fiji Military Forces	–	–	–	1	–	**1**
Kenya Regiment	–	–	–	1	–	**1**
Civilians	5	–	–	–	–	**5**
American Unknown Warrior	–	–	1	–	–	**1**
Total	**522**	**628**	**11**	**182**	**12**	**1355**

Appendix E
Other Gallantry Awards

Note: The gallantry awards below are those most frequently mentioned in this book. For a complete list, see Peter Duckers, *British Gallantry Awards: 1855–2000.*

From left to right: DSO, MC, DCM and MM

Distinguished Service Order (DSO)

The DSO, instituted by Royal Warrant of 6 September 1886, was an award for specific acts of gallantry and/or distinguished service in war by junior officers of the Army and Navy who were ineligible to be made a Companion of the Order of the Bath (CB). However, at the start of the First World War, DSOs were awarded to officers from the rank of Second Lieutenant to Brigadier-General. Once the Military Cross (MC) was instituted at the end of 1914, it was unusual for officers below the rank of Major to be awarded a DSO. After 1917 DSOs were more usually awarded for gallantry in action. In 1918 the award was extended to include officers in the RAF and in 1943 to include the Merchant Navy and Home Guard. Prior to 1943 a DSO could only be awarded to an individual who had already received a Mention in Despatches. In 1993 the DSO was superseded by the Conspicuous Gallantry Cross as an award for gallantry but has been retained as an award for leadership open to all ranks.

Military Cross (MC)

The MC, instituted by Royal Warrant of 28 December 1914, was an award for gallant and distinguished services in action by junior Army officers and warrant officers. In 1915 eligibility was extended to include Majors. In 1917 it was decreed that the MC should only be awarded for service in action and not, as sometimes had been the case, for meritorious war service. The Distinguished Service Cross (1914) and Distinguished Flying Cross (1918) were the Naval and Air Force equivalents. Since 1993 the MC has been open to all ranks.

Distinguished Conduct Medal (DCM)

The DCM, instituted by Royal Warrant of 4 December 1854, was an award for distinguished service and gallant conduct in the field by non-commissioned ranks in the Army. The Conspicuous Gallantry Medal (1855) and Conspicuous Gallantry Medal (Flying) (1942) were the Naval and Air Force equivalent. In 1993 the DCM became obsolete with the introduction of the Conspicuous Gallantry Cross open to all ranks.

Military Medal (MM)

The MM, instituted by Royal Warrant of 25 March 1916, was an award for acts of bravery whilst on active service by non-commissioned ranks in the Army, which were of a lower order than those meriting the award of a DCM. Women were eligible and several were awarded to women. The Distinguished Service Medal (1914) and the Distinguished Flying Medal (1918) were the Naval and Air Force equivalents. In 1993 the MM became obsolete when the MC was made open to all ranks.

PDSA Dickin Medal
'Tich', 1st Battalion, The King's Royal Rifle Corps

TICH
1ST KINGS ROYAL RIFLE
CORPS
N.AFRICA & ITALY
1941-1945
A.E.M.C. N° 1244
N° 53

The PDSA Dickin Medal awarded to 'Tich'

PDSA's founder, Maria Dickin, introduced the PDSA Dickin Medal in 1943. It is awarded to animals displaying conspicuous gallantry and devotion to duty while serving or associated with any branch of the Armed Forces or Civil Defence units, and is the animals' equivalent to the VC.

The medal, which is made of bronze, is embossed with the words *For Gallantry* and *WE ALSO SERVE*. The reverse is inscribed with details of the recipient. It is suspended from a ribbon of dark green, dark brown and pale blue, symbolic of the naval, military, civil defence and air forces.

To date (1 May 2006) there have been 60 awards of the PDSA Dickin Medal to 32 pigeons, 24 dogs, three horses and one cat. One of the dogs was a small black Egyptian mongrel terrier bitch called 'Tich', who was adopted by 1 KRRC before El Alamein. When the Battalion reached Algiers in 1943, Tich was placed in the care of Rifleman Thomas Walker, accompanying him on the front line usually on the bonnet of a Bren gun carrier or stretcher jeep.

During the fighting in Italy Rifleman Walker, a 'medic', was awarded the MM for a number of actions in which he either rescued or tended to injured men while under fire. On every occasion Tich remained by his side, being wounded on a number of occasions, once very seriously. Newspaper reports described Tich as the brave dog of an outstandingly brave man. In recommending Tich for the Dickin Medal, the Commanding Officer of 1 KRRC, Lieutenant-Colonel E.A.W. Williams, wrote: 'Her courage and devotion to duty were of very real and considerable value and her courageous example materially helped many men to keep their heads and sense of proportion in times of extreme danger. The sight of her put heart in the men as she habitually rode on the bonnet of her master's jeep and refused to leave her post even when bringing in wounded under heavy fire.'

The award of the PDSA Dickin Medal to Tich 'for loyalty, courage and devotion to duty under hazardous conditions of war 1941 to 1945, while serving with the 1st King's Royal Rifle Corps in North Africa and Italy' was announced on 1 July 1949.

During her life Tich gave birth to 15 puppies. The Battalion's Chaplain also said of her that: 'She can leap on to any type of truck or vehicle, will howl like a wolf, will cry, will remain standing against a wall until told to move. She will also smoke cigarettes, and never eat or drink until ordered to do so by her owner.'

After the War Tich lived with ex-Rifleman Walker in Newcastle, taking part with him in fund-raising activities for PDSA. She died in 1959 and is buried alongside many other PDSA Dickin Medal recipients in the charity's pet cemetery at Ilford.

Note: PDSA is the UK's leading Veterinary Charity and, since 1917, has cared for the pets of people in need by providing free veterinary care to their sick and injured animals. Today, the charity treats more than 4,650 sick and injured pets every working day from its PetAid hospitals, branches and practices nationwide.

Bibliography

The Regimental histories, annals, chronicles and archival records of the antecedent regiments of The Royal Green Jackets have been used extensively but are too numerous to be listed in this Bibliography. When quoted in the text, reference to the source may be found in the Endnotes.

Arthur, Max, *Symbol of Courage* (London: Sidgwick & Jackson, 2004).

Batchelor, Peter, and Matson, Chris, *VCs of the First World War: The Western Front 1915* (Stroud: Sutton, 1997).

Beckett, Ian F.W., *Johnnie Gough, V.C.* (London: Tom Donovan, 1989).

Caldwell, George, and Cooper, Robert, *Rifle Green in the Crimea* (Bugle Horn Publications, 1994).

Creagh, Sir O'Moore, and Humphris, E.M. (eds), *The V.C. and D.S.O.* (London: Standard Art Book Co., 1924).

Crook, M.J., *The Evolution of the Victoria Cross* (Tunbridge Wells: Midas Books, in association with the Ogilby Trusts, 1975).

David, Saul, *The Indian Mutiny* (London: Viking, 2002).

de la Billière, General Sir Peter, *Supreme Courage* (London: Little, Brown, 2004).

Doherty, Richard, and Truesdale, David, *Irish Winners of the Victoria Cross* (Dublin: Four Courts Press, 2000).

Duckers, Peter, *British Gallantry Awards 1855-2000* (Princes Risborough: Shire Books, 2001).

Glanfield, John, *Bravest of the Brave: The Story of the VC* (Stroud: Sutton, 2005).

Gliddon, Gerald, *VCs of the Somme* (Norwich: Gliddon Books, 1991).

Gliddon, Gerald, *VCs of the First World War: Arras & Messines 1917* (Stroud: Sutton, 1998).

Gliddon, Gerald, *VCs of the First World War: Spring Offensive 1918* (Stroud: Sutton, 1997).

Gliddon, Gerald, *VCs of the First World War: The Road to Victory 1918* (Stroud: Sutton, 2000).

Harvey, David, *Monuments to Courage*, 2 vols. (Privately published by the author, 1999).

Lucas Phillips, C.E., *Alamein* (London: Heinemann, 1962).

Marling, Colonel Sir Pecival, Bt., *Rifleman and Hussar* (London: John Murray, 1931).

Norman, Terry (ed.), *Armageddon Road: A VC's Diary 1914-16* (London: William Kimber, 1982) – The Diary of Billy Congreve.

Pakenham, Thomas, *The Boer War* (London: Wiedenfeld & Nicholson, 1979).

Percival, John, *For Valour* (London: Methuen, 1985).

Perkins, Roger, *The Kashmir Gate* (Chippenham: Picton, 1983).

Powell, Geoffrey, *Buller: A Scapegoat?* (London: Leo Cooper, 1994).

Roberts, Field Marshal Lord, *Forty-one years in India: From Subaltern to Commander-in-Chief* (London: 1898).

Snelling, Stephen, *VCs of the First World War: Passchendaele 1917* (Stroud: Sutton, 1998).

Sweetman, John, *The Crimean War* (Oxford: Osprey Publishing, 2001).

Thornton, Lt-Col L.H., and Fraser, Pamela, *The Congreves* (London: John Murray, 1930).

Toomey, T.E., *Heroes of the Victoria Cross* (London: Newnes, 1895).

Wilkins, Philip A., *The History of the Victoria Cross* (London: Constable, 1904).

Woolley, The Rev. G.H., *Sometimes a Soldier* (London: Ernest Benn, 1963).

Endnotes

Chapter 1 The Evolution of the Victoria Cross

[1] This chapter is titled the same as M.J. Crook's admirable book, *The Evolution of the Victoria Cross* (Tunbridge Wells: Midas Books, in association with the Ogilby Trusts, 1975), from which much of the material in the chapter is sourced.

[2] Captain Scobell served in the Royal Navy accepting the rank of Captain on half pay in 1843 - Crook, op. cit., 11.

[3] Crook, op. cit., 10-11, quoting Hansard, 3rd Series, cxxxvi, cols 505 *et seq.*

[4] Ibid., 7.

[5] Knight Grand Cross, Knight Commander and Companion of the Order of the Bath - GCB, KCB and CB.

[6] Authority to award the Indian Order of Merit (three classes) was initially vested in the Honourable East India Company but, following the Indian Mutiny, was assumed by the Crown in 1858.

[7] Crook, op. cit., 13, quoting Nottingham University, Newcastle Collection, NeC 9786, 33.

[8] Ibid., 15, and 276, quoting Nottingham University, Newcastle Collection, NeC 9701a and b.

[9] Ibid., 15-16, quoting Hansard, 3rd Series, cxxxvi, cols 1064/5.

[10] Ibid., 16.

[11] Ibid., 24-5, quoting Royal Archives, E6/69.

[12] Ibid., 25, quoting Royal Archives, E6/70.

[13] Ibid., 25-6.

[14] Public Record Office WO 98/1, copied from Crook, op. cit., 279-82.

[15] Crook, op. cit., 29, quoting the Panmure Papers, ii, 50.

[16] Although the implication was that eligibility for an award was dependent upon a single act, awards may relate to several.

[17] Royal Warrant dated 30 September 1961.

[18] Crook, op. cit., 64, quoting *Soldier*, Jan 1956, 13, which cites a letter contained in the VC Register which can no longer be traced.

[19] Ibid., 68.

[20] It is assumed that more Memoranda were not gazetted because commanders saw little point in submitting names of individuals for an award they would not receive.

[21] The detailed design of the VC carried out by Messrs Hancock is attributed to H.H. Armstead (b. 1828). The design bears similarity in shape to the Army Gold Cross awarded during the Peninsular War (1808-14), a number of which are on display in the RGJ Museum, Winchester. Messrs Hancock, trading as Hancocks & Co (Jewellers) Ltd., 52-53 Burlington Arcade, London, W1J 0HH (Tel: +44 (0)20 7493 8904) remains in business (2006) with continuing exclusive responsibility for the casting and engraving of VCs.

[22] Crook, op. cit., 33, quoting the Panmure Papers, ii, 94-5.

[23] Ibid., 34.

[24] Ibid., 37, quoting PRO, WO6/130.

[25] The decision to issue Crimean War Medals was taken in December 1854.

[26] Crook, op. cit., 40.

[27] Ibid., quoting the Panmure Papers, ii, 274.

[28] Ibid., 45, quoting the Panmure Papers, ii, 351-2.

[29] Max Arthur, *Symbol of Courage* (London: Sidgwick & Jackson, 2004), xii-xiii.

[30] Crook, op. cit., 51-2, quoting Queen Victoria's Journal, Royal Archives.

Chapter 2 **The Crimean War: 1854–6**

[1] John Sweetman, *The Crimean War* (Oxford: Osprey Publishing, 2001), 10.

[2] Sir William H. Cope Bart., *The History of The Rifle Brigade* (London: Chatto & Windus, 1877), 309. In February 1855 Norcott assumed command of 1 RB and received a CB for his services in the Crimea. He later became a Major-General.

[3] Cope, op. cit., 315.

[4] Ibid., 316.

[5] Sometimes spelt Inkermann.

[6] Cope, op. cit., 319.

[7] Cuthbert Fitzherbert, *Henry Clifford VC: His Letters and Sketches from the Crimea* (London: Michael Joseph, 1965), 88-9.

[8] Ibid., 25.

[9] Cope, op. cit., 322.

[10] Cuninghame's name is often incorrectly spelt with three 'n's, including in *The London Gazette,* an error verified by examination of his signature on documents held by the RGJ Museum and by his descendants.

[11] Cope, op. cit., 324.

[12] In September 1854, shortly after landing in Calamita Bay, Sir George Cathcart, commanding the 4th Division, presented each man in 1 RB with a piece of black oil-cloth to keep them dry – hence 'Cathcart's oilskins'.

[13] Cope, op. cit., 330.

[14] Ibid., 333.

[15] Sergeant in the British Army used to be spelt with a 'j' but is now usually spelt with a 'g'.

[16] Cope, op. cit., 333.

[17] Sir O'Moore Creagh and E.M. Humphris (eds), *The V.C. and D.S.O.* (London: Standard Art Book Co., 1924), 24-5.

[18] Cope, op. cit., 336-7.

[19] Ibid., 341.

[20] Ibid., 343.

Chapter 3 **The Indian Mutiny: 1857**

[1] The Meerut garrison included a second British regiment, the 6th Dragoon Guards (Carabiniers), and three native regiments: 3rd Light Cavalry and the 11th and 20th Bengal Native Infantry.

[2] Roger Perkins, *The Kashmir Gate* (Chippenham: Picton Publishing, 1983), 127.

[3] Ibid., 135.

[4] Lewis Butler, *The Annals of The King's Royal Rifle Corps, Vol. III* (London: John Murray, 1926), 121.

[5] Army Orders, 23 April 1859. Only 17 DCMs were awarded at Delhi compared to 43 VCs – Perkins, op. cit., 48.

[6] Crook, op. cit., 101 *et seq.*

[7] The Chandney Chouk was the main street running east to west from the King's Palace (Red Fort) to the Lahore Gate.

[8] Perkins, op. cit., 140.

[9] A serai is 'a stopping place for travellers, usually in the form of a square courtyard with animals inside and small rooms to sleep in'. Saul David, *The Indian Mutiny 1857* (London: Viking, 2002), 413.

[10] Butler, op. cit., 123-4.

[11] Doherty, Richard, and Truesdale, David, *Irish Winners of the Victoria Cross* (Dublin: Four Courts Press, 2000), 46-7.

[12] *KRRC Chronicle, 1912,* 52-3.

[13] Ibid., 54.

[14] Crook, op. cit., 235.

[15] Perkins, op. cit., 134.

[16] W.S. Moorsom (ed.), *Historical Record of the Fifty-Second Regiment* (London: Bentley, 1860), 370.

17 The correct spelling of Hawthorne, as shown in his service record and on his death certificate, is with an 'e'.
18 Field Marshal Lord Roberts, *Forty-one years in India: From Subaltern to Commander-in-Chief* (London: 1898), 126.
19 Perkins, op. cit., 64.
20 Lieutenant Home was killed destroying ammunition on 1 October 1857. Salkeld died of his wounds ten days later. Because General Wilson's awards required Royal assent and because the officers had died before it could be granted, a delay occurred while opinion was sought as to whether the awards should be discounted as 'posthumous'. In the light of General Wilson's Order and the fact that the awards were already public knowledge, such concerns were set aside and the awards announced in *The London Gazette* on 18 June 1858.
21 Perkins, op. cit., 120. The 75th (Stirlingshire) Regiment later became The Gordon Highlanders.
22 Quoted letters written by Lisle Phillipps are in the possession of his descendants.
23 From the original letter in the possession of his descendants.
24 Ibid.
25 David, op. cit., 308.

Chapter 4 **The Indian Mutiny: 1858–9**

1 Brigadier-General (later Lieutenant-General Sir Robert) Walpole was a Rifle Brigade officer who commanded a brigade at Lucknow.
2 Cope, op. cit., 377–8.
3 Doherty and Truesdale, op. cit., 59.
4 Bambrick's father fought at Waterloo. His uncle, Valentine, after whom Rifleman Bambrick was named, fought at Bhurtpore in 1825. His younger brother, Corporal John Bambrick, rode with the 11th Hussars (formerly 11th Light Dragoons) in the Charge of the Light Cavalry Brigade at Balaclava in 1854.
5 Butler, op. cit., 173-4.
6 Doherty and Truesdale, op. cit., 235.
7 Crook, op. cit., 66, quoting the VCR, i, 466-71.
8 Because of the similarity in Christian name Same (John) Shaw has sometimes been mistaken for Samuel Shaw, a Sergeant who served with 1 RB in South Africa and the Crimea, where he was awarded a DCM. However, Samuel Shaw never went to India. His Service Record shows that he transferred from The Rifle Brigade to the Royal Canadian Rifles in May 1858 and that on the date of Same Shaw's VC action, Samuel Shaw was in Canada. National Archives WO12/10169-10173 and WO12/10073-10091; 10539 Regimental muster rolls.
9 Cope, op. cit., 391.
10 Arthur, op. cit., 673.
11 Cope, op. cit., 398.
12 Ibid., 409, quoting William Russell's *My Diary in India*, ii, 370.
13 Sir Richard Levinge, Bart., *Historical Records of the Forty-Third Light Infantry* (London: W. Clowes & Sons, 1868), 276.
14 Indians today usually refer to the Mutiny or Sepoy Revolt as the First War of Independence.
15 Perkins, op. cit., 48.

Chapter 5 **Imperial Wars: 1864–84**

1 Levinge, op. cit., 281.
2 Ibid., 288.
3 From an original record dated 8 May 1905, held in the RGJ Museum Archives, in which the author, Mr E. Du Faur, states: 'My account of O'Hea's action in Canada … is from my notes of repeated conversations with him [O'Hea] in June 1874, and his statements made to and published in the public press'.

4 The other five VC awards 'not in the presence of the enemy' all arose from a single incident in the Andaman Islands on 7 May 1867 involving members of the 24th (2nd Warwickshire) Regiment.

5 A copy of the document is in the RGJ Museum Archives.

6 O'Hea's return to health and the record of his subsequent life in New Zealand and Australia have recently been questioned by a researcher who believes that Timothy O'Hea died in Ireland from tuberculosis between 1868–74 and that his brother, who was three years younger than him, assumed his identity in order to claim his brother's VC annuity. The assumption, therefore, is that it was O'Hea's brother and not O'Hea who went to New Zealand and Australia, possibly to escape discovery that he had been falsely claiming his brother's annuity, and that he took his deceased brother's VC with him. This version of events, for which there is some evidence, has yet to be verified.

7 The original affidavit is in the RGJ Museum Archives.

8 RGJ Museum Archives.

9 Crook, op. cit., 199.

10 Ibid., 146.

11 Geoffrey Powell, *Buller: A Scapegoat?* (London: Leo Cooper, 1994), 32.

12 Later Field Marshal Sir Evelyn Wood VC GCB GCMG.

13 Butler, op. cit., 299.

14 *The Essex Family Historian*, Number 113, September 2004, 32.

15 Lieutenant Howard-Vyse came from Stoke Poges, Buckinghamshire. He was commissioned into the 20th (East Devonshire) Regiment before transferring to the 3rd/60th on 14 January 1880. He was present at the actions at Ingogo on 8 February and at Majuba on 27 February 1881. He was the first officer killed during the Egyptian campaign, aged 23.

16 Crook, op. cit., 63.

17 Colonel Sir Percival Marling, Bt., *Rifleman and Hussar* (London: John Murray, 1931), 22 and 24.

18 Ibid., 107.

Chapter 6 Imperial Wars: 1899–1903

1 Major-General Sir Steuart Hare, *The Annals of The King's Royal Rifle Corps, Volume IV* (London: John Murray, 1929), 216

2 Six VCs were awarded for trying to save the guns and one to a Medical Officer for tending the wounded.

3 Lt-Col L.H. Thornton and Pamela Fraser, *The Congreves* (London: John Murray, 1930), 29.

4 Ibid., 31.

5 Crook, op. cit., 76–7.

6 Doherty and Truesdale, op. cit., 94.

7 Those present at Bergendal received the Queen's South Africa Medal clasp 'Belfast', the nearest place to Bergendal.

8 *Rifle Brigade Chronicle, 1900*, 180–2.

9 Acting Corporal was, until 1916, a rank in The Rifle Brigade equivalent to Lance-Corporal. The rank was retained in informal use by the Regiment thereafter.

10 Following the 1881 Cardwell Reforms, the Westmeath Militia was officially titled 9 RB.

11 An account of the Goughs leading role in the Curragh incident is included in Ian F.W. Beckett's excellent biography of Gough, *Johnnie Gough, V.C.* (London: John Donovan, 1989), 147–72.

Chapter 7 The First World War: 1914–16

1 Arthur, op. cit., 188. Five VCs were awarded for gallantry on 23 August 1914, the first of the War usually being attributed to Lieutenant M.J. Dease of the 4th Battalion, Royal Fusiliers.

2 Field Marshal Lord Grenfell was commissioned into the 60th, KRRC in August 1859. He became Governor of Malta in 1899 and Commander-in-Chief in Ireland in 1904. He was a Colonel-Commandant of The King's Royal Rifle Corps from 1898 until his death in 1925.

3 *The London Gazette*, 16 November 1914.
4 Lance-Sergeant was, and still is in the Brigade of Guards, a rank equivalent to Corporal.
5 *Deeds that Thrill the Empire, Volume 1* (Hutchinson, 1914–18), 270 *et seq.*
6 P.F. Batchelor and C. Matson, *VCs of the First World War: The Western Front 1915* (Stroud: Sutton, 1999), 27 *et seq.*
7 Ibid., 29.
8 Ibid., 41.
9 Woolley met the original 'Woodbine Willie', the Reverend G.A. Studdert-Kennedy, in France in 1916.
10 Batchelor and Matson, op. cit., 106.
11 Ibid., 125–6.
12 Arthur, op. cit., 212.
13 Ibid.
14 Creagh and Humphris, op. cit., 189.
15 Although the citation refers to La Brique being in France, it is in Belgium.
16 Reginald Berkeley, *The History of The Rifle Brigade in the War of 1914–1918, Volume I* (London: RB Club, 1927), 141.
17 John 15:13.
18 The middle son, Geoffrey, became a Lieutenant-Commander in the Royal Navy and was awarded a DSO. He also received the baronetcy intended for his father when his father died in 1927. The younger son, Christopher, was a Major in The Rifle Brigade.
19 Terry Norman (ed.), *Armaggedon Road: A VC's Diary 1914–1916* (London: William Kimber, 1982), 194, from which the two quotes in this paragraph originate.
20 The original letter resides in the RGJ Museum Archives.
21 Gerald Gliddon, *V.C.s of the Somme* (Norwich: Gliddon Books, 1991), 58, from which the two quotes in this paragraph originate.
22 General Sir David Fraser GCB OBE (b. 1920), who joined the Grenadier Guards and was Vice-Chief of the General Staff from 1973–5, is the elder son from their marriage.
23 There have been 24 instances of an individual being awarded a VC, DSO and MC, twenty-three during the First World War and one during the Second World War.
24 Ibid., 84–5.

Chapter 8 **The First World War: 1917–18**

1 Gerald Gliddon, *VCs of the First World War: Arras & Messines 1917* (Stroud: Sutton, 1998), 15.
2 Crook, op. cit., 147.
3 Gliddon, op. cit., 121.
4 The figure of 14 VCs on the first day of the Third Battle of Ypres (31 July 1917) may be compared with 12 VCs on the first day of the Gallipoli landings (25 April 1915) and 9 VCs on the first day of the Battle of the Somme (1 July 1916) and on the first day of the First German Offensive (21 March 1918).
5 Stephen Snelling, *VCs of the First World War: Passchendaele 1917* (Stroud: Sutton, 1998), vi.
6 Ibid., 79–81.
7 Ibid., 81.
8 Creagh and Humphris, op. cit., 252.
9 Snelling, op. cit., 83.
10 Ibid., 137.
11 Ibid., 142.
12 Ibid., 143.
13 Ibid., 127.
14 In 1922 the 7th and 8th (City of London) Regiments merged to become the 7th (City of London) Regiment at which point the Post Office Rifles ceased to be a part of The Rifle Brigade and became a Territorial battalion of The Middlesex Regiment.
15 Snelling, op. cit., 129.

16 Major-General Sir Steuart Hare, *The Annals of The King's Royal Rifle Corps, Volume V: The Great War* (London: John Murray, 1932), 248-9.
17 *RGJ Chronicle, 1966,* 267-8.
18 *KRRC Chronicle, 1933,* 198.
19 Anson (1857), Grenfell (1914), Borton (1917) and Grayburn (1944).
20 *Dictionary of National Biography* quoting D. Cooper, *Haig* (1935) 2.23.
21 William W. Seymour, *The History of The Rifle Brigade in the War of 1914-1918, Volume II: January 1917- June 1919* (London: The Rifle Brigade Club, 1936), 298.
22 Obituary, *RGJ Chronicle, 1969,* 227.
23 Ibid., 228.
24 Ibid.
25 There have been eight instances of an individual being awarded a VC, DCM and MM, all during the First World War.
26 Gerald Gliddon, *VCs of the First World War: Spring Offensive 1918* (Stroud: Sutton, 1997), 162.
27 Awarded to Acting Major B. Cloutman of 59 Field Company, Royal Engineers.
28 *The Oxfordshire and Buckinghamshire LI Chronicle, 1917-18,* 210.
29 Gerald Gliddon, *VCs of the First World War: The Road to Victory 1918* (Stroud: Sutton, 2000), 177.

Chapter 9 **The Second World War: 1939–45**

1 Christopher Wallace, *The King's Royal Rifle Corps ... the 60th Rifles. A Brief History: 1755 to 1965* (RGJ Museum Trust, 2005), 165-7.
2 Giles Mills and Roger Nixon, *The Annals of The King's Royal Rifle Corps, Volume VI* (London: Leo Cooper, 1971), 198-9.
3 Ibid.
4 Wallace, op. cit., 167.
5 Lieutenant-General W.H.E. 'Strafer' Gott CB CBE DSO* MC, a KRRC officer, was Churchill's preferred choice to command the Eighth Army. Unfortunately, before Gott could take command, he was killed on 7 August 1942 when two German fighter aircraft attacked the aeroplane in which he was flying to Cairo.
6 Captain G.E. Fletcher, killed commanding I Company 1 RB in Tunisia on 27 March 1943.
7 Major R.H.W.S. Hastings, *The Rifle Brigade in the Second World War, 1939-45* (Aldershot: Gale & Polden, 1950), 104-5.
8 A Committee of Investigation also compiled an authoritative report, an unexpurgated version of which is held in the RGJ Museum Archives. Lucas Phillips had access to the report, as well as first-hand accounts from participants, when writing his book.
9 C.E. Lucas Phillips, *Alamein* (London: Heinemann, 1962), 271.
10 Ibid., 267.
11 Ibid., 280.
12 Ibid., 287-8.
13 Captain Cecil Turner RN (d. 1978) and Brigadier Mark Turner DSO MC, Royal Horse Artillery (d. 1971).
14 *RGJ Chronicle, 1972,* 266-7.
15 *43rd Light Infantry War Chronicle, 1943,* 76.

Index